D1288891

MAJOR CASE MANAGEMENT

MAJOR CASE MANAGEMENT

A Guide for Law Enforcement Managers

By

DANIEL S. McDEVITT, B.S., M.S.

Chief of Police
Lansing, Illinois Police Department
Lansing, Illinois

CHARLES C THOMAS • PUBLISHER, LTD.
Springfield • Illinois • U.S.A.

Published and Distributed Throughout the World by

CHARLES C THOMAS • PUBLISHER, LTD.
2600 South First Street
Springfield, Illinois 62794-9265

This book is protected by copyright. No part of
it may be reproduced in any manner without written
permission from the publisher. All rights reserved.

© 2009 by CHARLES C THOMAS • PUBLISHER, LTD.

ISBN 978-0-398-07874-4 (hard)
ISBN 978-0-398-07875-1 (paper)

Library of Congress Catalog Card Number: 2009003954

With THOMAS BOOKS *careful attention is given to all details of manufacturing
and design. It is the Publisher's desire to present books that are satisfactory as to their
physical qualities and artistic possibilities and appropriate for their particular use.*
THOMAS BOOKS *will be true to those laws of quality that assure a good name
and good will.*

Printed in the United States of America
MM-R-3

Library of Congress Cataloging in Publication Data

McDevitt, Daniel, S.
    Major case management : a guide for law enforcement managers / by
Daniel S. McDevitt.
        p. cm.
    Includes index.
    ISBN 978-0-398-07874-4 (hard)–ISBN 978-0-398-07875-1 (pbk.)
    1. Law enforcement. 2. Management. I. Title.

HV7921.M314 2009
363.25–dc22   2009003954

ACC LIBRARY SERVICES AUSTIN, TX

PREFACE

Having spent the majority of my 35-year law enforcement career supervising or managing various types of investigative units, I had the opportunity to manage a number of what could arguably be considered "major cases." The definition of a major case will be discussed in Chapter 1, but most people could figure out on their own what it means. Where I come from, we call these "heater cases," and the name is very accurate. The reason we call them heaters is because whoever is tasked with managing these major cases is due to catch a great deal of heat (criticism, second-guessing, controversy, etc.) from a variety of sources—the media, the public, elected officials, and at times even other law enforcement personnel.

There are two very important things to remember when thinking about major cases: the first is that "Yes, it can happen here" and the second is "It's usually not a matter of **if**, it's usually a matter of **when** you'll catch a major case." The fact is that major case investigations have occurred in some very unlikely places, and there are many chiefs and many more former chiefs that found out the hard way that sometimes very bad things happen in very nice places. Unfortunately for them, this often resulted in situations in which law enforcement agencies were not prepared for major cases that have occurred in their communities. In many of these cases, the lack of preparedness has cost them dearly.

There are numerous examples of major cases that have occurred in communities that historically had very little serious crime, and the law enforcement agencies in those communities were sometimes lulled into thinking that major cases always happen in "the other community or on the other side of the proverbial tracks," and not in their community. These agencies lulled themselves into thinking that the types of "routine cases" that they are used to investigating are the only type they are likely to see.

Another sad fact relating to many of these major cases is the person managing them just can't win, no matter how well the case is investigated. This just seems to be the nature of the beast, and there seems to be very little that can be done to avoid it. There will always be someone who will criticize the type of response, the manner in which the investigative leads were followed, the way the police dealt with the media, and the list goes on and on.

Perhaps the best example that comes to mind involves what is arguably one of the most high-profile major cases in United States history, the "Beltway Sniper" investigation. In 2002, two individuals placed the states of Virginia, Maryland, and the Washington, D.C. area in the grip of real terror. There were ten murders and three people were critically wounded, and the crimes seemed extremely indiscriminate. The fact that the cases occurred within a year of September 11th, 2001 (the worst terrorist attack in American history), added an additional element to the scenario. Was this the work of a terrorist organization? Was this the beginning of widespread killings throughout the country by a radical group? People were afraid to leave their homes or send their children to school. Gas stations covered their driveway areas with opaque plastic so that their customers wouldn't become targets, and the terror continued.

The manner in which the investigation was addressed included the formation of a multiagency task force, which included several Federal, state, county, and local law enforcement agencies. The fact that agencies from several levels were included made the investigation more difficult, as did the media frenzy. In my opinion, the spokesperson for the task force, Chief Charles Moose of the Montgomery County, Maryland Police Department, did a superb job handling the media, in keeping the public informed of the progress of the investigation, and in assuring the public that the matter was being professionally handled. And yet, throughout the investigation Chief Moose was criticized for a variety of reasons. At one point Chief Moose became somewhat irritated with the media and was criticized. At another point when discussing a child who had been shot he became very emotional and in fact had tears in his eyes, and again he was criticized. Who could blame him for either? In fact, he was being criticized for being a caring human being and a conscientious cop. I have had personal conversations with members of the Beltway Sniper Task Force, which provided some material for this book, and I also recommend the publication *Managing a Multijurisdictional Case* by Gerard R. Murphy and Chuck Wexler, published by the Police Executive Research Forum (PERF), which outlines in detail many aspects of the investigation. Some of those details are also included in this text. Having been in the position myself of managing a number of major cases, case studies of many which are contained in this book, I was sometimes subjected to a great deal of criticism. As far as I'm concerned, this criticism seems to come with the territory, and it cannot seem to be avoided.

During a past assignment as Commander of a Child Sexual Exploitation Unit, our unit arrested one of the very first priests in a large Midwestern Roman Catholic Archdiocese for child molestation. His offenses were horrendous, as they involved victimization of young boys by someone who was in a position of spiritual trust and leadership. These offenses had taken place in two states, and this individual's activities were compounded by the fact that he had a fellow priest in the adjoining state, who was also molesting these same young boys. The case was very difficult, as some of the parents refused to cooperate with the investigation, which often happens in these types of cases. In addition, many members of the unit, myself included, were Roman Catholic. Many of us had attended Catholic schools ourselves, and some of us had our own children enrolled in Catholic schools and were active in our respective parishes.

While walking out of Mass one Sunday, I was confronted by a fellow parishioner, an older woman. She loudly asked how I could claim to be a "good Catholic" and still have participated in the arrest of this "fine priest." She continued to berate me, in front of a group of people, until I excused myself and walked away. It didn't seem to matter to her that the evidence against this individual was enough to convince both the prosecutor's office and a Judge that he had in fact committed the crimes in question, nor did it matter that the lives of these victims would be forever changed. The fact was, in her opinion, I was wrong for having done my job and managed this major case. Like I said, no matter how well you manage these investigations, sometimes you can't win.

Managing a major case is among the most challenging managerial functions that anyone in law enforcement can perform, and there are many pitfalls to avoid. It is the goal of this book to provide the law enforcement manager with some tools and strategies that they can use in managing their next major case. Most of these tools and strategies have been used by myself and my associates with some level of success, and many of the pitfalls that will be examined were learned the hard way, by actually making the mistakes that I will now attempt to caution the reader to avoid.

There are many operational and administrative elements of managing a major case, and if these are not addressed properly chaos can occur. The amount of chaos will be correlated directly to the gravity of the offense(s) being investigated. This too, can be avoided by insuring well-planned and organized efforts right from the start. This book will attempt to examine all the various elements that go into an appropriate response to a variety of types of major cases.

Managing a major case can be overwhelming to many law enforcement managers, but if the manager carefully considers all of the necessary functions and resources that go into a major case, it need not be overpowering. By conscientiously preparing as much as possible before the major case hits, these cases will be investigated from the onset in a much more organized manner.

This book contains a number of case studies, which will highlight both the good and the bad decisions and actions taken on a variety of major cases in a variety of settings. The names of the victims or any photographs will not be used, out of respect for them and their families. The victimology, geographics, and actions taken on each of these cases will be examined, and most importantly the "lessons learned," both good and bad, will be discussed.

Hopefully, this book will address many of these skills and strategies to better prepare fellow law enforcement professionals to successfully address the challenges of managing major case investigations.

D.S.M.

ACKNOWLEDGMENTS

About the time this book is being published, I'll be ending my 35-year law enforcement career. While I am very much looking forward to the next chapter of my life, the past 35 years have truly been a remarkable journey. A journey filled with some outstanding memories of some unbelievable situations. Being a cop for these many years affords one the opportunity and privilege to see and do things that other people just read about or see on movies or TV.

More important, however, than the situations one encounters, are the outstanding people that you work with and who also provide some wonderful memories. These outstanding people not only included my fellow law enforcement professionals at the Federal, state, county, and municipal levels, but also the dedicated prosecutors, judges, and their support staffs with whom I had the privilege to work.

I began my career right out of graduate school as a Special Agent with the Naval Criminal Investigative Service (NCIS), where I learned a great deal and worked with some true professionals, men like Special Agent Tim Dixon and Special Agent Stanley Pukelis.

I then worked 24 years with the Illinois State Police, where I was fortunate to experience a variety of great assignments, all of which afforded me the opportunity to learn from and interact with some of the finest people I've ever known in my life, way too many to mention here, but I would like to mention one, the late Sergeant Thomas W. Pritchett, Illinois State Police (Retired), an outstanding investigator and dear friend. Rest in peace, Tommy. Following my retirement as a Captain from the Illinois State Police, I became Chief of the Homewood, Illinois Police Department, and was able to work with some truly outstanding people.

I culminated the last eight years of my career by becoming Chief of the Lansing, Illinois Police Department, and this position provided me with the opportunity, for the first time in my career, to actually police the town in which I lived. I worked with some truly gifted individuals, and being their chief was a distinct honor, and a tremendous way to end my career.

Besides my fellow law enforcement professionals, however, some of the people who had the greatest personal impact on me also included the hundreds of victims and their families with whom I have interacted. I've been able to see people at their very best and at their very worst. I've seen the pain and agony of people losing a loved one in a variety of situations, some of which were very violent, and in many cases it fell to me to make the notification that their loved one would never be coming home again. I've sat in court countless times and watched as family members listened to testimony and viewed evidence, which unfortunately often caused them to relive the agony that their loved ones must have experienced. I've seen situations that I knew would result in many lives being inexorably changed, and in many cases there wasn't anything I could do for the victims or their families to make the pain subside. Nobody could witness and live through all of that and not be moved, and I can assure you that not only was I most certainly moved, in many ways I was permanently affected by much of it as well.

This is not an easy task, but then so much of what we do every day in the law enforcement profession isn't easy. If it were easy, anybody could do this. It takes a special breed of person to be admitted into this profession, and for those who make a career of it, the rewards that one receives from being able to actually help someone when they have nowhere else to turn are truly gratifying.

To the truly outstanding women and men with whom I've worked, thank you all from the bottom of my heart. Thank you for allowing me to be one of you, thank you for keeping me safe throughout my career, and thank you for the work you do every day. You are truly doing God's work, and never forget it. Please, my brothers and sisters in law enforcement, be careful out there and stay safe.

To my family who has been my support group throughout my career, I couldn't have done any of this without your love and support. I come from a very large family, too large to mention all of them without making this a "dedication book," but to my brothers and sisters, aunts and uncles, cousins and in-laws, thanks for always being there for me. To my little Italian mother, Mille grazie para tutti (she's Italian and she'll know what it means). She and my late father provided me with the two best role models that anyone could ever have.

To my children, our daughter Erika and her husband Jason, thanks for always being there and for giving us three beautiful grandkids, Kylie, Olivia, and Tanner Daniel.

To my son Christopher, thanks for always being a great son and a source of pride for your mother and me, and to your wife Kelly—we're very fortunate to have you in our family.

To my wife, well, you've been there with me since before the law enforcement chapter of my life began, and had it not been for you there's no way I could have accomplished anything that I've been fortunate to do in this career. I look forward with anticipation to the next chapter with you by my side. You will never know how much I appreciate having you in my life.

To the readers of this book, I wish you the best in your own careers, and I sincerely hope that you find this book both informative and useful when the next major case comes to your town.

CONTENTS

MAJOR CASE MANAGEMENT

Chapter 1

MAJOR CASES: GENERAL OVERVIEW

I 've had the privilege of teaching all over the world, and utilizing the Power Point presentations a great deal in my classes. Whenever I click on the overhead slide for the definition of "major case," I have the theme music playing from the 1985 Steven Spielberg thriller *Jaws,* based on the book by Peter Benchley. For those of you that saw the movie (which should be required viewing for everyone in the civilized world) you know that whenever you hear that familiar "ba-bump, ba-bump" sound, starting slowly but increasing in frequency, something very bad is going to happen, and somebody is going to get chomped by a great white shark. Besides the great special effects in this film, however, is the underlying story of Police Chief Martin Brody, excellently played by the late great actor Roy Scheider, who retired from NYPD to the quiet locale of fictitious "Amity Island." All this poor guy wanted to do was to forget the hustle and bustle of NYPD and end his career in this quaint tourist town on the ocean. But that was not meant to be. . . . Whenever the movie viewer hears that familiar theme, you know immediately that Chief Brody's whole life is going to turn upside down. He's going to start getting bothered by the tourists, the townspeople, the Mayor, the business owners, and everybody else. His quaint little town is going to go completely berserk, and it's up to him to take care of business.

The reason that I use this theme music in conjunction with the slide on the definition of a major case is because it is exactly what I want the students to think about when they get their next major case investigation. I want them to know what can happen to them is exactly what happened to Chief Brody on beautiful Amity Island. Their entire world can easily get thrown into turmoil, and both the immediate and the long-term impacts on them can be very substantial, and in some cases disastrous.

Where I come from, we call cases which could fit into the definition of major cases "heaters." We call them heaters because of all the heat that the person in charge of the investigation is going to feel coming down on them. They'll get heat from politicians, the community, business owners, and everybody else. Sometimes the heat is short-lived, usually it's not, and the heat can ruin careers. There are many (former) Chiefs and investigative managers out there whose careers ended with a major case going awry. There are some common obstacles for people who manage major cases, and those obstacles and methods to avoid them will be discussed in a later chapter. For now, let's define what a major case really is.

One definition that I've been using for years is *a real or suspected crime of such severity that it creates an intense public demand for identification, apprehension, and prosecution of the offender.* Major cases are serious crimes, and the degree of seriousness is a relative thing. In some communities which experience a great deal of violent crime, the crime would have to be very substantial to be considered serious. In other communities it might not have to be nearly as serious. There are some other definitions, however, and these should be considered as well.

Major cases also include *those crimes which necessitate a substantial commitment of resources for a prolonged period of time or which require the application of complex or unusual investigative techniques.* The mere fact that there will be the commitment of a huge amount of resources for a prolonged period of time could make almost any investigation a major case. Another element of a complete definition would be *any crime that induces significant public fear and evokes considerable media attention.* It is worth noting in this definition that the terms *significant and considerable* are based on your own definition, and these definitions will vary from community to community.

It must be made very clear that the definitions of major cases reflect absolutely a "relative concept." A murder in New York City or Los Angeles, in and of itself, might not constitute a major case, depending of course on who was killed and/or the circumstances of the murder. A similar crime in a community with little or no serious crime might just be the most significant crime that has ever taken place. In fact, in a community with little or no serious crime, an armed robbery or single sexual assault might fit into the definition of a major case–again, it's a relative concept.

The concept of "relativity," as it relates to major cases, is very similar to the relativity of drug enforcement efforts. A person selling ounces or even kilos of cocaine in some major cities in America might not be what could be considered a "big-time drug dealer," while someone selling dime bags ($10) of marijuana across the street from a Junior High in a smaller community might very well be an extremely important target for drug enforcement efforts.

COMMON ATTRIBUTES OF MAJOR CASES

Regardless of the type of crime involved, major cases seem to have some similar attributes which warrant exploration. These attributes might not all apply to the same cases, but usually one or more of them is present in virtually any major case. These attributes include the following:

- **A great deal of attention at the outset**. Many of these major cases immediately capture the attention of the public, and in some cases of the entire country. As printed media, TV, and radio transfers to the Internet, the speed with which news travels is phenomenal, and huge numbers of people can learn about any major crime in an instant.
- **Demand for additional resources**. The amount and type of resources that a law enforcement agency or agencies have to devote to the investigation of major cases can be very substantial. In fact, there have been many examples of major cases that have very quickly "broken" the budget of law enforcement agencies. There are ways to avoid this danger, however, which will be discussed in a later chapter.
- **Possibility of multiple agency involvement**. Many major case investigations involve multiple jurisdictions, and can also involve law enforcement agencies at the Federal, state, county, and municipal level simultaneously. Having a number of agencies involved in a joint investigation can result in some problems, most of which can be avoided, but the potential for problems is there nonetheless.
- **Stakeholder involvement outside of law enforcement**.

Similar to the example of "Chief Brody of Amity Island," the involvement of stakeholders outside the sphere of law enforcement, such as elected officials, business owners, the tourist industry, and other community organizations or individuals can also occur. If this is not addressed in an appropriate manner, it can be paralyzing for the law enforcement manager charged with investigating the major case. For the law enforcement command officer assigned to direct the major case investigation, this can be among the most significant areas of challenge.

• **Need for a modified organizational structure**. The investigation of major cases can necessitate the modification of an existing agency structure. If not handled properly, this can cause intra-agency and/or inter-agency friction that can negatively impact the investigation.

The investigation of major cases calls for complicated, demanding investigations that challenge the agencies tasked with solving them in unprecedented ways. They draw intense media and political attention, and are deemed to be "high profile cases," which causes significant internal and external pressures on the individual managing the investigative effort and on the agency itself. To effectively manage these major cases, the law enforcement profession must utilize expertise in two main areas:

Case Management. The utilization of effective case management skills in the major case investigation is critical. Of course, effective case management skills are necessary in the management of any type of investigation, but the problems inherent in not practicing effective case management are greatly exacerbated in the major case.

Incident Management. Since 9/11, police departments all over the country have become very familiar with the Incident Command System (ICS) for very good reason. The fire service has been managing incidents utilizing this system for many years, and it's about time that the law enforcement profession catches up. The Incident Command System allows for consistent responses to a variety of incidents, whether they be weather-related, criminal acts, or even terrorist incidents. The principles of ICS apply directly to many major cases, particularly those that started out as a very serious incident, such as a very high profile murder or other serious crime.

The law enforcement manager charged with the investigation of a major case will need to focus on creating order out of chaos. They must keep their options and agencies flexible in order to effectively respond to the ever-changing developments that typify major cases. The potential for chaos at the onset of the major case investigation is directly correlated to the gravity of the offense(s). In other words, the more serious the offense(s), the more potential there is for a great deal of chaos. This chaos can be overwhelming, but it can be avoided, but one must keep in mind that the potential is definitely there.

ROUTINE VS. MAJOR CASE INVESTIGATIONS

Most routine cases are conducted in a "bottom-up" manner, with the detective assigned to the investigation having primary responsibility for conducting the investigation. This means that the detective will be making many of the decisions regarding collecting and analyzing evidence, managing leads, and interviewing witnesses and suspects. The autonomy and freedom of movement necessary for detectives to perform their functions fits very neatly into this situation. The detective gets the case assigned, reviews the preliminary work done (usually by patrol officers) and then decides on an investigative plan of action. The really good detectives do this without so much as a second thought, it's almost as if they develop their plans and strategies on "autopilot."

In high profile or major cases, however, the investigation is usually conducted, at least to some extent, in the "top-down" manner, in which law enforcement executives and managers primarily control the investigation. The involvement of law enforcement executives and managers is necessitated to some extent by the notoriety of the case, and the larger the case it seems the more executive or managerial involvement will result. As you can imagine, this sometimes creates hard feelings for detectives, particular veteran detectives, who are used to running their own cases with little or no interference from their superiors. These hard feelings are exacerbated in situations where executives or investigative managers take total control or exert substantial influence over the case. This is significant because the usual "role" of the detective is being modified, and most competent people don't really care to have their professional roles modified.

The difficulties that can surface during major case investigations, although somewhat unavoidable, are not necessarily insurmountable, however, if the manager takes the time to recognize the disruption to the detective's routine and takes steps to avoid magnifying that disruption. These difficulties can emanate from the executives themselves, the detectives whose roles are being modified, or from both sides.

On the one hand, the personal involvement of the executive or manager in the investigation of the major case is quite frankly probably somewhat of a rarity, as their other duties preclude their personal involvement in the investigation of most cases. Their primary roles usually include providing leadership, support, and resources for the detectives who do this type of work every day. On the other hand, detectives must accept the fact that high profile and major cases truly "belong to everyone," not just to the detective assigned, as with routine cases. Sometimes even non-major case investigations take on a life of their own and start belonging to everyone for a variety of reasons. As an example, our agency was contacted for some minor vandalism to a residence in our community. The vandalism, which occurred during the high school football season, initially involved eggs being thrown at a residence. The family living in the residence had a teen-aged son, and the responding officer theorized that the vandalism might have something to do with the son. About a week later, the expensive vinyl fence surrounding the backyard of the same residence was spray-painted with obscenities, which was a significant increase in the amount of damage to the residence. In addition, the obscenities began to frighten the family, who continued to insist that the vandalism had nothing to do with their son. About a week later, a half-full bottle of vodka was thrown through the picture window, barely missing the family's 5-year-old daughter. At this juncture, the family called me as chief of police and demanded a meeting to discuss what was being done to investigate the matter. Prior to the meeting, I had a meeting with the detectives assigned and began making some suggestions as to what steps could be taken in the investigation. Of course, the detectives, all of whom were extremely competent investigators, took some offense at my involvement in the matter. Once I explained that the incidents had risen to the level where my involvement was being dictated by the escalation of the incidents, and that my personal involvement would continue until the matter was resolved, they began to understand. In other words, this investigation no longer belonged to the detectives investigating the matter, it now belonged to the entire department. Fortunately, we were able to determine who the three juvenile perpetrators were, and we made three arrests.

There are many major cases where chiefs and/or sheriffs feel that they must become more involved because of the enormous public pressure and community fear caused by the major case. This is probably true to some extent, but chiefs and sheriffs still need to balance their involvement so that it does not become counterproductive.

There's another problem inherent in the involvement of some chiefs or sheriffs in major case investigations, however, and this problem can become a sticky issue very quickly. The fact is that not every police executive is capable of being a primary investigator. Many police executives, many chiefs, and many sheriffs have never been a detective at any point in their career. While lacking any investigative background might not have a detrimental effect on their everyday duties, this lack of background will probably have an extremely negative effect on their ability to become personally involved in a major case investigation. They may be someone who has never conducted any type of investigation, and now they're going to start with a major case.

The bigger problem is that many of these law enforcement executives, chiefs, or sheriffs don't know (or won't admit) that they are not capable of being a primary investigator, much less the manager of a major case investigation. The best bosses I had throughout my career all had one thing in common, they were smart enough to know that they didn't know everything. Unfortunately, many law enforcement executives, chiefs, or sheriffs are still laboring under the delusion that they are *supposed* to know everything, and they spend a great deal of time trying to convince their subordinates that they do. This often ends in varying degrees of disaster.

PRIMARY GOALS AND KEY ELEMENTS OF SUCCESS

The primary goal of the major case investigation is to effectively manage all aspects of the major case investigation in order to achieve crisis resolution, a solution to the investigation, and, if warranted, successful prosecution of the case. Successful major case management includes the following key elements:

1. **Careful Planning and Preparation**. Not the first day of the major case, but well ahead of time. Prior planning for the major case will be discussed in a later chapter, and the necessity for careful planning and preparation for the next major case cannot be overemphasized.
2. **Defined Roles and Responsibilities**. The roles and responsibilities of all investigative and non-investigative personnel must be clearly defined. In addition, however, the roles and responsibilities of non-law enforcement personnel and other stakeholders must also be carefully considered, defined, and assigned. If this is not done properly, critical matters will not get addressed, and the chances to successfully conclude the major case investigation will diminish greatly.
3. **Managing Information Effectively**. This relates to incoming and outgoing information as well as the information provided to the personnel actually involved in the investigation itself. Each and every bit of information must be viewed as potentially critical to the investigation and handled appropriately.
4. **Maintaining Effective Communication**. This relates to internal and external communications, as well as interactions and communication with the media, the public, elected officials, and other stakeholders. Effective communications can spell the difference between a professionally managed investigation and a disaster.

As mentioned in the introduction to this book, sometimes it seems like "you just can't win" on these major cases, but in subsequent chapters a number of strategies will be discussed which will hopefully make the investigation of these major cases somewhat easier. There are a number of different responses that law enforcement agencies have used to address the various types of major cases, and there are a number of errors and obstacles that major case managers must avoid. These will be discussed in Chapter 2.

Chapter 2

TYPES OF MAJOR CASES
AND OBSTACLES TO SUCCESS

There are many types of major cases, and many obstacles to success. In addition, there are some "common errors" committed by major case managers that seem to happen all over the world. I myself have committed many, if not all, of these common errors at one point or another, and it is advantageous if discussing my own mistakes and errors can help someone else from repeating them.

Types of Major Cases

Major cases seem to fall into various categories, and although the basic responses and goals of major case management are common to all types, the manner in which these cases are investigated will vary to some extent. Types of major cases include:

Sensational Single Incidents. Once again, keep in mind the relativity of these types of incidents. In these single incident investigations, the police, particularly in areas of low crime, are under a tremendous amount of pressure to immediately solve the case, because "things like that just don't happen here." In addition, due to the fact that there may not be any similar crimes, the populous is terrified, which heightens their demand for a quick resolution, again putting the police under a tremendous amount of pressure. Although a sensational single incident might involve only one actual offense, these situations can become sensationalized by virtue of:

1. **Type of area in which the crime occurs**. When the incident occurred at Columbine High School in Jefferson County,

Colorado in 1999, the entire country was in shock to think that two high school students could wreak such havoc. Littleton, Colorado is an upscale community located in Jefferson County. According to conversations that I've had with Jefferson County law enforcement officials who were among the law enforcement personnel responding to the situation, many people in the area, including some law enforcement personnel, were astounded that something like that happened in a nice area like Littleton.

2. **Peculiarities of the offense itself**. Sometimes the heinous nature of the offense can sensationalize a single incident. A dismembered body, particularly brutal murder, or a totally senseless killing all fall into this category.

3. **Identity of the victim**. This can sensationalize a single incident, particularly if the victim is seen as "defenseless or vulnerable," such as an extremely young or elderly victim. In 1993, two ten-year-old abductors, Jon Venables and Robert Thompson, took James Bulger, a 2-year-old London boy, from a shopping mall in London. The toddler was led through streets to a railway siding where he was tortured, killed and his body abandoned across the track. For weeks following the murder, the grainy videotape from the mall of the young boy being led away by his killers was repeatedly shown on international television. The image of the defenseless young boy being led to his death was forever etched into the minds of the viewers of the video. The two killers were released from state custody in 2001, and in 2008, Bulger's mother, Denise Fergus, successfully sued a video game company that used the shopping mall footage that assisted the police in capturing the killers in a video game called "Law and Order." In the event that the victim is from a prominent family, a single incident might also be sensationalized.

4. **Identity of the offender**. There is perhaps no better example of this than the O. J. Simpson murder case. Although there were 1,811 murders in Los Angeles County in 1994, the attention of the world was riveted on just two of them, which had occurred during a single incident. In these cases the bulk of the media attention gets so focused on the offender that the victims become secondary. In fact, I have often asked my classes how many of them can remember the name of the second victim in the case, besides Simpson's ex-wife, Nicole Brown-Simpson. One might

be surprised that even many cops cannot remember the name of Ronald Goldman.

Multiple Incident or Crime Pattern Investigations. These types of major cases can involve either a series of crimes, large number of crimes, or a pattern of crimes, and include "serial type" offenses. A "spree" offender is someone who involves several victims in a short time in multiple locations. For example, the U.S. Bureau of Justice Statistics defines a spree killing as "killings at two or more locations with almost no time break between murders."

Serial offenders involve more than one incident, usually in different locations, with a "cooling-off" period in between incidents. "Mass offenders" may have multiple victims, but they typically stick to one location.

These multiple incident investigations are much more difficult for police, as the investigation is taking place while additional crimes are being committed. This can give the appearance to the public that the police are powerless to stop the perpetrator(s) and can lead to general panic, which in some of these cases, is exactly the message that the perpetrator(s) want the public to receive.

Extended Resource–Long Term Investigations. In these types of major case investigations, although the offense might not even be known publicly, the expenditure of resources on the investigation might be crippling to the agency or agencies involved, thereby making it a major case. An example might be a long-term narcotics conspiracy investigation, where huge amounts of manpower and resources are devoted to an investigation that might go on for years.

The expenditures on these extended resource/long-term investigations can also be the source of internal friction within the agency. The typical budget for any municipality can be viewed as a "pie," and each department in the municipality has their own slice of that same pie. If one department, the police, for example, uses up their own allocated "slice" of the budget pie and then goes asking for additional funding for a long-term investigation it's just a matter of time before some other department's slice gets impacted. This can cause hard feelings and friction, particularly if the expenditures for the major case are viewed as being made to the exclusion of everything else. Jealously often arises in these long-term investigations, as some people see involvement in a major case as a way to gain fame and notoriety, and sometimes careers have been made or broken on these cases. Many successful prosecutors have utilized their reputations as "crimebusters" in campaigns for other elected positions.

Even when the incident that initiated the long-term investigation has waned in importance, if the incident is serious enough investigative resources might still need to be dedicated to the investigation for a long period of time.

Multi-jurisdictional Major Cases. These can be among the most difficult major cases to manage, due to the variety of issues inherent in multiagency operations. In the next chapter we will discuss multi-agency response and investigative task forces.

Undercover and Sting Projects. Although not usually considered "major cases," I'm adding this category due to the massive expenditures of manpower and other resources. These are often of a very sensitive and/or dangerous nature.

HOW POLICE BECOME INVOLVED

The method in which police become involved in the investigation of major cases can vary from agency to agency, with some common attributes.

Primary Jurisdictional Roles. The majority of major case investigations start out as situations involving primary jurisdictional roles. The major case occurs in a single jurisdiction, and is initially handled by the patrol division. There is no question whose jurisdiction is involved, and the assignment of investigative personnel will probably come from a single agency. In cases such as these, uniformed personnel should be utilized as much as possible. Uniformed personnel can perform many functions that do not necessitate investigative personnel, such as conducting thorough preliminary investigations; crime scene protection; area and neighborhood searches; and to provide an easily recognizable uniformed presence in hostile areas.

- The biggest problem with major cases that involve primary jurisdiction is that these cases are often the cause of the most headaches, due to the fact that the law enforcement personnel who are charged with investigating the incident are known throughout the community, and in the event that the investigation is not cleared immediately, it is they who often bear the brunt of the criticism and second guessing.

Request for Assistance from Law Enforcement Agencies. Some major case investigations are initiated based on a request from the originating agency to another law enforcement agency. Many times these requests are made to Federal, state, or county agencies, due to their larger number of resources or their greater expertise.

The type of assistance requested can include a request to:

- Take over the entire investigation, with no involvement at all from the originating agency
- Work jointly in an informal cooperative effort with the originating agency
- Become involved in some type of a "task force" structure to handle the investigation
- Provide consulting services to the originating agency due to some perceived expertise

The problem in these situations for the agencies whose assistance is being requested is that they are often at a loss to turn requesting agencies down, particularly when assistance is requested by an agency with limited resources or expertise. These situations are not without their own unique problems, however, which usually emanate from the fact that the originating agency has sometimes already "handled" the case for a period of time, and another agency gets called in to "straighten it out." Having spent the majority of my career with a large state agency whose assistance was routinely requested, I've been in this situation on a number of occasions, with varying degrees of success. This often happens when agencies feel compelled to handle the matter themselves because the incident happened in their jurisdiction, but then find themselves "over their heads" and sorely in need of assistance.

- Crime scene personnel have already been over the scene, witnesses may be reluctant to speak with new investigator after having already been "handled," and the personnel from the originat-

ing agency may resent the introduction of outsiders to "their
case."

- In the event that an agency does agree to such a request for assistance, they must insist on receiving documentation of all work
accomplished prior to their entry into the investigation, to include
all reports, photos, interviews, notes, outstanding leads, and anything else that was done.

Request for Assistance from non-Police Agencies. In addition to
requests for assistance from law enforcement agencies, occasionally
requests are received from non-police agencies, such as prosecutor's
offices, based on their desire for a solid, prosecutable case, compounded by the fear that the originating agency might not provide
them with one. In cases such as these, you can usually count on resentment on the part of the originating agency, as their case is being
"stolen" by the assisting agency. Having the prosecutor's office make
it clear that this will be a "joint investigation" (if that is workable) may
decrease some of this resentment.

- In cases such as this, the agency providing the assistance must
insist on all reports, photos, interviews, and leads. They must not
settle for a review of the paperwork, however, they should also
insist on speaking to the personnel from the originating agency
who conducted the investigation. I can guarantee that in most
cases this will be a difficult and uncomfortable discussion. The
"new investigation" being conducted by the agency providing the
assistance must begin with the work done by the originating
agency. Unfortunately, the agency that is asked to provide the
assistance can't assume that the original work was done thoroughly, and in fact may have to (as much as possible) "start from
scratch" and re-do the previous work.
- I vividly recall being put into a situation in which young man was
kidnapped at the point of a shotgun in one suburb and less than
an hour later a murder occurred in an adjoining suburb. The victim was the kidnap victim from the initial suburb, and he was
murdered for his shoes, pants, and warm-up jacket in the adjoining suburb. It was immediately obvious that the murder was
merely a continuation of the kidnapping, but there was a major

problem—the detectives from the suburb in which the murder took place didn't trust the detectives from the suburb in which the kidnapping took place and vice versa, and therefore did not communicate with them. The prosecutor's office was at a loss and requested that the state police get involved in the investigation, and come to their office to "mediate" this stalemate and assign personnel to work with both agencies to investigate the kidnapping/murder. Fortunately for me, I knew detectives from both agencies very well, but even I wasn't prepared for walking into the prosecutor's conference room and seeing them refusing to face each other across the table. They all treated me cordially, but if I would address one agency the other agency wouldn't speak to me until I was done and began to address them directly. Fortunately, cooler heads prevailed, and we arrested the offenders (still wearing the shoes, jacket and blood-stained pants of the victim) for this and two additional murders.

Insertion/Injection Roles. This method, common to Sheriff's departments and state and Federal agencies, involves the forced "insertion" of the assisting agency into the investigation. This is among the most difficult types of major case scenario to manage, due to the hard feelings that are caused by an outside agency being forced into a case.

- The best method for avoiding a complete meltdown and getting the investigation rolling along is for an understanding to be reached with the originating agency's leadership and the "inserted" agency's leadership that although the investigation will be worked jointly, that the agency being brought in for assistance will be there for the duration. Perhaps the best method for immediate integration of the different agencies is for detectives from the originating agency to be "partnered up" with a detective from the outside agency. This will usually result in them finding a common ground and working together. It has been my experience that when you carefully examine most inter-agency relationships, the workers seem to get along pretty well, and often the problems stem from command personnel.

MAJOR CASE POLICE RESPONSE

- There have been a number of police responses to major case investigations over the years, and although they vary in sophistication, most are based on the idea of open communication and cooperation.

Investigative Conferences

The first investigative conference of which I am familiar is the one held at the Texas Department of Public Safety in 1980, which (unknowingly at the time) was looking at a series of murders later attributed to Henry Lee Lucas. The conference included representatives from 32 city 2nd county jurisdictions attended, and during the conference several new leads were developed. Following the arrest of Lucas, another conference was held at the Monroe, LA Police Department in October and January, 1983. Similar conferences have been convened in response to the "Green River Killings" in Washington, and by the Regional Organized Crime Information Center and other agencies in areas throughout the country.

Information Clearinghouses

Information clearinghouses are similar to investigative conferences, although they remain in operation over an extended period of time. The Texas Department of Public Safety hosted such a clearinghouse regarding Henry Lee Lucas from 1983–85. During this period they coordinated interviews of Lucas and provided information to agencies requesting assistance. They conducted preliminary interviews for interested agencies, and coordinated the interviews of numerous agencies. Ultimately, approximately 1,000 interviews took place by 600 different agencies. Numerous criminal cases were cleared, many of which were alleged to have been committed by Lucas.

Investigative Consultants

To my knowledge, the first time that the idea of investigative consultants was used was during the Atlanta Child Murder Case. The Atlanta child murders, were a series of murders committed in Atlanta, Georgia from the summer of 1979 until the spring of 1981. Over the two-year period, twenty-nine African-American children, adolescents and adults were killed. During the investigation, in an effort to provide the Atlanta investigators with some outside assistance, five investigators were selected from a nationally-nominated pool. They traveled to Atlanta, working for two weeks alongside Atlanta area detectives. While the consultants didn't actually solve the case, they were able to provide some different direction and leads.

The case doesn't have to be as high-profile as the Atlanta Child Murder case, however, and I have been involved in similar consultations for investigations that were major cases but much less noteworthy. The idea behind these consultations is to get a group of trained and experienced professionals together to look at an incident or series of incidents and provide their professional opinions.

Centralized Investigative Networks

Perhaps the best known such network is the Violent Criminal Apprehension Program (VICAP) of the Federal Bureau of Investigation, which collects, collates, and analyzes information on unsolved and potentially serial murders and searches for similar pattern characteristics across reporting jurisdictions. Once the data is submitted by a law enforcement agency and analyzed, the analysis can be sent back to the contributors to determine if patterns or similarities exist with other open cases. The technology that is now in use for VICAP submissions has taken a very good system and made it much better and more "user-friendly." The latest version allows law enforcement agencies to input data and receive responses on-line, which is extremely convenient.

ERRORS AND OBSTACLES IN THE
MAJOR CASE INVESTIGATION

Although the following seven errors have often been committed by major case managers, myself included, they are not inexorably linked to major case management, and in fact they can all be avoided. When teaching the class on "Major Case Management," after discussing these common errors I usually ask students if they themselves have ever committed them, or if they know of other investigative managers who have. I have yet to have a class where someone wasn't "intimately familiar" with at least some of these errors, and in most cases all of them. These common errors include:

1. **The complexity of the investigation is initially underestimated.** The problem with this common error is that eventually the person managing the major case investigation will come to the realization that they have underestimated their response. Once they do make a proper assessment of the complexity of the investigation, however, the disparity, the actual complexity of the investigation, and the inadequacy of their response to the investigation has become too substantial to offset.

As an example—the person managing the major case investigation should have responded with twenty investigators, they instead responded with five. When they realize that they don't have enough personnel they put out a frantic call for additional manpower. The problem is that now they're playing "catch-up," and the time that it will take to bring the additional fifteen investigators up to speed and to the same level of knowledge about the case as the original investigators can become insurmountable.

This error is particularly commonplace in communities with little major crimes or incidents. They can become so overwhelmed by the gravity of the offense that they underestimate their response, reasoning "things that bad just don't happen here." Another pitfall is their reluctance to appear as "alarmists" and in doing so "water-down" their response by utilizing smaller numbers of personnel or other resources.

This is also very common in communities where the police department (or the chief) is unwilling or reluctant to request assistance, or sometimes too pig-headed to accept it when offered. I am familiar with a multiple murder case that occurred in a community with an extremely small amount of serious crime. When the murder occurred, several agencies at the Federal, state, county, and municipal levels all offered assistance to the department in whose jurisdiction the multiple murders had occurred. Even though this department had never handled anything this complex, and even though they had no investigators who had ever handled anything remotely similar to this investigation, they flatly turned down all offers of assistance. Comments were made by the chief of this agency that although he thanked the other agencies for their offers, he told them that they would be called if and when the need arose. This response reminded me of a quote that I once read in the July 1996 issue of *Police Chief Magazine,* the official publication of the International Association of Chiefs of Police: "Certainly the traditional safeguarding of turf is a problem in many jurisdictions. Some chiefs feel threatened by the suggestion that they are unable to successfully investigate a major crime without the assistance of outside experts. Unfortunately, they may be protecting their egos at the victim's expense as the crime goes unsolved."

Many communities (and chiefs) have learned the hard way that sometimes it is better to swallow some pride and accept the assistance that is offered for the good of the investigation. Some of the most high profile murder cases in the U.S. have involved similar responses by chiefs (usually *former* chiefs) who have learned this lesson the hard way.

The best way to avoid this error is to assume nothing, and err on the side of safety. Look at the major case as a complex investigative effort and plan accordingly. If later it becomes apparent that this is not a complex incident but instead is something much simpler, you'll be very well (if not overly) prepared to address it. It's like investigating what initially appears to be a suicide, which most really good investigators treat as if they are a homicide investigation until proven otherwise.

2. **The investigation proceeds too quickly without adequate planning and control.** In major cases, the typical police response to "quickly react" might not be the best approach, but unfortunately these cases are sometimes treated as "crimes in progress" calls, rather than the complex investigations that they in fact are. Without adequate planning and control right from the onset, the major case manager runs the risk of the investigation sinking quickly into chaos.

I always advise investigative managers that the first thing that they need to do when confronted with a major case is to sit down with a legal pad and start making some notes regarding what they intend to do. Better than the blank pages of the legal pad, however, would be to utilize a planning document that forces you to keep on track, such as the one suggested in *Appendix 1,* which will be discussed in detail in Chapter 4. This plan includes such elements as manpower allocation, crime scene response and management, location of resources, and operational, support, and investigative personnel considerations. Sometimes just the fact that you're sitting down in a quiet location (assuming you can find one amid the chaos) and thinking things through can calm you down and help you think more clearly.

One of the biggest considerations that the major case manager must confront is manpower acquisition and allocation. Planning for the acquisition of personnel is something that must be handled immediately, particularly if the investigation involves a multiagency response and personnel are going to come from more than one agency. Having enough personnel on hand to initiate investigate efforts, in my opinion, is like carrying a gun off-duty. It has always been my personal philosophy that I'd much rather *have* the gun and *not need it* than to *need* the gun and not have it. If you initially overestimate the number of personnel that you need and seek to acquire more than you need, so what? You'd be much better off having too many personnel and sending some home the next day than having too few and having to play "catch-up" to get more.

I once read where a (former) chief justified his turning down of offered manpower by saying that additional personnel would result in too many people stumbling over each other, confusing the issue, and going in all directions. I can't understand how any major case manager utilizing effective planning and control would allow personnel assigned to a major case to stumble over each other or go off in all directions. With proper planning and control, these things are much less likely to happen.

3. **The investigation moves too quickly from the evidence gathering phase to the investigative phase.** There are only so many people that can be utilized in the evidence gathering phase, and that leaves idle detectives who want to get something started. The evidence gathering portion of the major case investigation might not be the "fun" part (except perhaps to the crime scene investigators), but the information and leads gained at the crime scene during the evidence gathering phase can provide needed direction for personnel involved in the investigative phase. Without that direction, investigative time and effort can be wasted.

Having a roomful of detectives "chomping at the bit" to get the investigation started and then having to "rein them in" for a short time until you know in which direction you'd like to point them can be frustrating for both the detectives and the major case manager, but it is sometimes necessary in order to utilize your resources in the most efficient and effective manner possible. Making certain that any and all immediate information available from the crime scene or evidence gathering phase is available and utilized in assignment of activity will preclude the major case manager from committing this error.

4. **Too many, or in some cases all of the resources are initially spent on the obvious investigation "avenues or theories."** It is human nature to sometimes quickly come up with a "theory" of how a crime happened. It is also good investigative practice to follow the investigative "avenues" that the evidence presents, but one must keep in mind that if these theories or avenues end up reaching a dead end, it's often too late to go back and re-do the primary steps.

Oftentimes, the first or most obvious investigative theory becomes the focus of all of the attention, even though it may be a faulty theory. This is particularly true if the theory presented happens to be the theory of the chief or sheriff. In these cases, there may be some investigative personnel (or even investigative managers) who want to curry favor with the law enforcement executive and will direct too many (or all) resources at their theory. In one of the case studies that will be examined, a (former) chief wanted all resources directed at his theory, which, it was ultimately discovered, had little if anything to do with what actually happened.

The best method to avoid committing this error is to assume nothing and verify everything. While theories can be helpful to the major case manager, it is more prudent to continually look at theories from the perspective of the fact that while they might be viable, they might also turn out to be wrong. Keeping this in mind and focusing resources on other avenues at the same time that you are exploring your investigative theories or avenues should keep you from committing too many resources to something that might backfire and leave you hanging.

5. **Too many people make too many incorrect assumptions about who is responsible for what and what's being done.** As was mentioned earlier, there is a great propensity for a major case investigation to become chaotic, and that propensity is directly correlated to the gravity of the offense. Without a firm control and organized efforts right from the start, incorrect assumptions can be made, which can result in work being duplicated, not accomplished, or never even considered. Rather than make assumptions, documenting the work that is being done and to whom that work is assigned should help you to avoid committing this error.

6. **Too often, the first viable suspect that emerges becomes the**

"be all . . . end all" suspect," and valuable time pursuing other leads is lost as all efforts are directed at the suspect of the moment. This error is extremely difficult to avoid, particularly when investigating a case that is very heinous or emotional. In these cases, it is easy to get frustrated to the point of somehow wanting to "will" the suspect to be the offender. In a similar manner to error #4, this is the time for the major case manager to continually ask themselves what additional efforts they should be making on the chance that this is not the offender. There aren't too many situations in life where it is a good idea to "second-guess" oneself, but if it is ever appropriate, this is the time to do it.

The best example I can think of was a multiple murder investigation in which one of the theories was that the crimes might have been committed by a disgruntled employee, who had somehow come back to wreak revenge on the business owner and employees. Imagine the surprise of the investigators assigned to the case when the day after the discovery of the bodies they developed information on a disgruntled employee who had, a month earlier when he was fired, threatened to "come back and get" the manager. Unfortunately, as with many "too good to be true" situations, this was not the offender. Of course, it was good sound investigative practice to pick up the disgruntled employee for questioning, but it was not good sound investigative practice to cease all other efforts because of being convinced that the suspect "had to be the guy." When it turned out that the disgruntled employee had nothing at all to do with the murders and he had to be released, the nearly five days that he was held and questioned turned out to be wasted time, and the valuable time that should have been devoted to other investigative efforts was lost forever.

7. **Managers or executives who, for whatever reason, become personally involved in investigative responsibilities.** Particularly with very serious and high profile cases, many law enforcement executives, whether they are capable of actually investigating anything or not, have a tendency to become personally involved in the operational aspects of the major case investigation. In addition, sometimes the major case managers, who should be supporting the efforts of investigative personnel and acquiring resources for them to be able to perform their duties, also begin performing detective's tasks. This usually leaves detectives uncertain about their role and how to make a meaningful contribution to the investigation, and causes a great deal of frustration.

In the next chapter we will explore some responses of police agencies to major cases, including the formation of task forces to address these situations.

CASE STUDY #1: MULTIPLE MURDER TASK FORCE

VICTIMOLOGY: This was a multiple murder case, which involved six victims.

Victim #1–54-year-old Black Male owner of a grocery store
Victim #2–20-year-old Black Male, stock clerk at the store and nephew of Victim #1
Victim #3–17-year-old White Male gas station attendant
Victim #4–25-year-old White Male gas station & mini-mart attendant
Victim #5–21-year-old White Male manager of a "Radio Shack" store, located in a "strip mall" at a shopping center
Victim #6–28-year-old Male White customer of the "Radio Shack" store

MAJOR CASE CONSIDERATIONS: This was considered a "Major Case" due to the following elements:

- Number of victims (6)
- Extensive media coverage
- Climate of terror within the impacted communities
- Multiagency task force involvement

GEOGRAPHICS: Victims #1–#4 were all killed in a mid-sized (65,000) Midwestern city. Victims #5 & #6 were both killed in a small shopping center just over the state line in a neighboring state.

SPECIFIC FACTS: These six murders took place over an 7-day period.

Incident #1: Victims #1 & #2 were both shot several times (head & body) with two different weapons–two days later,
Incident #2: Victim #3 shot twice with the same weapon–two days later,
Incident #3: Victim #4 shot five times with the same weapon–two days later,
Incident #4: Victim #5 & #6 shot several times with two different weapons

Some of the victims had post-mortem gunshot wounds, and in most of the cases some cash or items were taken. In the last incident a police scanner was taken. There were no witnesses to any of the incidents, and no physical evidence recovered at the scene, with the exception of the projectiles, recovered from the bodies during autopsies.

IMMEDIATE ACTION TAKEN: The local police launched an extensive investigation after the first incident, and had the majority of their Investigative Division assigned to the case. Although assistance was offered from Federal, state, and county law enforcement agencies, all offers of assistance were refused.

Every time that the investigation started moving along, another murder would occur, and throw the investigation back into "response mode." This was not only frustrating for the investigators assigned, but it made the community wonder if the police department, which was extremely professional, were equipped to handle this type of a series of murders. In addition, the media was totally negative, highlighting the multiple murder aspects, publicly stating that the police department was "over its head" at best, and inferring incompetence.

The community was terrified, sales of weapons went up, rumors ran rampant, and many citizens began openly arming themselves, particularly persons working at gas stations, mini-marts, and other business of that type with a high amount of pedestrian traffic. When an ex-con suspect was finally developed, it was learned that he had left the area shortly after the last murders and traveled to a southern state. Investigators were sent to the southern state, where they located and arrested the suspect. Two weapons were recovered from the personal property of the suspect, which were lined through ballistics to the murders.

There was still no hard evidence to put the suspect in the city at the time of the murders however, and this link was not made until a cash register receipt, left in a car once used by the suspect, led to his being positively identified as having been in the city at the time of the murders.

MAJOR DIFFICULTIES: Following several weeks of investigative effort, the Governor of the state sent the director of the state police agency to meet with the mayor of the community in which the first five murders had occurred. Following the meeting, and against the strong objections of the chief of police of the city, the state police was (forcibly) "injected" into the investigation.

Ten state police detectives were selected for the assignment, with the promise of as many additional detectives as it would take to solve the case. The state police personnel selected for the task force had never worked together before, and most were completely unfamiliar with the area in which the crimes had occurred.

LESSONS LEARNED:

1. When dealing with an unknown subject murder, make certain that an absolutely thorough background is conducted on the victim(s). Following the final murders, a thorough background investigation was conducted on the first two victims. The grocery store owner, a fixture in the community, had, approximately eight years earlier, called the city's police department when a customer that the store owner knew to be wanted in an armed robbery entered his store. The city police department responded to the scene and arrested the customer, who was convicted and sentenced to 10–20 years in prison. When he was released after serving eight years of his sentence, one of the first things that he did was to go to the store and kill the store owner. The store owner's nephew was apparently in the "wrong place at the wrong time," as there was no connection between the killer and the nephew.

2. When dealing with multiple victims of separate incidents, consider using the "team approach," assigning a team of officers to separate victim investigations. In this investigative task force, the investigators were divided into four teams, with one incident assigned to each team. This allowed the investigators assigned to the individual incidents to become intimately familiar with the individual incidents and the victims. When strategic briefings were held (twice per day), all personnel were able to be briefed on the specifics and particulars of these individual investigations, thereby keeping them appraised of what was occurring in the overall investigative effort.

3. When dealing with situations in which a law enforcement agency is forcibly "injected" into an investigation, it is critical that to immediately establish a positive working relationship

between the agencies involved. One method of doing this is to "partner" members of the agencies together. This will allow them to become acquainted with each other, to share investigative expertise, and to share the intimate knowledge of the geographic area, the community, and the criminal element in the community.

4. Don't allow personnel to overlook or trivialize minor leads, insist on thorough completion of all leads, no matter how seemingly insignificant they may appear. In this investigation, there was no hard evidence to place the suspect in the city in which the murders occurred when they happened. The discovery of a cash register receipt in a vehicle used by the suspect led to his being positively identified as having made a purchase in a store located approximately two blocks from the scene of the first double murder, approximately an hour prior to the murders. This cash register receipt, which bore no store name or address, was very instrumental in linking the suspect to the area, in a manner very similar to the parking ticket which helped capture the "Son of Sam" serial killer in New York.

5. Don't allow investigators to relax prematurely once the offender is identified/caught, oftentimes that's when the real work begins. Once this suspect was arrested and brought back to the city, there was a great deal of work left to be done to "firm up" the case against the suspect.

CASE RESOLUTION: The suspect was convicted for all four of the murders which occurred in the original state, and both murders which occurred in the neighboring state. The first four convictions resulted in the suspect receiving the death penalty, and after almost fifteen years of appeals he was executed by lethal injection. Some of the family members of his victims attended the execution, and although the law enforcement personnel who had worked the case were invited, I know of none who attended.

Chapter 3

THE USE OF TASK FORCES IN
MAJOR CASE INVESTIGATIONS

Throughout my career, I have been involved with a number of multiple agency operations, other work groups, and task forces. Many times these methods are designed to increase the amount of available manpower to address whatever crime problem or incident has occurred.

It seems that whether economic times are good or bad, municipal, county, and sometimes even state law enforcement agencies are often strapped for personnel, which can negatively impact the management of major cases. It is also true that individual law enforcement agencies, particularly small to mid-sized agencies, are beginning to realize that "we can't always do it alone," and as a result are seeking non-traditional approaches to incidents, crime problems, or even major case investigations.

One of the most common approaches to address the lack of personnel and sometimes the lack of expertise is to become involved in multiagency Mutual Aid Agreements, Memoranda of Understanding, or the use of Task Forces. These approaches often allow the municipal, county, or state agency to augment manpower with which to address the major case investigation.

As with any agreement between units of a single agency or between multiple agencies, the keys to success involve preparation and careful planning. It is strongly recommended that this planning and preparation take place long before the major incident occurs, not the first day of the major case investigation to address the incident. The chaos which often accompanies a major incident and the difficulties which

30

are involved with initiating the response to investigate that incident(s) usually do not allow enough time for much planning or preparation.

If your agency has any inclination to become involved in either a Mutual Aid Agreement or a Memorandum of Understanding with other agencies that would be used to address major case investigations, the planning of these documents should take place well in advance of any plans to activate these agreements.

In order to start planning for such an agreement, the agencies which are interested in initiating such an agreement need to carefully research their own policies as well as state laws relating to such agreements. There are states which have restrictions on mutual aid agreements or memorandums of understanding between agencies. As an example, in the state of Virginia the only agencies that can enter into mutual aid agreements are those that share a common border. Other states have their own regulations which need to be researched.

MUTUAL AID AGREEMENTS

Law enforcement agencies often find themselves in positions where a method is needed which allows officers to assist one another across jurisdictional lines with full police powers. These occasions are becoming more frequent in situations when communities/agencies are close together geographically, which occurs with some regularity during "urban sprawl," where large numbers of suburbs spring up overnight as people leave major cities. As an example, there are over 100 separate police agencies in Cook County, IL, whose borders nearly overlap in some areas. Each of these agencies has their own policies and procedures, and for any mutual assistance to take place, there must be some documentation that would permit it. Without this documentation allowing such a mutual effort, questions with regard to liability would no doubt arise, as would questions relating to: officer's compensation due to personal injury, death, pension, insurance, workmen's compensation, salary, expenses, and other benefits.

Law enforcement needs only to look to the fire service for guidance on the best manner in which to design these agreements. The fire service has been "light-years" ahead of law enforcement with regard to mutual aid and assistance. The Mutual Aid Box Alarm System (MABAS), in use throughout the United States, is an excellent example. When the MABAS system is activated or put into place, the requesting fire agency knows immediately how many fire departments are going to respond, what the type of apparatus will be arriving, and the number of personnel and specialists that will be included. I have been on several fire scenes when firefighters and equipped arrived from outside jurisdictions, and the speed and efficiency with which these firefighters are able to assist each other is virtually seamless.

In recent years the law enforcement profession has seen the benefits of such a system. In the state of Illinois, law enforcement agencies have formed the Illinois Law Enforcement Assistance System (ILEAS), which has proven very valuable for a variety of natural disasters, crowd control, civil disturbances, and other events.

It seems that although agreements are commonplace for natural disasters, such as weather-related incidents, they are not as common for "law enforcement emergencies," such as those generated by a major incident which would result in a major case investigation. By appropriately utilizing a mutual aid agreement or memorandum of understanding, agency heads can address a broad range of situations, including major case investigations.

Types of Mutual Aid Agreements

There are basically two types of mutual aid agreements, Voluntary Cooperation and Requested Operational Assistance.

- **Voluntary Cooperation:** Mutual aid agreements are written agreements between two or more law enforcement agencies which permits voluntary cooperation and assistance for natural disasters or matters of a "routine" law enforcement nature across jurisdictional lines. Often, agencies with mutual boundaries are involved in these types of agreements. As an example, many agencies become involved in "Emergency Communications Agreements," which allow for one agency to take over the communications for another during power outages or other loss of communications equipment.
- **Requested Operational Assistance:** Mutual aid agreements are written to include language to address what could be considered "law enforcement emergencies," and usually included occurrences, which might be accidental, natural, or caused by man, and

which result or may result in substantial injury or harm to the population or substantial damage to or loss of property. These incidents might include exceptional "single event" situations such as protests, dignitary visits, hostage situations, air crashes, and/or natural disasters. As an example, I was involved in a number of KKK and Nazi demonstrations which involved multiple agencies. These multiagency incidents were usually very short duration (1–2 days), and usually involved a single or perhaps a few locations.

Required Elements of Mutual Aid Agreements

Prior to entering into a mutual aid agreement, agencies must research their own regulations and policies, as well as any applicable local, county, or state laws to make certain that participation in such an agreement is permitted. Most mutual aid agreements that allow for agencies to address the types of "law enforcement emergencies" that involve major case investigations have certain required elements, to include the following:

1. The nature of the law enforcement assistance to be rendered. This can be specific to the point where specific criminal acts are mentioned as being covered by the agreement. Without such wording and setting of some parameters, assistance from participating agencies could be requested for not only major incidents like murders, but for more mundane duties such as parking enforcement. This could become very cumbersome very quickly.

2. The agency that shall bear any liability arising from acts assumed under the agreement. This might be worded so that the agency making the request for assistance, or the agency in whose jurisdiction the activity occurs would assume all liability for acts taken under the agreement. On the other hand, some agreements address the question of liability by stating that liability for the actions of the individual participants in any mutual aid response would fall to the individual agencies employing those individuals.

3. The procedures for requesting and for authorizing assistance. Without such wording, mutual aid agreements are sometimes abused. Situations can arise where the agreement is being used for law enforcement assistance that is either not needed or not truly warranted. Agreements often mention specific situations in which the agreement can be utilized, sometimes getting specific enough to list criminal activities that would apply, and who is authorized to request and authorize assistance. In some agreements, only Chief Executives are permitted to request or authorize assistance, in other agreements, designees are authorized to do so.

4. The agency that has command and supervisory responsibility. Without such wording, the chaos which could ensue from not having someone in charge could become overwhelming very quickly. The idea of "well, we've always worked well together in the past" usually doesn't work when a major incident occurs, and the idea of command and supervisory responsibility needs to be clearly spelled out from the beginning to avoid conflict or chaos. The command and supervisory responsibility might be restricted to the chief executives, or it may extend to supervisory personnel who are on-duty at the time the agreement is activated.

5. A time limit for the agreement. Seldom are these mutual aid agreements "open-ended," and most have some type of time limit. Many of them, however, have "sunset clauses," which allow for the agreement to remain active until formally renegotiated or extended by agreement between agencies or governmental entities.

6. The amount of any compensation or reimbursement to the assisting agency or agencies that provide assistance. The amount of money that can be expended during either a natural disaster or some type of "law enforcement emergency" can be astronomical, and can be absolutely crippling to the budget of many agencies. The need to address any type of compensation, whether it be overtime, equipment rental, fuel for vehicles, or any other expenses must be clearly spelled out in the agreement.

7. Any other terms and conditions necessary to give it effect. Some governmental entities require that the agreements in which their law enforcement agencies become involved are approved by the city council, mayor, or other official(s). Some require that the agreements be filed to become legal, while others limit the signatory authority for agreements to a specific individual, such as a mayor or city manager, authorized to enter into such agreements.

It is best to address these types of concerns proactively in a non-stressful environment so that when the crisis of the major case occurs, the police response can be immediate.

MEMORANDUMS OF UNDERSTANDING

In addition to Mutual Aid Agreements, some agencies become involved in "Memorandums of Understanding," also known as "Intergovernmental Agreements," with other agencies, to address major case investigations and other incidents or events, and sometimes they are used to establish major crimes task forces. The advantages of memorandums of understanding is that they are more formalized agreements, and as such are more suitable for long-term operations, such as major case investigations. With a memorandum of understanding, little if anything is left to chance, and if applied to major case investigations, all aspects of the investigative effort are covered in the memorandum. The elements of the memorandum of understanding (MOU) usually include:

Parties. The names of agencies who will be signatories to the agreement, as well as provisions for the addition of other agencies.

Purpose. A general statement regarding the purpose of the agreement.

Authority. This section discusses liability for the actions of the personnel included in the agreement.

Costs/Expenses. This section outlines costs for which task force member agencies are responsible, as well as costs that shall be borne by participating agencies.

Liabilities/Insurance. This section discusses liabilities for signatories to the agreement when working under the agreement.

Termination/Modification of Agreement. This section details the length of time in which the agreement is valid.

Signatures. Those personnel authorized to sign the task force agreement.

HISTORICAL PERSPECTIVE ON TASK FORCES

One of the first task force operations was the U.S. Department of Justice's Organized Crime Strike Forces, which were established in the late 1960s as a result of U.S. Attorney General Robert Kennedy's frustration with organized crime involvement in the Teamster's Union, then under the leadership of James Hoffa. The manner in which Attorney General Kennedy began the strike forces was that high-ranking representatives of all Federal agencies dealing with organized crime were assigned to a particular city to attack organized crime in that geographic region. These Organized Crime Strike Forces matched representatives of the FBI, IRS, Secret Service, Narcotics and the Department of Labor together with a number of highly-experienced Justice Department lawyers.

These strike forces were based on the theory that you would take these experienced agents and lawyers out of their daily routine and have them concentrate solely on organized crime. They would work together as a team, across jurisdictional lines, placing inter-agency rivalries aside. The idea behind the inclusion of attorneys in the strike force was based on the thought that if these attorneys were involved with these cases from the onset that "vertical prosecution" would result. In this type of prosecution, the attorneys assigned to the strike force began planning the prosecution phase of the investigation simultaneously with the investigative phase. The same attorneys assigned to the strike force would also prosecute the case, ensuring a seamless transition between the investigation and the prosecution.

Another example of successful task force operations are the National Transportation Safety Board (NTSB) "Go Teams." These teams consist of a group of NTSB personnel representing a range of investigative skills. They are on 24-alert, and they can arrive at accident scenes anywhere in the country on very short notice. Each team consists of approximately six specialists and experts directed by an "investigator-in-charge." In addition, an NTSB board member always accompanies the team to the site, while a public affairs officer coordinates media activities.

These Go-Team members get used to working together and accustomed to working within an already established power structure, which avoids the time-wasting turf wars and the uncertainty over roles that sometimes seems to torment "ad hoc" task forces. In addition to the investigative elements, the NTSB operates its own technical laboratory to ensure proper and unbiased analysis of evidence.

MAJOR CASE TASK FORCES

In recent years, many law enforcement agencies have come to the realization that major cases often require the type of response that they can barely meet. With the exception of very large agencies, most small to mid-sized law enforcement agencies can't always "go it alone," and must depend on each other for assistance.

One method of addressing major case investigations is to form some type of a task force to address the major case. Some task forces are designed to be in operation for a number of years, and some are initiated for a specific investigation and designed to only be up and running for as long as that investigation is being conducted. At the conclusion of the investigation, the task force is disbanded.

Some task forces, particularly the "Major Case Task Forces" that have been initiated throughout the country over the last twenty years, are designed to be operated in an "on call status." When the personnel are not activated and actually being utilized as members of the task force, they return to their routine duties at their own agencies until the next time they are activated.

The simple definition of a task force, as it relates to a major case investigation, is *a group of personnel, from either a single agency or multiple agencies, who are removed from their routine duties, to devote their time and efforts specifically to either a single investigation or to a group of related investigations.*

Task Force Memorandum of Understanding

While the task force memorandum of understanding contains all of the elements of any such document, the memorandum of understanding for a major crime task force includes some additional elements. Memoranda of understanding for major crime task forces usually include the following elements:

- **Parties.** The names of agencies who will be members of the task force, as well as provisions for the addition of other agencies to the task force are outlined.
- **Purpose.** A general statement regarding the purpose of the agreement, i.e., "The purpose of this agreement is to provide comprehensive investigative services to member agencies including, but

not limited to those cases outlined in the "Case Acceptance Guidelines" when requested to do so by the chief of police of member agencies or their designee, with the approval of the board of directors.

- **Case Acceptance Guidelines.** It is imperative that case acceptance parameters are set in the memorandum of understanding or the task force will be overutilized by some member agencies.
- **Authority.** This section discusses liability for the actions of the personnel assigned to the task force.
- **Board of Directors/Policy Board.** This section outlines the responsibilities of the governing body of the task force, usually consisting of the chief executives of the participating agencies. The board's responsibilities are also listed in detail.
- **Costs/Expenses.** This section outlines costs for which task force member agencies are responsible, as well as costs that shall be borne during task force activations by all participating agencies. Provisions for additional fees and costs are usually listed in this section. Most task forces charge a minimal annual fee to each member agency, which can be adjusted by vote of the board of directors as the need arises.
- **Liabilities/Insurance.** This section outlines the requirement for liability insurance, workmen's comp insurance, and vehicle insurance for task force members when conducting a major case investigation following task force activation.
- **Task Force Personnel Requirements.** This section outlines the personnel requirements for task force member agencies, and also binds the members of the task force to the policy and procedures of their own agencies as well as task force policy and procedures.
- **Administrative/Operational Procedures.** This is an agreement by member agencies that the investigation of crimes within the member agencies' jurisdiction that have been accepted by the task force and Board of Directors shall be conducted according to the procedures of the task force.
- **Asset Forfeiture on Task Force Cases.** In the event that assets are seized during task force cases, this section outlines how those assets will be divided among task force member agencies.
- **Misconduct.** This section outlines what actions will be taken in the event of misconduct by members of the task force.
- **Termination/Modification of Agreement.** This section details

the length of time in which the agreement is valid.
- **Signatures.** Those personnel authorized to sign the task force agreement. Appendix 1 is a sample "Memorandum of Understanding/Intergovernmental Agreement" for a Major Crimes Task Force. Appendix 2 is a sample set of "By-laws for a Major Crimes Task Force."

PROS AND CONS OF THE TASK FORCE APPROACH

There are many benefits to the task force approach, but perhaps the two most compelling are the fact that a task force greatly enlarges the body of manpower available for the investigation, and the fact that a task force brings in high-quality individuals to share experiences and approaches.

The positive aspects and benefits of task forces include:

- There is more manpower available on short notice, which is of particular benefit to the small or mid-sized law enforcement agency. Rarely does a police agency other than a large municipal department such as Chicago, New York, or other major cities have enough personnel to address a manpower-intensive major case investigation. Most suburban agencies cannot do so alone.
- Multiple agency task force investigations mean that the costs of running the investigation might be more likely to be shared among participating agencies. Many agencies would be crippled by the costs associated with a major case investigation, and this approach allows them to address the major case without expending all of their financial resources.
- The task force approach provides the ability to generate fresh perspectives quickly due to the larger number of personnel involved in the investigation. Sometimes an outside perspective will allow investigators from the originating jurisdiction to see the case in a different light in that outside experiences and perspectives are brought into the investigation.
- If the task force utilizes a pre-planned response, administrative complications associated with major cases and multiple agency operations will be minimized. Memoranda of understanding address financial, liability, and other issues prior to activation.

- Involvement in a major case is something exciting and often stimulates the initiative/performance of officers, particularly in multiagency task forces. Most police officers sincerely want to do a professional job, and when they are surrounded by like-minded professionals, their desire to do so is multiplied.
- The competitive nature of police officers can be a positive element in a multiagency task force, in that the desire to successfully conclude the investigation can drive investigators to perform extremely well.
- The task force approach allows the law enforcement agency or agencies in whose jurisdiction the incident(s) occur to address the problem without draining all of its manpower for day-to-day operations. Just because a major case occurs in a jurisdiction doesn't mean that the routine burglaries, thefts, and robberies are going to stop. These crimes are important to the victims and to the police department and must be addressed, even while a great deal of effort and resources are devoted to the major case.
- As the investigation progresses, even personnel from multiple agencies begin to think more and more alike (if the basic goals and objectives are clearly established from the onset of the operation). It is gratifying to watch a major case task force in action–the personnel seem to feed off each other's efforts and the "team spirit" of task forces can lead to very successful investigation. This is very similar to "elite" military units, where not just anyone can become a member and membership is something to which many people aspire. I am aware of one suburban major crime task force which prides itself on a near perfect solution rate on some very difficult investigations. I believe it to be true that "success breeds success," and the more successful some of these task forces are, the better they become.

There are also some negative aspects to the task force approach, however, which should be considered, and these include:

- Variations in report writing format/skills among personnel assigned to the task force can cause delays in reporting. Not everyone is an excellent report writer, and when one considers the importance of reports, this can lead to problems.

- Individuals occasionally have difficulty in taking direction from outside agency personnel when assigned to multiagency operations. Even when the chain of command of the task force is clearly spelled out on paper and verbalized from agency executives, some people still don't seem to "get it," and resist taking orders from someone not in their normal chain of command. Provisions must be made to deal with these individuals immediately.
- Some agency officials are reluctant to cede any of their authority over the investigations of incidents in their own jurisdictions, and this reluctance sometimes filters down and is adopted by investigative personnel. Entering into a task force requires giving up a portion of your authority and autonomy, and chiefs who are unable to do these things should think carefully before entering into task force agreements.
- Unless there is a task force selection/screening process of some type, there is no real way of determining the talent/expertise level of unknown personnel from other agencies. While most law enforcement executives have enough pride in their organizations to assign competent professionals to task force operations, in some cases there is no real "selection" taking place and you "get what and who you're given," which means that you might get "stuck" with a "less than stellar performer."
- The competitive nature of police officers can be a negative element in a multiagency task force if the level of competition allows jealousy and the accompanying problems to surface. If the desire to "personally solve the case" outweighs the desire for "the group to solve the case," problems can ensue.
- Unless a pre-planned and organized response is in place, the costs incurred during the investigation can often be the subject of disagreements regarding who will provide funding to cover them. This is why the agreement setting up the task force is so critical, to avoid later arguments and disagreements regarding payments.

INFORMAL "AD HOC" TASK FORCES VS. FORMALIZED TASK FORCES

Task forces used to address major case investigations, can be from a single agency or from multiple agencies, and they can be ad hoc or formalized. In the single agency task force, personnel from several units within the agency are assigned together to concentrate their efforts on the investigation of the major case. In a multiagency task force, personnel from several different agencies are actually removed from their agency and their normal duties and assigned to a task force. Some multiagency task forces can be permanently established, like the Drug Enforcement Administration (DEA) and U.S. Customs Task Forces in operation in major cities throughout the United States. Most major case task forces, however, are designed to be activated when a case that meets their stated criteria occurs and then deactivated when the case is concluded. There are many types of task forces currently in operation, with pros and cons to each. The problems associated with ad hoc or informal task forces can be extremely detrimental to the major case investigation, however, and should be carefully considered.

Informal task forces occur when individuals and equipment from various jurisdictions are pieced together based on allegiances, friendships, traditions, associations, business and personal relationships, and whatever assistance may be available at any given time. Problems develop quickly in this response, and include the fact that the organization of the ad hoc task force can be haphazard. Sometimes issues not related to the case may interfere with investigative work, resulting in power struggles between agencies.

The decision to participate in a formal or informal task force agreement for use in major case investigations needs to be considered thoroughly and immediately. While sometimes informal or ad hoc multijurisdictional or multiagency groups are suitable and work, they are usually unpredictable. Some of the disadvantages of informal task forces include the following:

1. Informal task forces often waste valuable time getting the agreements down, time which could be spent actually working the investigation. Since there are no formal written agreements in place when the informal task force begins work on a case, these agreements must be hammered out "on the fly" during the onset of the case.

2. The delay in assembling a group and organizing it can hinder the investigation from the outset. If one or more agencies are very busy at the time, it could be several days until the person-

nel from those agencies are ready to go to work with the informal task force.

3. With an informal task force, no two responses are ever the same, and sometimes agencies participating are based on who the police chief feels is currently available and in a position to help, rather than on which agencies offer the most expertise.

4. People and technology are often incompatible, which can lead to confusion and wasted time. If personnel are not using compatible communication or data processing technology, problems in communication and report preparation can occur. In formalized task forces, communications issues are determined at the time the agreement is formulated.

5. The roles of the assembled investigators are not based on specific training and experience relevant to the crime that needs to be solved. Most formal task forces have personnel train together so that their responses and procedures are consistent.

6. Informal task forces might suffer from loss of manpower due to other "important matters" at one's parent agency, whereas formalized task forces/mutual aid agreements have provisions for loss of personnel.

7. Informal task forces are often canceled when the overtime begins to pile up, particularly in agencies that have fiscal issues, unless some provisions have been made.

8. Informal task forces have a tendency to "break apart" as soon as a problem arises, which usually involves a question of some type of liability. I once commanded a unit that was involved in a multiagency fugitive task force. Agencies at the Federal, state, and county level had banded together to address the issue of wanted fugitives, and a memorandum of understanding was established that allowed for a six-month investigative project. After about two months, during which the investigators assigned made numerous arrests and truly did an outstanding job, a situation arose in which a Sergeant assigned to the project shot and killed a wanted subject. Although the media attention was extensive, the task force merely "stood down" for three days, regrouped, and went back to work without missing a beat. Had it not been for the memorandum of understanding (intergovernmental agreement) the task force might have ceased to exist.

Formalized Task Forces

One of the mechanisms for making sure the issues above are avoided is to form semi-permanent task forces which will activate during major case investigations. The clearly defined roles and responsibilities associated with these task forces can allow these task forces to immediately begin investigating the major case, rather than spend time on administrative matters. The various jurisdictions involved in the task force agree in advance in the matter of how to assemble the major crime investigation unit, specifying the duties of its personnel and protocols for the conduct of the investigation, including the specific role of the prosecutor's office.

TASK FORCE PLANNING

The planning that goes into a major case task force is critical, and must be given a great deal of thought. Thoughtful planning can lead to coordinated responses to major case investigations, and can also preclude administrative problems. The following agencies should be included in the planning stages:

- Municipal, county, state, and Federal law enforcement agencies—whichever agencies are interested in the formation of the task force should take part in the planning of the task force. The personnel assigned to the planning stages should be command personnel, with decision-making authority. The time wasted in having to "seek permission" by personnel not empowered with decision-making capability can become very distracting. In addition to the command personnel, however, I feel that the inclusion of a major case investigator from each agency involved is a good idea. Without the inclusion of personnel who actually *investigate* major cases, decisions regarding policy and task force operations might be made by someone in a command position who is too far removed from actual investigations to see the implications of a faulty policy or procedure.
- Crime Lab Personnel at the command level should be involved in the planning of the major crimes task force. The laboratory assets are probably going to be intimately involved in many of the

The Use of Task Forces in Major Case Investigations

matters under investigation and getting lab command in on the ground floor of the planning can avoid someone else setting policies and/or procedures that the lab cannot follow.

- Medical Examiner/Coroner personnel will probably also be involved in at least some of the major case investigations that will be handled by the task force, and having them involved in the planning stages can be extremely beneficial to the task force. Their input will be very pertinent, particularly as it relates to violent crimes, and having them involved in the planning stages can sometimes gain "priority status" later for task force cases.
- Prosecutor's Office—is a very important stakeholder in any major case investigation, and they need to be involved in the planning and formation of the task force from its inception. Many task forces have a specific assistant prosecutor assigned to work with the task force on any case to which they respond. This affords the task force, in some cases, the benefit of "vertical prosecution," where the same prosecutor assigned to assist in the investigative phase is also involved in the prosecution phase.
- Local government officials should have some involvement in the planning stages of a major crime task force, as their approval is usually required for agencies to participate in the task force. In addition, in the event that additional funding is needed for operations the fact that these government officials are aware of the task force operational concepts might assist when it comes to acquiring necessary funding and/or equipment.
- Media representatives should have some involvement in the planning stages of a major crime task force, as this allows the buildup of rapport and will also assist in the development of a media policy that is workable and effective. In addition, the positive publicity that the task force will receive during its formation will send the message to the public that law enforcement agencies in their area are professional enough to put jealousies aside and band together in a major case task force for the common good.

CASE SCREENING

Another aspect of task force planning is to determine what type of crimes or incidents the task force will investigate. If there are no parameters set on cases to be investigated, task forces have the propensity to be "overused," that is they are called out for everything and anything. Most multiagency "on-call" type of task forces do not have the luxury of enough manpower to be activated continuously, and therefore some type of case screening mechanism must be in place. In addition, most task force agreements include policy on how cases will be referred, what type of crimes will be investigated, and what types will be referred back to the requesting agency.

Time limits are usually set for requesting task force activation, which precludes the member agencies from trying to solve the case on their own and when they get over their heads calling the task force to "bail them out" of their predicament.

Most task forces have it written into their intergovernmental agreement or memorandum of understanding that in the event that the task force commander feels that a particular crime is not suitable for a task force investigation, his decision, pending review of the board of directors or advisory council, is considered final.

Most task forces investigate the following offenses:

1. Homicide
2. Non-Parental Kidnapping
3. Serial Arson, Rape, Sexual Assault
4. Police Involved Shooting/Deadly Force/In-custody Deaths
5. Other exceptionally heinous offenses

The last category allows for some leeway in the event that a crime occurs that the agency cannot investigate by itself and really requires task force assistance to investigate.

TASK FORCE FUNDING

It has been well documented that the expenses incurred during major case investigations cam be absolutely crippling for many agencies. The costs of running a major case investigation go well beyond the salaries and benefits of those personnel involved, and can include a variety of expenses:

• **Overtime.** This is a serious concern with any agency, but for agencies with collective bargaining agreements it can be critical. I know of no union contract that permits the management of a law enforcement agency to avoid paying overtime strictly because a case reaches major case status.

- **Additional support personnel.** In the event that additional support personnel must be acquired, as in the case of clerical staff from temporary service companies, the costs can be tremendous.
- **Additional equipment.** In the event that the major case investigation necessitates the use of specialized and/or technical equipment, the costs associated with the equipment can become very difficult for agencies to manage.
- **Facility rental.** In the event that the agency hosting the task force activation does not have a suitable facility for use as a command post, a facility will have to be acquired. In addition, storage facilities might be required for large items of evidence or other storage.
- **Travel/per diem expenses.** In many major cases, investigative personnel may have to travel out of the area to investigate leads, and travel and per diem expenses must be considered.
- **Additional communication costs.** In the event that suitable communications equipment is not available, this equipment will have to be rented/leased if it is critical to the major case investigation.
- **Printing expenses.** In the event that flyers or other informational documents (such as those needed in missing persons cases) are needed for the major case investigation, expenses for printing and distribution of these documents will be an added expense.
- **Vehicle rental/maintenance.** In the event that suitable vehicles are not available for specialized use such as surveillance operations, suitable vehicles will have to be acquired, usually as rental vehicles.
- **Fees for "experts" which are otherwise unavailable.** On occasion, the services of experts who are not part of the law enforcement agencies involved might be necessary, with their associated costs.

Funding Sources

Although the costs associated with the above expenses can be very high, thought should be given during the planning stage to potential sources of funding for these expenses are usually:

1. **Sharing of expenses by all task force members.** This is probably the most common method of funding task forces. Each agency with personnel assigned pays the salary and overtime expenses for their own personnel. (In some Federal task force arrangements the overtime is paid by the Federal government.) The individual agencies are required to equip their personnel with a suitable vehicle and other necessary equipment. This method of funding is aimed at seeing that no single agency has to bear the burden of expenses for personnel other than their own, and it is a good way to spread the pain of the extra costs that could otherwise cripple an individual agency.
2. **Identifying and acquiring grant of similar money.** Some states, and to some extent the Federal government, may have grant money available for multiagency efforts on major case investigations. Research into the availability of such funding should take place during the task force planning stage.
3. **Obtaining federal/local/state emergency funding.** Many states have emergency funding available for natural disasters, and some may have funding available for law enforcement emergencies, such as those encountered in major case investigations. This must also be researched during the planning phase, and even if the amount doesn't cover all of the expenses it might still be beneficial.

TASK FORCE ORGANIZATION

The organization of a multiagency task force involves the cooperative efforts of agency heads and the other personnel and organizations mentioned in the section on "Task Force Planning." Having helped form major crimes task forces in a number of locations, the key element of task force formation is that the agency heads involved must actually see the value in the task force approach and be willing to give up a little bit of their autonomy and authority to make the task force work.

The formation of the major crime task force, if agency heads are truly interested, need not be painful, and instead can be an excellent team-building exercise that can have long-term benefits for all the agencies involved. It is essential that officials from agencies who are joining a task force understand the leadership structure, decision-making protocols, and investigative methods that the task force will use. These methods might differ from the methods with which they are familiar. In addition, they must be flexible enough to balance the needs of the task force with the many different priorities that can arise during a major case investigation and be able to adjust to the investigation's changing demands and conditions.

Multiple agency task forces, in addition to the functional positions that will be discussed in Chapter 4, are usually led by a group consisting of command level representatives from agencies with personnel assigned to the task force. They can be called the "Task Force Advisory Council, Board of Directors, or Task Force Policy Board." They are critical to the formation of the task force agreement or memorandum of understanding, and other elements of the task force such as the task force by-laws, setting operating policies and procedures, and overseeing the operations of the task force. The duties of the task force advisory council/board of directors, include the following:

- Determine all major policies and procedures of the task force
- Establish financial controls
- Make decisions on problems
- Make final decisions on when the task force will be activated and de-activated (pursuant to discussion with the task force commander)
- Review task force activities and manpower once activated
- Meet regularly to discuss task force issues, problems, manpower, activities, etc.
- Determine who will hold the position of task force commander
- Determine training needs

Depending on the type of task force in use, the advisory council/board of directors may meet periodically to discuss task force activities and address any issues. They set policy and procedures for the task force operation, and will enforce any violations of those policies. The following example will outline the formation of a multiagency task force which I was asked to design, train, and implement. The experience was beneficial to all agencies involved, and the task force, currently in operation, has conducted many successful investigations. This task force was initiated by a local college "Public Safety Institute," which had received a federal grant to develop law enforcement strategies that would benefit the community. The formation of the major crime task force was one of the first grant projects for this institute. To provide some idea of the time frame in which the formation took place, Phase 1, the "Introductory Meeting" took place in early February and Phase 5, the "Task Force Training" took place mid-May. In less than five months the major crime task force, the first of its kind in this particular state, was fully operational.

- **Phase 1–Introductory Meeting:** Chiefs and investigative commanders from all agencies within the geographic area to be covered by the task force met for an informational luncheon meeting which included a presentation on the value of major crimes task forces.
- **Phase 2–Questionnaire and Examination of Results:** A questionnaire was sent to all chiefs to determine the level of interest in forming the task force. Individual calls and meetings were scheduled with chiefs who had questions or concerns about becoming involved in the task force. At the end of this phase, 18 of 19 area police departments chose to join the task force.
- **Phase 3–Task Force Development Meeting:** At this meeting a board of directors was selected from among the chiefs, and discussions were held on the types of policies and procedures that would be necessary. There were a total of three (3) such meetings, which included selection of a task force commander and assistant commander, approval of an intergovernmental agreement (memorandum of understanding), determination of personnel selection strategy, and review of written policies for the task force.
- **Phase 4–Task Force Personnel Selection:** Examination of applications and interviews were held to determine the personnel to be assigned to the task force.
- **Phase 5–Task Force Training:** All personnel assigned to the task force underwent a three-day course of training in "Major Case Management." Following the training a general meeting was held with all task force personnel, during which they were provided with their identification and equipment. Following this

meeting the task force was operational, and within three weeks they received their first call-out to a double homicide in a member community.

Whether an agency decides to approach a major case investigation individually or as part of a single or multiagency task force, there are certain functional positions and responsibilities that need to be seriously considered. These will be covered in the next chapter.

CASE STUDY #2: MULTIPLE OFFENDER MURDER

VICTIMOLOGY: White Male, 42 years of age, married father of two children, worked as a factory worker.

MAJOR CASE CONSIDERATIONS: This was considered a "Major Case" due to the following elements:

- Location where the crime occurred—gang-infested suburban area
- Specifics of the crime—this was a senseless beating in which the victim was beaten to the point of being unrecognizable
- Motive—appeared to be the result of a "road rage" incident
- Racial implications—white victim brutally murdered in a black neighborhood
- Involvement of a corrupt police agency which led to involvement by the Prosecutor's office

GEOGRAPHICS: The area in which the crime occurred is an extremely low-income suburb, known for a great deal of violent crime as well as drug and gang activity. The local police department was extremely poorly staffed, poorly trained, and rife with corruption. Several officers had been indicted, others provided protection for narcotics dealers, and on more than one occasion the state police or county sheriff's police had to take over law enforcement duties in the community due to the arrest of many of the local officers for their involvement in armed robberies and narcotics offenses.

SPECIFIC FACTS: The victim had worked the 3–11 shift at a factory in a nearby suburb. Following work, he stopped at a bar with some co-workers, and then proceeded home. There were two routes from the bar to his residence—one stuck to the main roads and the other went through an extremely economically depressed Southern suburb, which is the route he chose. The victim was over six feet tall and over 300 pounds, and was driving a Ford Ranger, which is a small pickup truck. The victim was found in his vehicle, which had crashed through the iron fence of a senior citizens housing complex near an intersection in the suburb. The victim had received extensive trauma to the back of his head and neck as well as to the sides of his head, and the injuries were such that they could not have occurred during the vehicle accident.

IMMEDIATE ACTION TAKEN: The aforementioned local police department arrived at the scene and began their "investigation," which consisted of arresting four persons standing near the truck, who were witnesses to the crash, and holding them for several days prior to releasing them without charges. No neighborhood canvass of any kind was conducted, and no reports were prepared, other than the names of the arrestees. The only positive action taken on scene was to call for a state police crime scene technician.

Following two weeks of attempting to get information on the murder from the local police, the family of the victim contacted the prosecutor's office and demanded some assistance. The prosecutor's office responded by contacting the state police and requesting that they take over the investigation. A squad of investigators was assigned to the investigation.

MAJOR DIFFICULTIES: It became immediately apparent that the local police department wanted nothing whatsoever to do with the State Police investigation, and in fact refused to cooperate in any way. The Victim's family, who had been stonewalled for two weeks by the local police department, began putting pressure on the local media for a quick solution to the murder.

The investigation was dramatically hampered by the fact that the people in the community were not only fearful (terrified) of possible suspects, but just as fearful of the local police department, based on their past performance. The four "witnesses" who had been arrested by the police had no desire to cooperate with the state police investigation, and intelligence information was received that they had been cautioned against doing so by the local police department. It took approximately eleven months to develop any potential witnesses. Two witnesses were uncovered—the first was a 35-year-old woman who lived in the community. While on a date with her boyfriend (she was married to someone else) they had driven by two vehicles in the intersection, a Ford Ranger pickup truck and a mid-sized car. The front left corner of the car was locked into the wheel well of the pickup truck, prohibiting the truck from moving even though the driver of the pickup truck (victim) was attempting to move the vehicle and get away. The four offenders exited the car and, using a tire jack assembly, a tire iron and a piece of 4 x 4 lumber, were beating the driver of the pick-up truck (victim) as he attempted to get away. When they were done beating him to death, they moved their car, thereby freeing up the pickup truck to career across the intersection into the fence of the senior citizen's complex. This witness knew two of the four offenders by name. Needless to say, the fact that this married woman was out with her boyfriend didn't exactly make her eager to speak with us, but once the investigator got past that he was able to convince her to "do the right thing" and cooperate. To this day, I don't know how he did it, but he did.

The second witness, who observed the entire incident and knew three of the offenders, had been one of the "witnesses" originally picked up by the local police department. Through some very skillful questioning and witness handling, one of the state police investigators was able to convince both witnesses to come forward and testify before a grand jury which led to indictments on three of the four offenders. When the arrests of the offenders were to take place, the local police provided alibis and attempted to thwart the arrests of the suspects. Two of their officers (sic) who had been fired upon by one of the offenders when the arrest warrants came out suddenly changed their stories and denied that the incident took place, even though the shooting was captured on the emergency channel of the police radio when the officers (sic) called for help.

The three offenders were all ranking gang members, and when they were developed and the community learned of their involvement, area residents were reluctant to cooperate, due to the (well-deserved) reputation of the suspects. One of the offenders, whose nickname was "Mad Dog," had used a fully automatic weapon to spray the attendees at a family picnic when one of the children at the picnic had splashed him while opening a can of soda. Another of the offenders was reportedly among a group who had made attempts to purchase Light Anti-tank Weapons (LAW Rockets) with which they planned to assault district stations of the Chicago Police Department. This offender's father was a Lieutenant with the local police department in whose town the murder had taken place.

When the charges against the offenders were filed and through discovery their attorneys received the identities of the two witnesses, the attorneys and their clients sent gang "enforcers" out to locate our witnesses, in an obvious attempt to either get them to change their testimony or to somehow make sure that they did not testify at the trials. Threats on the lives of our witnesses caused us to move them both several times, seek employment for them, and provide protection for their extended family members who remained in the community.

At the time of the trial, we received intelligence information that the friends of the offenders had planned to assault the court building in an effort to free their associates. Based on their backgrounds, we mounted an extensive witness protection/escort operation at the time of trial.

LESSONS LEARNED:

1. When handed an investigation that another agency has already started, it is usually advisable to start from "square one" and begin the investigation all over, as much as possible. While many of the things that should have been done, such as a thorough neighborhood canvass at the time of the offense, could not be done after the fact, we were able to re-interview some people who we knew were in the immediate area. It wasn't anything that led to important information, but it was a logical investigative step that had to be completed.

2. When dealing with a "less than trustworthy" police agency, do not provide any more information than is absolutely necessary. As indicated, when it came time to arrest these offenders, the chief of police for the local department informed us that his two officers who were shot at by the offenders had been mistaken and the sounds on the emergency radio channel was probably a "car backfiring" or something else. Trust among law enforcement agencies is something that most of us take for granted, but there are agencies who do not warrant any trust at all.

3. Spend as much time and effort as it takes to provide for witness protection. When the case got to trial for one of the most violent offenders, I was able to sit in court and watch the testimony of our female witness. This was the most frightened I've ever seen anyone in not only my police career, but in my life. When she was asked to identify the offender in court, she got so terrified when she looked at him that she immediately vomited all over herself. After a short recess and a change of clothes, she came back into the courtroom carrying a Bible (which I learned later had been loaned to her by the investigator who had gotten her

to come forward). When asked to identify the offender this time, she stood, pointed at him and identified him as the murderer.

4. Prior to providing moving/living or any other expenses to witnesses, obtain approval from the prosecutor. One of the tactics of the defense attorneys at trial was to try and establish that our two witnesses, who had been moved approximately three times each in the 18 months that the case took to go to trial, were only testifying because we were paying them to do so. The fact that the prosecutor knew about all of the payments (moving expenses, living and rent expenses, and other subsistence) and that each of the payments was well-documented precluded any problems with the fact that money had been spent on these witnesses.

CASE RESOLUTION: All three offenders were tried separately, and all three offenders received sentences of eighty years each. One of the offenders was later murdered in prison.

Chapter 4

MAJOR CASE MANAGEMENT
PLANNING AND ORGANIZATION

In one of my past assignments I was the officer in charge of a regional Tactical Response Team (TRT) for a large state police organization. Although not an actual member of the team, I was responsible for seeing to it that they had the proper management support with which to perform their very hazardous duties. I had a great deal of tactical experience, which included both military and civilian law enforcement which included high-risk tactics, search warrant entries, etc., so I was very comfortable working with this outstanding and elite group of operators.

The things that always struck me as essential when dealing with these types of high risk operations were: the critical need for good, sound, and thorough planning prior to the operation, the need for sound management and leadership throughout the operation, the necessity for discipline by all personnel during the operation, and the need for a thorough debrief after the operation was concluded. Particularly when dealing with high-risk situations, there wasn't much room for error. There are many similarities between the management of high-risk operations and the management of major case investigations. All major cases begin with an accurate preliminary assessment of the situation, followed by the development of investigative goals and objectives and an investigative plan. When these goals and objectives are coupled with a solid plan and good management, the chances for success of the investigative efforts are heightened.

PRELIMINARY ASSESSMENT

Before launching into a major case investigation, I would strongly recommend that the manager take time to conduct a preliminary assessment of the situation. Considering the following:

1. Has a crime been committed, or is the occurrence of a crime suspected?
   - If so, what specific crime or crimes are to be investigated?
   - Do the elements of that crime exist?
   - Does your agency have jurisdiction over the situation or incident?
2. Have adequate personnel been allocated?
   - If additional personnel are needed, what is their availability and source?
   - Are there available investigative specialists that will be required?
   - Is the span of control over personnel manageable?
   - Is there a need for additional resources?
   - If so, has the availability and source of the resources been identified?
3. Is there a need for stakeholder involvement outside the law enforcement agency?
   - Have pertinent outside stakeholders been identified? (Note that stakeholders are groups and individuals who may not be directly involved in the major case investigation but may have a vested interest in the investigation.)
4. Stakeholders may include:
   - Community members, groups, organizations
   - Governmental representatives
   - Non-governmental organizations
   - Security or military agencies
   - Healthcare organizations, systems, and regulators
   - Business, tourism, and infrastructure organizations

INVESTIGATIVE PLANNING

Once the situation has been assessed and a determination made that a crime has been committed under an agency's jurisdiction, the major case manager can take these initial findings and develop an investigative plan that specifies the priorities, tasks, and required resources for the case.

An investigative plan:

- Provides a foundation for the investigation of any incident classified as a major case.
- Ensures key personnel are involved and adequate resources are allocated from the onset.
- Identifies critical components of the major case management team.
- Outlines procedures for implementing a coordinated and effective response to the investigative needs of the case. Appendix 3 is a sample "Major Case Management Checklist."

Plan for the Long Term

In developing an investigative plan, the major case manager should plan for the long term and avoid setting time limits on goals or tasks. While a quick resolution of the investigation may be predicted, the prediction may be inaccurate due to:

- The investigation may be more complex than initially assessed.
- The investigation may involve a crime pattern or organized criminal enterprise groups.
- The investigation may have extra-jurisdictional or even international connections.

Major case managers should not request initial resources on a short-term basis. When resources are requested it should be done with the idea that the resources will be needed until the investigation is concluded, which might involve a great deal of time. Do not cause irreparable harm to the investigation by insuring those entities who are providing resources, whether those resources are personnel or equipment, that they will have those resources returned in a short time. It is much easier to disengage resources when no longer needed than to have to start over and reacquire them.

Avoid Time Limits

There is enough pressure on the major case team to solve the case without adding the burden of time limits. Artificial time limits can cause frustration to the investigative personnel, to the case managers, to agency executives, and can destroy public confidence in law enforcement efforts. Major case managers should resist outside pressure to predict when the investigation will be concluded. In addition, sloppy investigation, incomplete coverage of leads, a lessening of standards, or even unethical or illegal lapses in judgment or investigative techniques may arise when time limits are imposed. Tasks within the mission may have time limits imposed, but managers need to make sure that any deadlines for those tasks are realistic.

GOALS AND OBJECTIVES

Major case managers must develop attainable goals and objectives to ensure that all personnel involved in the investigation understand the focus from the outset of the investigation. These goals must be audibly communicated to all personnel. Similar to the "Mission Statements" that are developed and advertised throughout organizations, the goals of the major case team must be internalized by all team members to insure the greatest chance for success in the investigation. While the main objective in any major case is obviously successfully solving the case, there are additional management objectives that should not be overlooked. These objectives can include:

- **Identifying and arresting those responsible.** It is not enough to merely solve the crime, the ultimate goal of crime solution is to identify and apprehend the perpetrator(s).
- **Disrupting perpetrator's future criminal activity.** Particularly with regard to repeat or serial offenders, disruption of the perpetrator's opportunity to commit crimes in the future should also be an objective.
- **Allaying public fears.** The public fear that accompanies a major case can be paralyzing to a community. The elimination of those fears is something that should be considered as an important objective of the investigative effort.

- **Identifying related crimes.** The major case investigation might uncover and identify related crimes committed by this perpetrator or their associates while conducting the major case investigation.
- **Meeting prosecution needs.** The successful meeting of all of the objectives listed above will be meaningless if the prosecution is not effective. The needs of the prosecutor, throughout the investigative phase and also throughout the prosecution phase must be considered as critical to the overall success of the major case investigation.

CHAIN OF COMMAND

- Effective plans need to be administered in an effective manner, which calls for the proper exercise of authority and responsibility. The best method to insure the proper exercise of authority and responsibility is to have a clearly defined and effective chain of command, which is communicated to and understood by all assigned personnel. (Note: The person who is ultimately responsible for the overall major case investigation can be called the major case manager, commander, or officer in charge. For purposes of simplicity, this person will be referred to hereafter as the major case manager.)
- The major case manager will insure activation and operational control of the major case management team. In that capacity he/she will insure development of an overall strategy for resolving the major case. That strategy will guide the major case team throughout the investigation and into the prosecution phase.
- The component/function leaders will devise specific tactics to support the major case manager's strategies. The tactics and strategies that these component/function leaders develop will be specific to their functions and to the personnel assigned to them to perform those functions. At no time should the tactics and strategies developed and implemented by one component/function leader be in conflict with those of another component/function.
- All operational plans and/or tactics must be approved by the major case manager or his/her designee. Without such approval

and oversight, conflict between component/function elements might occur, and adherence to the original investigative plan might not occur.

- It is important to immediately identify who is in charge of the overall investigation and the different functional teams, such as administrative and logistical matters, personnel, and resource acquisition.
- The chain of command contains designated personnel to act in the absence of the major case manager, to insure managerial and investigative continuity.
- Participants in the investigation need to be made aware of the chain of command so they understand the legitimacy of instructions they receive and the organization of the investigative effort. One of the methods to insure that participants in the investigation are aware of the chain of command is to provide them with a written document outlining the chain of command, all component/functions, and the personnel assigned to those component/functions.

KEY TASKS OR FUNCTIONS

1. An effective investigative plan must determine key tasks or functions that need to be met in the investigation.
2. The major case manager must:
   a. Assess what is known about the crime or incident, including:
      - The type of crime, where it occurred, and comparisons with similar crimes.
      - Whether the crime or incident is part of a crime pattern or ongoing criminal enterprise.
      - Any ongoing investigations on this crime pattern or criminal enterprise.
   b. Assign key tasks:
      - Carefully define roles and responsibilities of personnel.
      - Identify roles, limitations, and influence of stakeholders.
      - Ensure that information and communications are managed effectively.

Stakeholders

In the development of an investigative plan, the major case manager must identify stakeholders and detail their involvement in the investigation. The major case manager must take an eclectic view to the definition of "stakeholders," and not limit his or her view to strictly law enforcement personnel. Many stakeholders in major case investigations have nothing to do with law enforcement but are personally impacted by the major case investigation.

As an example, a number of years ago in the Orlando, Florida area, a large number of tourists, many of whom were from foreign countries, were being attacked and robbed by a group of offenders. These tourists had come to Orlando to visit many of the attractions such as Disney World and other entertainment venues. Needless to say, the entertainment venues, hotels, airlines, were all stakeholders in the successful resolution of this series of incidents which compromised a major case investigation. When it was determined that these tourists were being targeted by the license plates on their cars which somehow designated those license plates as belonging to rental vehicles, the car rental companies became a huge stakeholder, as did the Florida Division of Motor Vehicles, which immediately did away with the special designator for rental car license plates.

Law Enforcement Resources

1. Very few major cases can be investigated without additional resources. Management personnel need to quickly make an assessment—are the existing resources I have available, sufficient to achieve case solution in an effective and efficient manner?
2. The investigative plan should be based on needed resources. In the event that additional resources are necessary, they must be immediately identified and efforts to acquire them initiated.
3. Management personnel must estimate the following resource needs:
   • Personnel functions and numbers
   • Logistical support
   • Equipment
   • Budgetary or fiscal considerations
4. The case will suffer if there are needs that are not properly iden-

tified. Once the resources are identified, obtained, and put to use, the plan must anticipate how they will be administered and for how long. Once again, the major case manager should plan "for the long term," and not be pressured into predicting a rapid solution time for the investigation.

5. In the event that resources are acquired that are not adequately prepared for the task assigned, provisions must be made to bring these resources up to an adequate level of performance.

Non-Law Enforcement Resources

- Depending on the nature of the case, medical doctors, psychiatrists, university professors, reporters, and others may be of assistance in the investigation.
- In the case of multijurisdictional investigative efforts, personnel including security, diplomatic, and intelligence representatives and officials can be actively involved in some facets of the investigation. As an example, in multinational investigations, diplomatic protocol must be followed when coordinating jurisdictional efforts. While serving as Commander of a Child Sexual Exploitation Unit with a state police agency, I had occasion to send an investigator to Europe on a child abduction investigation. Having to deal with the State Department was a new experience for someone with no prior exposure to international treaties, embassy protocol, etc.

In developing the plan, the major case manager must consider the implementation of that plan, including how the plan will be communicated to personnel and how the plan will be monitored.

Communicate the Plan

- Using existing standard operating procedures and protocols, the plan must be communicated to all involved personnel. In Chapter 8 the topic of strategic briefings will be examined. The investigative plan should definitely be clearly and thoroughly discussed at the initial strategic briefing so that all personnel become intimately familiar with the plan.
- Meetings designed to discuss the plan and identify areas of potential confusion will assist in having the participants understand

their assignments and the role they play in connection with other participants. In addition to the investigative plan, organizational charts detailing the chain of command and the major case investigative team organization need to be communicated to all participants.

Monitor Plan Through Investigative Results

- Effective plans are flexible as planners cannot anticipate every event influencing the case. The results of the investigation need to be tracked from the inception, thus allowing for investigative results to direct plan maintenance or plan change. Major case management personnel should not view the investigative plan as a document that is "written in stone," but rather as a "living document," which can be subject to modification or change as the need arises during the investigation.
- Investigative results and plan effectiveness can be monitored during strategic briefings in which investigative results are immediately discussed.

MAJOR CASE ORGANIZATION

No matter how well-written and well-communicated an investigative plan may be, without proper organization from the start the major case investigative effort will most certainly suffer. The organization of the major case can be something very foreign to the major case manager who is inexperienced in these types of cases, but it need not be overwhelming. The problem with organizational structures of many law enforcement agencies is that they are so complex and complicated that they become ineffective. The organization of a major case investigative effort need not be overly complex, no matter how complex the actual investigation might be.

The initial stages of a major case investigation involve a great deal of confusion, often directly correlated in degree to the gravity of the offense. Without a proper organizational structure right from the start, the investigative efforts, no matter how professionally accomplished, might suffer from the confusion and disruption that occurs during disorganized efforts. There is a critical need for visible order and the appearance of control to be established immediately, and a need for all information to be channeled through the appropriate channels. When dealing with your own agency's personnel, this is usually not a problem, but it can become a major problem when dealing with outside agency personnel.

1. A proper organizational structure:
    *   Helps coordinate the work of individuals, teams, or units from within or outside the originating agency.
    *   Enables the appropriate delegation of responsibility, function, and authority.
    *   Allows for effective information sharing and communication.
    *   Minimizes errors as key considerations are less likely to be overlooked.
2. Using the organizational chart as a guide will ensure:
    *   Lines of authority are direct.
    *   Unity of command and chain of command are not violated.
    *   Information flow is not hampered.
3. Any organizational structure should be flexible and able to be modified as investigative requirements or developments dictate.
4. A chain of command:
    *   Must be established early in the investigative planning.
    *   Must be followed.
    *   Serves as a filtering system designed to ensure transmittal of critical information to decision makers.
5. In developing a command structure for multiple agency operations, consider:
    *   The agency with the most resources.
    *   The agency with jurisdiction over the most cases (in the case of multiple victims/incidents).
    *   The agency with the highest profile or most critical incidents.
    *   The agency with the best evidence.
    *   The agency with the most investigative expertise.
    *   The agency with the most experience in multiagency investigations.
    *   The agency with a pre-existing command center.
    *   The jurisdiction that will prosecute the case.
6. Once the lead agency and command structure is determined, the scope and nature of their authority must be established, includ-

ing which decisions they will make on their own, and which decisions will require the consultation with other involved agencies.

An excellent example of the development of a sound organizational structure took place on the east coast of the United States in October 2002, when a sniper team terrorized the suburban Washington, D.C. and Central Virginia regions, leading to 14 shootings that resulted in 10 deaths. The manhunt and investigation that led to the capture of two suspects eventually included more than 20 local, 2 state and at least 10 federal law enforcement agencies. The first decision to be made was whether to investigate these matters separately or as part of a task force. The task force was quickly formed, and it was determined that due to the fact that Montgomery County, Maryland was the site of the first shooting that the command post for the task force should be located there.

The next consideration for the task force was how to design the chain of command for such a large undertaking that consisted of over 30 separate law enforcement agencies. It was determined that three individuals would share leadership of the task force, which quite frankly was somewhat of a novel approach which appeared to fly in the face of the usual insistence on "unity of command" with one person in charge. In the sniper task force, however, three individuals shared the sniper task force leadership–Montgomery County Police Chief Charles Moose, Federal Bureau of Investigation Special Agent in Charge Gary Bald and Alcohol, Tobacco, and Firearms Special Agent in Charge Michael Bouchard. Chief Moose acted as the primary spokesman because of his agency's legal authority to investigate the murders.

The chain of command and organizational structure of the sniper task force was tested under a variety of circumstances, but the chain of command and the organizational structure held fast, even under tremendous pressure. Even when a shooting occurred in the District of Columbia on the evening of Day 2, Chief Ramsey of the Washington Metropolitan Police Department did not question that the task force was headquartered in Montgomery County, agreeing that it was the logical location. It should be noted that Chief Ramsey's experience in command positions with the Chicago Police Department included a well-deserved reputation for his ability to work in cooperative efforts with a variety of law enforcement agencies. His ability to work with the sniper task force, therefore, was not at all surprising.

Major Case Organizational Structure

1. Most major cases are organized with two major components: operational and support functions. No matter how complex the investigation might be initially or how complex it may become during the investigation, this simple "bifurcated" structure seems to work well in a variety of circumstances.
2. Operational functions may include:
   - Investigations
   - Intelligence and information management
   - Crime scene management
   - Legal coordination
3. Support functions may include:
   - Logistics
     a. Facilities
     b. Transportation
     c. Equipment
     d. Supplies
     e. Administrative/clerical support personnel
   - Technical support
   - Media
   - Intelligence
   - Surveillance (if needed)
   - Emergency services (medical, tactical operations teams, negotiators- if needed)
4. Whether the investigation involves single agency, multiple agency, or task force involvement, all of the above listed functions should be considered. In the case of smaller agencies, several of these functions may be assigned to one individual, due to personnel limitations or expertise of an individual to manage several functions.
5. Once this is determined, the scope and nature of their authority must be established, including which decisions they will make on their own, and which decisions will require the consultation with others.

OPERATIONAL FUNCTIONS AND POSITIONS

Major Case Manager

The selection of the major case manager is critical to the success of the investigative efforts. The leadership that will be exercised by the person in this position is going to set the stage for the efforts of all subordinate personnel. This is not the position for someone who is being "tested" or "groomed" for higher command. This is not the position for someone to be placed in solely on political considerations. I have seen both of these things occur with disastrous results. The person in this position must have *proven ability,* and not just "good potential." The road to hell, in my opinion, is paved with unrealized potential and unfulfilled good intentions. Actual strategy for selection of this individual will be discussed in Chapter 8, but the responsibilities of the major case manager include:

1. The major case manager has operational authority (and responsibility) over all major case personnel.
2. The major case manager:
   - Makes the final decision on all major operational issues.
   - Keeps assigned personnel and stakeholders apprised of case progress and developments.
   - In a multiagency operation, operates independently without interference from and with the support of the agencies that make up the major case team.
   - Provides prosecutors with whatever assistance is necessary during the prosecution phase.
   - Balances the needs of the entire investigation with the needs of the involved communities.
3. The major case manager must:
   - Have extensive investigative and management experience, proven leadership ability, technical expertise, and the ability and willingness to delegate duties and responsibilities.
   - Remain detached from the fundamental responsibilities of the investigation to be able to manage the overall initiative.
   - Possess well above average oral and written communication skills.
   - Be able to lead under extreme stress and criticism.

- Use proper teambuilding skills to manage the overall investigative effort.
- Remain focused on all priorities, sometimes emphasizing certain ones over others to meet changing demands and conditions.
- Distinguish between executive and operational responsibilities.

Deputy Major Case Manager

1. The deputy major case manager:
   - Assumes the duties of the major case manager in his or her absence.
   - Supports the efforts of the major case manager.
   - May be assigned responsibility over specific functions, teams, or groups of functions.
2. The deputy major case manager must:
   - Have extensive investigative and management experience, proven leadership ability, technical expertise, and the ability to delegate duties and responsibilities.
   - Possess well above average oral and written communication skills.
   - Be able to lead under extreme stress and criticism.
   - Have the appropriate technical expertise to be able to manage specific functions if necessary.

Primary Investigator (Case Officer)

1. This position is normally selected by the major case manager. With direction from the major case manager, the primary investigator:
   - Supervises daily activities related to the investigation.
   - Assigns tasks to investigative personnel and exercises oversight to ensure task completion.
   - Ensures the investigative plan is followed, and makes adjustments to the plan as required.
   - Maintains oversight over leads and investigative results.
   - Provides situational briefings to the major case manager or other stakeholders as needed.

- Coordinates the compilation of the investigative report.
- Coordinates liaison during the prosecution phase.

2. The primary investigator must:
   - Be an experienced investigator with proven ability to coordinate, organize, and control a complex, multifaceted investigation.
   - Be highly motivated with a great deal of initiative and stamina.
   - Possess well above average oral and written communication skills.
   - Be capable of multitasking in a highly stressful environment.

Lead Coordinator

1. The lead coordinator:
   - Acts as the central repository for all leads generated.
   - Processes and evaluates all investigative leads.
   - Prioritizes each lead according to potential importance, ensuring that the highest priority receive immediate follow-up.
   - Prepares and reviews leads for accuracy and ensures appropriate distribution.
   - Reviews all leads with the primary investigator and appropriate team or function leaders.
   - Obtains information necessary to augment incomplete leads.
   - Assists the primary investigator in lead assignment.
   - Ensures investigative leads reporting documentation is completed.
   - Tracks lead assignments and completion.
   - Indexes lead information for later retrieval and coordination.

2. The lead coordinator must:
   - Have extensive investigative experience.
   - Be able to recognize the potential importance of a lead.
   - Have excellent organizational skills.
   - Be capable of multitasking in a highly stressful environment.
   - Be able to prioritize and objectively scrutinize individual items of information received while maintaining focus on the overall investigative effort.
   - Be able to maintain continuity and attention to detail as the investigation develops and the number of leads increases.

Crime Scene/Evidence Coordinator. It is strongly recommended that this position be filled with someone having a background in crime scene analysis and processing, such as a crime scene investigator. It is felt that such a background would better equip the crime scene/evidence coordinator to better communicate with crime laboratory, medical examiner/coroner or crime scene personnel.

1. The crime scene/evidence coordinator:
   - Coordinates all operations and activities at the crime scene (if any).
   - Develops the evidence recovery strategy.
   - Supervises evidence recovery personnel.
   - Coordinates evidence recovery operations with other functional components.
   - Ensures compliance with chain of custody requirements.
   - Prioritizes items submitted for analysis.
   - Coordinates and ensures proper storage and transmittal of evidence.
   - Disseminates analytical results to appropriate personnel.
2. Acts as liaison and coordinates the efforts of any specialized personnel, including:
   - Criminal profilers
   - Crime scene specialists
   - Medical examiner/coroner's office
   - Divers
   - Explosives ordnance disposal teams
   - Forensic pathologists/odontologists/anthropologists
   - Psycholinguists
   - Psychiatrists
   - Psychologists
   - Search and rescue units
   - Canine search teams
3. The crime scene/evidence coordinator must:
   - Be aware of the necessity for crime scene protection and the value of potential items of physical evidence.
   - Know principles and applications of evidentiary chain of custody requirements.
   - Know evidence collection and processing techniques.
   - Be capable of completing complex evidence collection and

analysis reports to reflect activity accomplished.
- Possess well above average oral and written communication skills.
- Be capable of multitasking in a highly stressful environment.

Legal Coordinator. It is strongly recommended that this position be filled with someone from the prosecutor's office, such as an assistant prosecutor, and that this position be selected and assigned immediately, so that the person assigned may become a working part of the major case investigation. If at all possible, the concept of "Vertical Prosecution" should be considered, where the initial prosecutor assigned to the investigative phase follows the case all the way to the prosecution phase.

1. The legal coordinator:
    - Coordinates all legal matters that arise during the major case investigation.
    - Coordinates investigative and prosecution strategy with prosecutors.
    - Prepares legal documentation during the investigation and prosecution phases.
2. The legal coordinator must:
    - Have extensive knowledge of criminal law and procedure.
    - Be familiar with the investigative process and prosecution requirements for major crimes.
    - Be able to prepare specialized legal documents necessary to the major case.

Investigator. Strategies for selection of investigators in the major case investigation will be discussed in Chapter 8.

- The investigator conducts investigative activity as determined or assigned, to include:
- Interviewing or interrogation of witnesses, informants, suspects, victims, and others.
- Participating in physical and/or electronic surveillance.
- Preparing comprehensive investigative reports.
- Conducting liaison with other investigative and legal agencies.
- Assisting in trial preparation.

- Testifying in court.
- The investigator must:
- Know the nature of potential crimes and relevant legal requirements and regulations.
- Be well versed in investigative techniques and operations.
- Be capable of accurately describing investigative efforts in complex case reports to reflect activity accomplished.
- Be capable of working complex, long-term investigations.
- Be highly motivated with initiative and stamina.
- Possess well above average oral and written communication skills.
- Be capable of multitasking in a highly stressful environment.

SUPPORT FUNCTIONS AND POSITIONS

Although the operational functions and positions might appear to be more "glamorous" and "important" to the investigative effort, nothing could be further from the truth. If it were not for the work of the support personnel, many major case investigations would never have been successfully concluded. The support functions and positions include:

Logistics Coordinator

1. The logistics coordinator:
   - Arranges for and secures suitable command post facilities.
   - Arranges for adequate food and lodging for personnel.
   - Establishes and coordinates a transportation and supply system.
   - Establishes and coordinates maintenance services.
   - Facilitates acquisition/hiring of specialized items or personnel required for operations.
   - Maintains complete records of supplies and equipment used.
2. The logistics coordinator must:
   - Have a thorough knowledge of equipment and supply acquisition policies, procedures, and sources.
   - Have experience with facility acquisition, utilization, and maintenance.

- Be able to screen, select, and employ support personnel.
- Have excellent organizational skills.
- Be capable of multitasking in a highly stressful environment.

Technical Support Coordinator

1. The technical support coordinator:
   - Arranges for and secures appropriate technical equipment and services as needed.
   - Facilitates hiring of specialized personnel required for operations.
   - Maintains complete records of technical equipment and specialized personnel used.
2. The technical support coordinator must:
   - Have a thorough knowledge of technical equipment and supply acquisition policies, procedures, and sources.
   - Be able to screen, select, and employ technical personnel.
   - Have excellent organizational skills.
   - Be capable of multitasking in a highly stressful environment.

Media Coordinator

1. The media coordinator:
   - Formulates and implements a media relations policy for the major case governing all participating agencies and personnel.
   - Develops and maintain a collaborative relationship with media representatives.
   - Implements a process for receiving, routing, and processing media inquiries and requests.
   - Develops a process to eliminate or reduce leaked information.
   - Prepares and conducts regularly scheduled press briefings at designated locations.
   - Prepares and disseminates press releases.
   - Develops and maintains a log documenting media inquiries and police responses that describes specific information released regarding case progress.
   - Collects and files media releases regarding the case.
2. The media coordinator must:
   - Have a thorough knowledge of media policies and procedures.

- Have experience with preparation of press releases and preparation and delivery of press briefings and interviews.
- Be capable of developing and maintaining ongoing positive relationships with media personnel.
- Have excellent written and verbal communication skills.
- Be capable of multitasking in a highly stressful environment.

Intelligence Coordinator

1. The intelligence coordinator:
   - Formulates and implements an intelligence collection plan for the major case.
   - Implements a process for receiving, routing, and processing intelligence information and requests.
   - Prepares and conducts intelligence briefings for investigative command.
   - Prepares and disseminates intelligence reports.
   - Develops and maintains a database of intelligence related to the investigation.
2. The intelligence coordinator must:
   - Have a thorough knowledge of intelligence gathering methods, policies, and procedures.
   - Have experience with preparation and delivery of intelligence briefings.
   - Be capable of developing and maintaining ongoing positive relationships with media personnel.
   - Have excellent written and verbal communication skills.
   - Be capable of multitasking in a highly stressful environment.

Surveillance Coordinator (If Needed)

1. The surveillance coordinator has direct control of all physical and technical surveillance operations. The surveillance coordinator:
   - Determines feasible options within surveillance capabilities and makes recommendations.
   - Formulates and implements a surveillance plan for the major case in conjunction with the overall investigative plan and strategy.
   - Directs implementation of surveillance operations and coor-

dinates with other functional components.
- Ensures that intelligence developed through surveillance activities is communicated rapidly and accurately to appropriate major case personnel.
- Prepares and conducts situational briefings regarding surveillance to appropriate personnel.

2. The surveillance coordinator must:
   - Have a thorough knowledge of surveillance methods, policies, and procedures.
   - Have experience with preparation and delivery of surveillance briefings.
   - Have thorough knowledge of available surveillance equipment.
   - Have excellent written and verbal communication skills.
   - Be capable of multitasking in a highly stressful environment.

Emergency Services Coordinator (If Needed)

1. The emergency services coordinator:
   - Briefs major case manager on the continuing or future needs of emergency personnel.
   - Ensures appropriate emergency services personnel are available.
   - Ensures appropriate equipment is available for emergency personnel.

2. The emergency services coordinator must:
   - Have a thorough knowledge of emergency services policy and procedures.
   - Have a working knowledge of the activity and operations of medical, tactical, and negotiations personnel.
   - Be capable of multitasking in a highly stressful environment.

CASE STUDY #3: MULTIPLE OFFENDER ROBBERY/MURDER

VICTIMOLOGY: White Female, 32 years of age, Mother to four children. She was employed as the Manager of the gas station/mini-mart where the crime occurred.

MAJOR CASE CONSIDERATIONS: This was considered a "major case" due to the following elements:

- Political promises to "clean up the violence" in the community shortly before the crime
- Status of the victim—very well-known in the community, active in school programs with her children
- Location in which the crime occurred—although there was much violent crime in the area, there had not been any in the immediate area of this business
- Specifics of the crime—this was an "execution-style" shooting
- Motive/Proceeds of the crime- there was a total of $80 taken during the robbery/murder

GEOGRAPHICS: The robbery/murder occurred at a gas station/mini-mart located on a major street in a Southern suburb of Chicago. The community is bordered on the North by the City of Chicago, and includes residential areas, business/industrial areas, and some sections of economically depressed housing. The community is located on the Illinois/Indiana state line, and on the Indiana side is a large city with some areas that are severely economically depressed and crime-ridden.

The city in which the robbery/murder occurred had been known for years as having a "sin strip" of prostitution and bars, which for the most part were connected to organized crime along the state line. This had given the city an extremely bad reputation, coupled with the political and occasionally police corruption which interacted with the organized crime elements. The "sin strip" had been virtually eliminated by tearing down square blocks of buildings. The mayor who had been instrumental in the decimation of the sin strip, had promised "reform" from the city's violent past, took this crime very personally as a "slap in the face" to his administration.

SPECIFIC FACTS: The victim, as the manager of the station, had been scheduled off for the evening but volunteered to work in order that a female teenaged employee could attend a school dance. The victim had worked many night shifts at this location, and was well aware of the safety precautions available, which included bullet resistance glass on all outside windows, and a tray system for taking in receipts. The victim, however was not using the tray to take in receipts, and had the left the entry door open due to the warm weather.

The investigation revealed that at 10:19 the victim sold gasoline and cigarettes to a patron who was later identified. At 10:37, another regular patron came into the station and didn't see any employees. The patron, aware of the fact that the station had a back room, after unsuccessfully calling for an employee entered the back room and noticed the victim lying on her back in a puddle of blood and brain matter in the storeroom.

Cause of death was a contact GSW (gunshot wound) to the back of the head, "execution style," and the weapon was described as a .380 caliber weapon. The projectile was recovered at the front of the cranial cavity. Inventory of the station revealed that approximately $80 had been taken. The location had no security cameras, nor were there any cameras in any adjoining businesses or in the immediate area of the station.

IMMEDIATE ACTION TAKEN: The city's police department, which had some truly talented investigators who were well-versed in investigating violent crimes, were under a tremendous amount of political pressure to immediately solve the crime. They began their investigation, which included all five of their Investigators, and although the investigation was professionally conducted, no formal information management system was initiated.

The police department, through the media, established a "hot line" to gather tips and other information regarding the crime. The owner of the station, Mobil Oil Company, immediately offered a $25,000 reward for information on the murder, and this information was provided to the media. The police department, augmented by volunteers, supervised the distribution of nearly 1,000 flyers announcing the reward, which was also featured in the local newspapers. As the case progressed, very few if any leads and information were developed, and even usually reliable and very active informants had no information to provide.

After two solid weeks of virtually round the clock efforts, the police department requested assistance from the state police. The state police responded with a squad of investigators and entered into a joint investigative effort. A formal information management/leads system was put into place.

Approximately three weeks after the murder, the victim's purse was found by Chicago Streets and Sanitation workers in a garbage can in an alley on the South side of Chicago in an economically depressed area. The area in which the purse was found was approximately five miles from the scene of the crime.

MAJOR DIFFICULTIES: Following the discovery of the purse, the (former) chief of the department suggested that we mount a three-week 24-hour surveillance of the immediate area in which the purse was found. His plan called for all young black male subjects in the area of the house in whose garbage can the purse was found to be picked up, transported to the department, and questioned. Although this was the only promising lead to have emerged on this investigation, it was the chief's intention to assign all available manpower to the surveillance, which would have precluded the work on other leads. When it was explained that it would probably not be prudent to focus on one lead to the exclusion of everything else, he relented and only took half of the available personnel for the surveillance.

After another week, while continuing to work other leads and angles on the case all investigators were encouraged to contact their informants for anything that might be related. One of the Investigators was contacted by an informant who had an interest in the reward and who had driven past the station at approximately 10:20 pm. This informant related that he observed a car similar to that of a subject whom he knew as "Todd," but that he had not observed anyone in the vehicle. The informant described Todd as a small-time cocaine and marijuana dealer. Records checks of Todd revealed a minor criminal history, mainly for drug offenses, with no violent crime background. Not knowing whether Todd was involved in the robbery/murder, but considering the possibility that his vehicle might have been there around the time of the murder, a plan was developed in which the informant would introduce an undercover officer to Todd with the intention of purchasing a small quantity of cocaine. The reason for this approach, rather than simply picking Todd up and questioning him, was that we felt that if we had something with which to pressure Todd (cocaine delivery charges) that in the event that he did have something to do with the robbery/murder he might be more likely to provide us the information.

The introduction was made, and over the course of the next two weeks two small cocaine purchases were made from Todd. Once the second purchase was made, Todd was brought in for questioning. Although he initially denied any involvement with the sale of cocaine, when the undercover officer was brought into the room he knew that he had a problem. The questioning then switched to the robbery/murder, and after extensive questioning he indicated that he had indeed been at the location on the night of the murder but that his two friends, "Sammy" and "Danny" had gone inside and committed the crime. He identified Danny as the shooter, and agreed to testify against both men in exchange for leniency on the cocaine delivery charges. An assistant prosecutor had been assigned to the investigation and was able to tentatively approve the agreement.

It was learned that Sammy had left the area shortly after the crime and was residing in California. A warrant was secured and Sammy was picked up and brought back to be questioned on the robbery/murder. Of course when he was questioned he indicated that it was he who stayed in the car and that Todd and Danny had entered the station, and that Danny had been the shooter.

It was also learned that Danny, at the time of the murder, had been convicted of an attempted murder a week before the robbery murder, but was released for two weeks by the Judge to "get his affairs in order" prior to reporting to prison for his 20–40 year sentence. He had become involved in this robbery/murder while "on leave" from having been convicted of an attempted murder in the neighboring state. It was also learned that Danny had a violent past, having killed his first victim at the age of 15 while running from a restaurant for not paying his bill. The victim was a cook who had chased him from the restaurant, and Danny had stabbed the cook to death. He had been sent to a "youth authority" facility until he reached the age of 19 and was released.

Shortly after the arrest and ensuing publicity on the case, another witness came forward. After leaving the crime scene, the trio of offenders had stopped in an alley on the south side of Chicago to relieve themselves and had dumped the victim's purse in a nearby garbage can. In reality, the location of the evidence had no real connection to the offense, other than the offenders having passed through the area. Following their dumping the purse, the trio went to a friend's house to smoke marijuana after which they and their friend, returned to the suburb where the crime had occurred. While driving across a bridge spanning a river on their way back to the suburb where the crime had occurred, Todd, who was driving his car, threw the weapon used in the robbery/murder into the river. The friend asked what had been thrown from the car and the trio bragged about the murder, even going so far as to drive past the station, which was now saturated with police. The friend, who was terrified of all three offenders, didn't mention his observations to anyone until they were arrested, and then only to seek the reward.

LESSONS LEARNED:

1. Don't fall into the trap of assigning all available personnel to focus on one "hot" lead to the exclusion of all others, no matter how hot that lead might be at the moment. Although the discovery of the purse would cause one to wonder how it got there, to have assigned all available personnel to mount a round-the-clock surveillance to the exclusion of all other leads would have been foolhardy. In reality, as it was learned, the hot lead basically fizzled out and didn't amount to much of anything.

2. In the event that a suspect is developed who is involved in any other criminal activity, don't ignore the possibility of seeking charges on other crimes in order to "put pressure" on the suspect. Use your imagination, and try whatever angle you can think of to gain information. Don't limit yourself to "traditional" investigative work, if you can see an opportunity to utilize another facet of law enforcement, as in this case undercover operations, consider using it. Had it not been for the cocaine delivery charges on Todd, he would have had no reason to speak to the police, and probably would not have.

3. The assignment of an assistant prosecutor at the onset of the investigation, particularly in a system wherein "Vertical Prosecution" is allowed can be a definite plus. The fact that an assistant prosecutor was intimately familiar with the case not only

streamlined the "plea agreement" with Todd, it certainly assisted at the trial stage.

4. Don't let the acquittal or unsuccessful prosecution of one of a group of offenders dissuade you from vigorously prosecuting on additional suspects. Needless to say, everyone involved in this investigation was upset with the acquittal of the first offender, but we also felt that the most violent of the trio had probably pulled the trigger.

5. Maintaining focus of personnel is often best accomplished by "humanizing" your victim(s). In this case I had a large family photograph of the victim, her husband, and their four children displayed in the command post. Next to this photo I displayed a photo of the victim at the crime scene, laying face up on the floor of the station, with blood and brain matter on the floor. The message to the investigators working the case was simple: Take a good look at this photo and realize that this Mother will never be there to care for her children as they grow up. The daughters will never have Mom there to teach them about becoming young women and the son won't have Mom there to fix his knee scrapes and make them better. And this poor guy, the husband, will be without the companionship of his wife because of what these bastards did in the next photo. Look at this photo and tell me how tired you are, or that you're upset because you're missing your son's baseball game, or that you're frustrated and don't want to go on.

CASE RESOLUTION: The case went to trial and the defendants were tried separately, with Sammy's trial going first. Even with testimony from Todd, the jury acquitted Sammy, who then flatly refused to stick around to testify against Danny. Needless to say, the assistant prosecutor, who had been involved with the investigative phase and now took the case to trial, was devastated.

Shortly thereafter, Danny was brought to trial, and once again Todd testified against him, as did the witness who had been with the trio and observed them disposing of the weapon (which was never recovered) after the crime. Danny was convicted and sentenced to Life Without Possibility of Parole, which is scheduled to begin when he completed his 20–40 year sentence in the neighboring state.

Chapter 5

EFFECTIVE MANAGEMENT STRATEGIES

The management strategies and techniques that are utilized during the management of a major case aren't really that much different from those used during everyday management. The difference is that these strategies and techniques usually differ in degree and intensity. The pressures placed on major case managers can be and sometimes are overwhelming. Maintaining focus on the ultimate goals and objectives which were discussed in Chapter 4 can assist greatly in managers not succumbing to the tremendous pressure, criticism, and second-guessing that occurs during major cases. Operating in a task force environment with a predetermined memorandum of understanding or intergovernmental agreement as discussed in Chapter 3 can make the entire process run much smoother.

KEY MANAGEMENT TASKS FOR THE MAJOR CASE MANAGER

An awareness of **key management tasks** can help managers identify and perform their job requirements, while avoiding the pressures which can cause loss of focus. Some of the most critical management tasks for the major case manager are discussed below.

Planning

Major case managers function as planners. Successful organizations have objectives and develop appropriate strategies for achieving those objectives. In the role of planner, the major case manager is looking to current and future organizational needs. In the management of major cases, although planning might seem to be too much of a long-range concern, this is not necessarily true. Considering the fact that the major case manager has no real idea and therefore cannot predict how long the major case efforts will continue, planning for the future is sound management. Planning in the major case includes making certain that adequate resources are going to be available for as long as the investigation continues. Without this planning, the amount of available resources and even the number of available personnel might dwindle to the point where there aren't enough resources to continue the investigation.

Organizing

Management involves the coordination of different activities to achieve high quality results. Success in this endeavor requires organization. By organizing activities, management assigns identified tasks to individuals and groups within the organization. This enables objectives to be achieved. In Chapter 4, the topic of organization in the major case was examined, and the simple "bifurcated" organizational model of Operations and Support Services was utilized for illustration purposes. In a particularly complex and multifaceted long-term major case investigation a more elaborate organizational structure might be necessary. The actual type of structure, however, is not that important, more important is that the operation is well-organized and that the organizational structure is clearly communicated to all participants at the onset of the investigative effort and reinforced during the investigation.

Commanding

Commanding involves using assigned personnel in an organized manner to achieve goals and objectives of the mission. This can be accomplished through motivation, influence, and effective leadership. Managing a major case is a true test of the leadership capabilities of all personnel who are selected to supervise components/functions, but the biggest and most critical test of leadership ability relates to the person chosen as the major case manager. Any deficiencies in leadership ability of the person chosen for this position will become evident very quickly, and will have a dramatic impact on the overall operations of the major case investigation. This is why the selection of the major case manager is critical to the success of the major case investigation. The criteria and selection strategy for selection of the major case manager will be discussed in Chapter 8.

Controlling

Managers are required to establish systems of checks and balances, monitor plans for effectiveness, modify plans when and where appropriate, and implement the changes. Checks and balances must be utilized not only by the major case manager, but by all personnel assigned the supervision of the various components/functions, whether those components/functions are operational or support. In addition to these functions, to be truly effective major case managers must also be able to perform the following duties:

1. **Act as a role model for personnel.** Actually lead by example, rather than merely "talking a good game," the major case manager must actually perform to the level and in the manner that is expected from subordinates.
   - **Delegate responsibility and rely on those delegates.** Delegation for the sake of delegation is meaningless. Tasks which are delegated should be those tasks that are actually relevant and necessary to the investigative effort, and the appropriate level of authority should be delegated along with the tasks.
   - **Be proactive versus reactive.** Rather than waiting for things to happen to improve the investigative effort, the major case manager should be "making things happen" by getting out in front of potential problems rather than allowing these problems to paralyze the investigation.
   - **Be consistent.** Consistency in how the investigation is viewed, consistency in how personnel are treated, and consistency in being able to effectively read what is going on in the major case investigation is critical.
   - **Be flexible.** Rarely does anything go exactly according to plan, and contingency planning is important for the major case manager. Flexibility can mean the difference between seeing a low point in the investigation as an omen of doom or as an opportunity to attempt to overcome it.
   - **Recognize achievements and work efforts.** People often

behave in a manner for which they are rewarded, and behavior that is rewarded will usually increase in frequency. The difficulty with rewards during a major case investigation is that the major case manager or other supervisor cannot wait until the end of the investigation to provide positive reinforcement, it should be provided throughout the investigation.

- **Monitor fatigue and maintain motivation.** Fatigue can lead to poor decisions and slipshod work, and it is virtually impossible to motivate people who are suffering from fatigue. Personnel (and management) must be monitored continually to make certain that they are not working themselves to the point of exhaustion and fatigue.
- **Have and display confidence in the process and personnel.** The major case manager, to be effective, must at times be a "cheerleader" for the investigative effort, constantly exhorting the personnel involved to give their very best efforts to the investigation.
- **Display personal attention to the case while letting others work.** People like to feel as if they are unique and even special, and the good major case manager can recognize and reward the uniqueness of individuals, but not to the point where that extra attention gets in the way of their performing their duties.

2. **Work with those outside the case.** The interactions with outside entities and stakeholders, such as political figures or community members is an important part of the major case manager's duties, and cannot be ignored simply because it isn't "law enforcement related."

- **Act as a buffer from outside pressures.** Part of the function of the major case manager is to make certain that a working environment is established and maintained that allows the personnel assigned to the major case to perform their duties to the best of their ability. Having to worry about supplies, relief, equipment, or virtually anything else can divert the attention of the personnel assigned from their duties and cannot be tolerated.
- **Maintain positive relationships with outside agencies.** Particularly in multi-agency operations, the major case manager must see to it that all participating agencies and their

chief executives are kept abreast of major developments and that their needs are met.

As important as these management functions and abilities are, however, it is worth noting that even the most experienced major case manager cannot solve a case without a well-organized team of investigators and other personnel. Many of the challenges in a major case investigation come from managing the investigative personnel. Successful management of the major case leads to successful resolution and prosecution.

GUIDELINES FOR MANAGING A MAJOR CASE

- **Plan for the long term.** Although this has been mentioned before, it does warrant repeating. Plan and organize for the long term, rather than anticipating a quick resolution. It is easier to cut back on resources when it is determined they are not needed, rather than attempt to reorganize and get additional resources.
- **Organize by task/function (specialty).** In developing a major case organization, focus on organization of functions and not personnel. The organizational model discussed in Chapter 4 is based on functional responsibilities, not personnel. When assigning personnel to functions, assign tasks by expertise and experience.
- **Establish teams to address components/functions.** Once a mission is established and goals/objectives identified, designate teams of skilled personnel who can contribute to mission. The specific team goals will relate directly to the component/function to which the team is assigned, and will be geared toward achieving their support of the overall mission. It must be clearly communicated that all positions, components, and functions are critical to the overall effort. As an example, the component/function of "Logistics Coordinator," or those personnel working in that component/function might not appear as "critical," but if the logistics of the overall effort are not properly addressed the efficiency of the investigative effort will surely suffer. If the location being utilized as a command post is not suitable, a host of issues, including morale of the personnel assigned to the major case, will certainly suffer.

- **Share information.** Hold regular meetings with appropriate audiences to share or discuss meaningful information. Sharing information relates not only to investigative personnel, but to the many stakeholders that have a personal interest in the major case investigation. Strategic briefings will be discussed in Chapter 8, but those are not the only method of sharing information.
- **Separate investigative functions from administrative functions.** Ensure that assigned personnel are directing their efforts appropriately, and that all of those efforts are not only seen as critical to the overall effort, but that they are also appreciated. Don't burden investigative personnel with administrative functions, as this will divert their attention from investigative duties, and just as important, allow those personnel assigned to administrative functions to focus on their duties.
- **Remember case prosecution.** Managers may be pressured to take premature action or make careless decisions in the resolution of a case, jeopardizing the ultimate prosecution of a case. Develop a relationship with the prosecutor early in the investigation to ensure that prosecution needs are being met during the investigative stages. The fact that the investigation and prosecution of any major case is a "team effort", should be constantly reinforced throughout the investigation.

MAINTAINING SITUATIONAL AWARENESS AND DECISION-MAKING

Situational awareness includes having an awareness of what is happening around you, which enables you to understand how information, people, events, and your own actions can affect your goals, objectives, and decision-making, both now and in the near future. Lack of situational awareness can lead to mistakes, such as improper prioritization of tasks and erroneous decision-making, either of which can be devastating to the major case investigation. If both are occurring, disaster can occur. Situational awareness is something that the military uses in a variety of situations, from fighter pilots having "dogfights" with other aircraft to ground unit commanders about to engage the enemy. As a (retired) intelligence officer, we practiced situational awareness routinely when analyzing terrorist operations and incidents.

That awareness assisted greatly with not only the analysis but also with the predictions of possible future scenarios that resulted from the analysis.

Establishing and Maintaining Situational Awareness in Major Case Management

- **Analyze issues** as they arise. As information is obtained it must be analyzed for content, completeness, thoroughness, and applicability to mission. Never take anything for granted. There's an old motto in military intelligence that says "In God we Trust, All others We Monitor." This means that when something is important enough to analyze it is also important enough to monitor.
- **Seek input** from subordinate personnel and other stakeholders. Without this input, it is easy to lose focus on the reality of the situation you are in. The input might come from the least experienced personnel assigned to the major case investigation, and that lack of experience should not dissuade the major case manager from seriously considering the input. The input might also come from non-law enforcement stakeholders, and potentially valuable input should not be disregarded because of their non-law enforcement status. If they are stakeholders, they have a personal interest of some type in the investigation, and their input might be extremely valuable to the overall goals and objectives of the investigative effort.
- **Use analysis results** to assess goals and objectives, and strategic and tactical operations. Following analysis, modifications to organizational structure, investigative planning, goals and objectives, and operational activities may be made. Don't get locked into one structure, one plan, or one method of operation. The process of criminal investigation is by nature a fluid and flexible process. The management of a major case oftentimes necessitates more fluidity and flexibility than is necessary for routine investigations.

Management of Decision Making in the Major Case Investigation

The cold hard truth is this faulty decisions made during routine operations are usually not of the magnitude that they are irreparable. Faulty decisions made by management during a major case investigation, on the other hand, may be devastating to the overall effort.

Having made some faulty decisions myself, I can attest to the fact that even years later, long after everyone else has forgotten about the case, the person in charge who made the faulty decision will remember it clearly. In some cases they are even "haunted" by it to some extent.

As an example, while commanding the brutal gang murder of a young woman who had been tortured, sexually assaulted, and beaten before being killed, the time came to make a decision on whether or not to conduct a round-up of gang members who hung out at a local strip mall. The purpose of the round-up would be to conduct interviews in an investigation that was beginning to stagnate due to lack of information and leads. It was felt that a large number of interviews of gang members and their associates might provide that one bit of information that could kick-start the investigation. After carefully considering the totality of the circumstances, however, which included the volatile nature of the neighborhoods, residents, and the political climate, I decided against the round-up, and agonized over the decision while the investigation continued. Even though we ultimately solved the case and arrested and convicted the offenders, the number of hours of dogged investigative work that resulted from my decision and that might have been saved played on my mind for quite a while after the investigation was ended.

Decisions made during the management of a major investigation:

- Have shortterm and long-term impact on the case as well as the organization.
- Must be based on an adequate communication process.

Proper major case management results in an organization that is able to obtain, receive, analyze, and pass on information to decision makers so that sound decisions affecting case outcome can be made.

Decision making is the process in which managers act to achieve the organization mission. Decision making involves a certain amount of risk taking, which cannot be avoided. The fact is you might end up making a wrong decision even after carefully considering all the available alternatives and after receiving as much competent input as is humanly possible. You still might fall on your face and be remembered forevermore as the person who made the wrong decision that blew the major case. Quite a scary possibility, isn't it? But after all, that's why the person in charge is paid the big bucks, right?

Over the years, I have been to more classes than I can remember that taught various decision-making strategies, some good and some not-so-good or even impractical. Based on some of those lessons, and more importantly based on having made some bad decisions during major case investigations myself, I'll offer a simple process for making decisions in the management of a major case that have worked for me and many of my associates.

For purposes of illustration, I will use the real-life example of having discovered "leaks" to the media during a major case investigation. Unfortunately, even on very sensitive cases, this has occurred in many locations, so it is a very possible problem for the major case manager to have to overcome. In this particular case, the leak was so blatant that copies of actual investigative reports somehow ended up on the evening news being reported by an investigative reporter. Needless to say, the fallout following the newscast was huge.

Step One: Decide if There is a Problem

The first step in the decision-making process is to decide if there is in fact a problem that must be acted upon. If so, describe and understand the problem, and accept the challenge to tackle the problem. Questions to ask include:

- Is there a problem?
- Am I exaggerating or minimizing the problem?

In the case of a leak of information during a major case investigation, this is obviously a serious problem, and if a leak exists it is hard to minimize or exaggerate. Leaks during major case investigations can cause irreparable harm to the investigation, and can result in the loss of confidence on the management of the investigation by participants, the public, victims, and other stakeholders.

Step Two: Define the Problem

Before reacting to what you think the problem might be, seek to understand more about why you think there's a problem. Questions to ask include:

- What can you see that causes you to think there's a problem?

- Where is it happening?
- How is it happening?
- When is it happening?
- With whom is it happening?
- What is the risk to the major case investigation if the problem is not solved?

If the problem seems overwhelming, break it down into several smaller related problems. Verify your understanding of the problem by conferring with a peer or someone else. If there are several related problems, prioritize and determine which ones to address first. Understand your role in the problem to determine if that influences your perception of the problem.

In our example, the risk to the major case investigation if the leaks continue could be disastrous. This would be particularly true if the specifics of investigative methods, the identity of potential suspects, the use or identity of confidential informants, information regarding surveillance activities, or a host of other items of information were leaked.

Step Three: Look at Potential Causes for the Problem

- Collect and review information available.
- Write down your assessment and information from others.
- Write down a description of the potential causes of the problem in terms of what is happening, where, when, how, with whom and why.

In this example, one could consider, as best you could, which officers are known to have interactions with the media, either on-duty or as part of their personal life. Once those determinations were made, those personnel who could be considered the identities of the most likely sources of the leaks could be determined.

Step Four: Identify Alternative Approaches to Resolve the Problem

Brainstorm for alternate solutions to the problem, using command and supervisory personnel most closely associated with the issue. In a major case, the major case manager, his/her deputy, the primary investigator, and whatever other component/function supervisory staff would be directly related to the issue at hand would be included in these discussions.

In our example, the meeting to determine a prudent course of action included the above personnel as well as the media and legal coordinators. It was felt that the media coordinator had the closest relationships with the media, and the legal coordinator could provide information on the most appropriate manner in which to address any major case personnel who might be ultimately identified as having leaked the information. In this situation the alternatives discussed were either talking directly to the most likely source of the leaks or planting false information with the suspect to see what happened.

Step Five: Make a Decision

Questions to ask include:

- Which approach is the most likely to solve the problem for the long term?
- Which approach is the most realistic to accomplish for now?
- What is the extent of risk associated with each alternative?
- What personnel, money, and facilities are needed?
- How much time is needed to implement the solution?
- Who will primarily be responsible for ensuring implementation of the decision?

In this case, the decision was made to confront the likely source of the leaks. It was felt that the problem of the leaks, if not immediately addressed, could have long-term consequences on the overall investigative effort.

Step Six: Verify if the Problem has been Resolved

If the problem has not been resolved, questions to ask include:

- Was your decision correct?
- Were sufficient resources allocated?
- Should you reevaluate information or evidence and make a new decision?

If the problem has been resolved, questions to ask to prepare yourself for the next problem include:

- What changes should be made to avoid this type of problem in the future? Should the operational plan be modified?
- What did you learn from this problem solving? Are there any steps that could be taken to preclude the same issue from reoccurring?

In our leak example, the verification included monitoring the news coverage of the investigation to determine if any additional leaks existed. Fortunately, there were none, and the individual responsible for the original leak, who fully admitted his culpability, was removed from the major case investigation and returned to his parent agency for disciplinary action.

The problem with decision making is that it is by no means fool proof, and sometimes it has to be repeated until the appropriate or correct decision is ultimately made. There are, however, some common errors of decision makers, all of which can be avoided. These errors include situations in which the decision maker fails to:

- Take action when a decision is required. Putting off a necessary decision, particularly if it is in response to a problem or issue, will not make that problem or issue correct itself or go away. Decisive action usually needs to be applied, and sometimes the wrong decision is better than no decision at all.
- See the whole picture. Managers make errors when they do not take available information into consideration or when they discard information out of bias. Never assume that you have all the facts, continually seek additional information that might be beneficial for decision making.
- Gain team support for the process. Involve as many people as possible who must live with the impact of the decision.
- Learn from previous decisions, particularly your mistakes.
- Make a decision at the lowest possible level or as close to the scene of action as possible.
- Consider new ideas. Managers who stifle communication, reject ideas, or belittle recommendations, find themselves with few alternatives.

BUILDING AND MAINTAINING TEAM UNITY

I have used the term "major case investigative team" throughout this text, and it is purely intentional. The participants in a major case investigation are truly members of a team, each with a specific purpose, function, and duties, but each also focused on the overall goals and objectives of the investigative effort. In order to effectively manage such a team, the major case manager must practice not only solid and effective team building, but also effective team maintenance. There are several qualities that any effective functional team leader should possess, which include the following:

- **Flexibility.** Functional team leaders must be able to adjust to change. Their approach to even the most disconcerting matters must be unflappable. A team leader must realize that he or she cannot make everyone happy all the time. Leaders must endure criticism and still maintain their composure. Flexibility is the foundation for innovation and keeping pace with change, which is routine in the major case investigation.
- **Credibility.** A common downfall of management personnel is to pretend to always have an answer for everything, based on the fact that they truly believe that they have to know everything. A functional team leader that can admit that he or she does not know an answer builds and sustains credibility among team members. Truly believing that there are members of the team who know much more about particular topics than you (the manager) does can help establish and maintain the credibility of the functional team leader and the major case manager.
- **Integrity.** A functional team leader who tells one person one thing and another something else loses both credibility and integrity when these two people compare notes. A leader without credibility and integrity cannot lead effectively, and the efforts of the major case team will certainly suffer in an atmosphere lacking in integrity.
- **Delegation.** The more a functional team leader delegates, the more people involved who may generate new ideas and approaches. A team leader who does not empower employees to make decisions is merely positioning the organization for a crisis. An effective leader is willing to empower others to lead in certain

situations. Personnel are (hopefully) selected for assignment to major case investigations based on their individual talents and expertise, and to not allow them to exercise that talent and expertise is counter-productive.

One of the most critical aspects of any major case investigation is the management of information and leads. Many major investigations have faltered or failed because of poorly managed information, and missing a critical lead or lead connection can be devastating to an investigation.

Chapter 6

INFORMATION MANAGEMENT

In Chapter 2, some common obstacles or errors committed by major case managers were discussed. One of the most critical errors was that the investigation proceeds too quickly without proper planning and control. Nowhere is this more problematic than when it relates to the management of information. If both incoming and outgoing information are not managed properly, that one bit of information that could "blow the investigation wide open" and lead to a quick solution will be missed. No major case manager would want the fact that an investigation was blown because they didn't insist on professional, thorough, and effective management of information on their conscience. As with many other problems and all of the common errors discussed throughout this book, however, most problems associated with information management can be avoided.

The types of information likely to be encountered during a major case investigation and which need to be managed include:

- Incoming information and intelligence from various sources
- Investigative leads and related information
- Information regarding key decisions and events
- Administrative information, such as scheduling, overtime, payments to informants
- Logistical information necessary for management of the major case investigation

In order to be effective, the information management system must include the following considerations:

- A central repository for all information gathered
- Appropriate analysis of information and intelligence must be conducted to determine relevance and importance
- Appropriate dissemination of information and intelligence must take place
- Prioritization of incoming information must be accomplished for operational decision-making.

In the event that information is not properly managed, the following could occur:

- Faulty decision-making. Decisions regarding operational activities and other elements of the major case must be based on best possible information.
- Failure to properly prioritize operational activities. In the event that information is gathered requiring investigative activities, prioritizing those activities is essential. Improperly managed information can lead to inaccurate prioritization.
- Missing connections or associations. Improperly managed information can lead to missing connections or associations between individuals or groups which might be pertinent to the matters being investigated.

MANAGEMENT OF AN INVESTIGATIVE LEADS SYSTEM

A lead is any item of information that will generate an activity or provide a direction for the major case to follow. Leads come from a variety of sources, to include:

- Witnesses, victims, and other community members
- Crime scene analysis
- Confidential sources (informants)
- Police or intelligence agencies
- Media representatives
- The investigation itself (leads generated by leads completed)

The investigative leads system which is utilized *is the very heart of the investigative effort,* and if it is unworkable, the investigation will surely suffer.

When setting up your investigative leads system, keep it as simple as possible, in order that personnel will understand the system and comply with it. Keep in mind that many of the personnel assigned to this investigation may have never worked on a *major case,* and some of the personnel may have never worked on *any* investigations, so the system selected must be easily understood and easily followed.

The investigative leads system should consist, at a minimum, of the following elements:

1. **A method of integrating new leads into the investigation.** Any and all information that could generate a lead must be included in the investigative leads management system. Failure to do so could result in missing a significant lead which could be critical to the investigation.

2. **Documentation of assigned leads including to whom they were assigned and the date of assignment.** If this is not done, confusion over responsibility and timeliness of investigative activity would occur.

3. **A method for evaluating and prioritizing each lead with its relative potential importance to the investigation.** Some leads are potentially more important than others and it is imperative that a proper analysis of leads is completed to determine relative importance.

4. **Providing a routing system for each lead as it is assigned for further investigation.** Once the raw information is transformed into a lead, a system of routing must be developed to preclude lost leads or information.

5. **Establishing a common format for investigators to include new leads.** If a procedure is not developed and followed for inclusion of new lead information, consistency of analysis and prioritization of leads will not be able to take place. Investigators could begin to independently follow leads without making those leads part of the investigative leads management system and hamper the major case effort.

6. **Providing a method of information storage that allows for easy retrieval and cross-referencing.** Lead information may need to be quickly retrieved during the investigation, and cross-

referencing with existing leads or information may reveal connections between individuals, groups, and organizations.

7. **Report preparation system for completed leads.** Once leads are completed, reports must be generated. If this is not done in a consistent manner by all personnel, information may be lost.

Discretion and examination of any new leads will dictate whether or not they must be handled immediately, which highlights the desirability of having one individual assigned to manage the investigative leads system. This can ensure adherence to the system, consistency and better continuity.

PAPER-BASED LEADS MANAGEMENT SYSTEMS

In the event that a paper-based leads management system is used, individual items of information obtained and assigned will be captured on lead sheets. It is the purpose of the lead sheets to capture the information, act as a mechanism for assigning leads to investigators, and act as a means of documenting the information gathered during investigation of the lead.

Lead Sheets

In order to be complete, lead sheets must contain the following at a minimum:

1. Sequential lead number
2. The date the lead was received
3. Source of the information (this can be coded for reliability purposes)
4. The individual to whom the lead is assigned
5. The date the lead is completed
6. Cross-references to related leads
7. Summary of the information gathered

Copies of the lead sheets should be disseminated:

• To case file

- To investigator assigned the lead
- To intelligence analysts
- To clerical staff for cross-referencing and indexing

Sometimes the use of multi-part forms will make this dissemination easier. Appendix 4 is a sample "Paper-based Lead Sheet."

Master Leads Directory

In many major case investigations the number of leads generated can become extremely large very quickly, and if not consistently and carefully organized, it can become very confusing. Lead connections can be missed, duplicate leads may get pursued, and investigative continuity may suffer.

It is very beneficial for the leads coordinator to maintain an ongoing record of lead assignments, which will allow the leads coordinator, major case manager, primary investigator, or other participant or stakeholder to get a very quick summary of the leads that have been assigned. The master leads directory and the lead assignment control log also permit investigative personnel to get a quick overview of lead assignments. Appendix 5 is a sample "Master Leads Directory." Appendix 6 is a sample "Lead Assignment Control Log."

COMPUTER-BASED INFORMATION
AND LEADS MANAGEMENT SYSTEMS

In addition to paper-based leads management, there are many commercially produced computer-based investigative leads systems available. These systems are built around data base programs, and can provide the major case manager with numerous advantages over the paper-based systems. Occasionally, law enforcement managers look at computerized investigative leads system as some type of panacea that will basically run the case for them, however, which is not true. Computerized information and leads management systems are simply sophisticated data base programs, which can assist in the major case investigation in a number of ways, but which will not allow shortcuts of good, sound, investigative activity. Although it might not yet exist, the ideal computerized leads management system should:

1. Serve as the electronic **repository** for all tips, leads, and other case information;
2. Be **compatible** with other leads management systems so as to be able to transfer information on related investigations;
3. Is **web-based** for authorized personnel to be able to access the system off-site;
4. Feeds **multiple** information systems based on one-time data entry;
5. Performs data **analysis,** such as cross-checking and indexing; and
6. Provides **action tasks** for investigators to consider completing.

Although computer-based leads management systems are a mechanism for charting leads on a computer, they can also be used for cross-indexing subjects, documenting vehicles, items of evidence, and so forth. Ease of access to data and user-friendliness is critical for any computerized leads and information management system. A major problem associated with computerized information management systems, however, is they can be cumbersome unless someone trained in the system use is available for a long-term assignment to the major case investigation. It is imperative that if used, the computerized system be in place and initiated as soon as the investigation begins. The advantages of computerized investigative leads systems for major case investigations lie in their capacity for storing vast amounts of information and speed in processing that information. There are other advantages of computerized systems, which include:

1. Rapid identification of linked information, including information from multiple-related investigations and sometimes even "cold cases."
2. Elimination of duplicate leads/investigations, the computerized system will catch the fact that the name, vehicle, or phone number in the new lead has already been examined as part of the investigation.
3. Reduction in lost leads or information, it is much easier to lose a piece of paper than it is to lose data on a backed-up computerized system.
4. Rapid data response as time consuming hand searches are eliminated, rather than going through hundreds of lead sheets by

hand, the computerized system is capable of doing the same process in seconds or minutes.

5. Adaptability of system to specific case needs, such as analysis of phone records, or generation of time lines.
6. Useful for non-investigative functions, such as budgeting, personnel scheduling.
7. Possibly compatible with other leads management systems, which opens up communication opportunities with other jurisdictions working on related investigations.

As beneficial as computerized information systems can be, however, there are some disadvantages, which include:

1. **High cost of hardware, software, programming, training, storage.** many agencies are not fiscally capable of purchasing the hardware or software
2. **Lack of existing computer expertise.** Utilization of computerized leads systems requires training or skills which many agencies do not possess
3. **Lack of appropriate facilities for the computer system.** Some agencies don't have suitable facilities for their investigators, much less for additional computer systems
4. **Lack of capability for converting present records to computerized format.** Information, to be useful in a computerized leads management system, must be stored in a compatible format, and at present many agencies do not store their data in such formats
5. **Data security.** Unless data stored in computerized leads systems is thoroughly protected and backed-up, data security can be an issue

Perhaps the biggest problem with computerized investigative leads systems is that oftentimes they're purchased well ahead of time and never utilized until the major case begins. When the major case begins it is way too late to learn the system. People that are not used to using a system become reticent about using it, especially during a high profile case, and it is unrealistic to expect personnel to learn a new system in the middle of a crisis.

In the event that a computerized investigative leads system is available and will be used in the major case investigation, I would strongly recommend that the agency **practice using it beforehand on non-major investigations**, such as police backgrounds, burglaries, etc. so that your personnel become familiar with the system. By doing so, the ability to work with the computerized system on the major case will be enhanced. As with any computer system, make certain that all essential data is adequately backed up, preferably in an off-site secure location.

LEAD ASSIGNMENTS

The major case manager must avoid the appearance of unfairness by assigning more noteworthy leads to a selected group of personnel. This may cause hard feelings, jealousy, and create the perception of unfair or disparate treatment. It is, however, the responsibility of the major case manager to make certain that the investigation is being handled in the most efficient manner possible, with the most capable person assigned to the task.

Knowledge of one's subordinates and their respective strengths and weaknesses is imperative, but this is very difficult if not impossible when outside agency personnel are being used. In these cases, the only method of learning the talents and skills or strengths and weaknesses of assigned personnel may be to make discrete inquiries from their home agencies. This is not perfect, but it may be better than making the wrong assignment on a critical portion of the investigation.

The idea that all leads are vitally important to the overall investigative effort must be constantly reinforced, so that personnel will approach even the most mundane leads, such as large area searches, apartment building canvasses, or other non-glamorous leads with the proper attitude and attentiveness. Making all of these leads important to investigative personnel is the job of the major case manager, and is an extremely important part of their function. Probably the best example I can think of was the Son of Sam serial murder investigation which took place in New York City between 1976 and 1977. The offender, David Berkowitz, confessed to killing six people and wounding seven others in the course of eight shootings. The interesting thing was that Berkowitz was linked to the murders by a parking citation which had been placed on his vehicle near one of the murder scenes. A few years ago, in the twenty-five-year anniversary of what became known as the Summer of Sam, one of the original NYPD detectives who had been assigned the task of examining thousands of parking citations was interviewed. He joked that when he and his partner were told they were going to be examining a roomful of boxes of parking citations they both groaned. The example of a serial killer being caught largely on the basis of a parking citation should convince even the most cynical investigator of the necessity for treating all leads as potentially critical.

INTELLIGENCE ANALYSTS IN THE MAJOR CASE

The use of intelligence analysts in the major case, if available, should be seriously considered. Intelligence analysts can provide a great deal of input to decision makers and can conduct research that otherwise would probably not be accomplished. The use of experienced analysts can provide management of the major case with critical thinking to objectively scrutinize facts and suppositions. They can provide a great deal of information and data that can benefit the major case investigation in many ways, to include the following:

- **Providing information useful in resource acquisition.** They can research the availability of resources, which can be very time-consuming, and provide that information to either operational or administrative functional team leaders
- **Providing information regarding criminal groups or organizations.** Through the examination of data bases and contacts with agencies at every level, they can provide up-to-date information useful for the investigation
- **Identifying relationships between individuals/groups/organizations.** Analysts can create organizational or linkage charts to illustrate relationships, which can be very helpful to investigative personnel
- **Generating timeline information for sequencing of events.** When long periods of time must be analyzed to determine activities of suspects or persons of interest, analysts can provide timeline charts which illustrate this information
- **Generating and testing investigative hypotheses.** Analysts are very adept at working with partial information and creating

hypotheses utilizing known parameters, which can be very useful when dealing with limited information

The only caveats that I could recommend to a major case manager to consider when utilizing intelligence analysts would be: make certain that you are using experienced criminal intelligence analysts who are comfortable working with and around police; and don't expect miracles from them—they can provide directions to go, things to examine, but rarely will they provide you with the name, address, and location of the offender.

In addition to using intelligence analysts, however, major case managers should view every law enforcement officer from any agency involved in the major case investigation as a source of intelligence, which will be discussed in Chapter 8.

MAJOR CASE REPORTING

Regardless of the quality and professionalism of the investigative efforts exerted during a major case investigation, if the efforts are not thoroughly and professional documented the prosecution of the case will certainly suffer. In major cases, particularly those involving multiple agency investigative efforts, this can be extremely difficult, where personnel are preparing investigative documents in a variety of different formats and styles. The primary investigator, who is ultimately responsible for the investigative written product, must see to it that policies and procedures are put into place to standardize case reporting as much as possible. This will result in consistency of reporting and ease of review, which will definitely enhance the investigative effort.

While some task forces are sophisticated enough to have their own report writing format, most are not. One method of seeing to it that the best possible work product is produced is to allow each person assigned to complete investigative reports to write them in whatever format they normally utilize for their home agency. These reports are then combined into some type of investigative summary report. It is not reasonable to expect investigators to suddenly learn an entire new format of writing reports when called into a major case investigation. In addition, the actual *format* of their reports isn't nearly as important as the *content*. Writing in a format that is comfortable to them will usually result in better written reports.

Styles of Case Reporting

There are basically two types of investigative reports being written: "Compilation of Effort" and "Individualized Reporting of Each Event." In the "Compilation of Effort" style, the entire investigation is completed and one report is written at the end to reflect all investigative activity. In the "Individualized Reporting of Each Event" style, a separate report is written for each activity completed, shortly after the activity is concluded. For example, an interview is conducted and a report is written, a surveillance is conducted and a report is written. There are advantages and disadvantages to each of these styles of reporting:

Compilation of Effort

Advantages:

1. The report consists of one single document.
2. Some people think it's easier to sit and write the entire report at one sitting.

Disadvantages:

1. Procrastination—forgetting details, as reports can be written long after the activity
2. Incompleteness—minute details might be omitted
3. Tendency to "synopsize" rather than report specifics

Individualized Reporting of Each Event

Advantages:
1. More detailed reports
2. Timeliness usually means better recollection
3. More chance that minute details will be included

Disadvantages:

1. More time is spent writing

2. Some investigators feel that it is possibly harder to write this way as investigative activity must cease to generate reports
3. Probably more time-consuming

Investigative Report Routing

There must be a procedure in place that insures that documents and information related to the investigation are not misplaced or lost. Making certain that all personnel adhere to consistent and strict investigative report routing will insure thorough documentation of investigative effort, reduction in missing documents, and a thorough, professional, and complete work product. Typical investigative report routing includes:

1. Lead information received
2. Lead sheet generated
3. Lead checked against other leads or information
4. Lead logged and numbered
5. Lead assigned
6. Completed lead sheet returned
7. Draft report of activity generated
8. Draft report reviewed
9. Final report prepared and submitted for analysis/indexing
10. Final report submitted to file.

Security of investigative documents and reports is critical in any investigation, but particularly in the major case. Throwing draft or rough reports into the trash can be extremely embarrassing when they show up intact on the evening news. I have personally observed a reporter going into a dumpster looking for rough reports near the command post of a major case investigation in which I was involved. I would strongly recommend taking a cue from the military regarding sensitive documents and to consider the use of either cross-cut shredders or "burn bags" for disposal of sensitive documents which are no longer needed. In addition, access to and copying from investigative files must be documented and controlled, so that sensitive information doesn't become lost or fall into the wrong hands. Insistence must be placed upon entering all case documents into the case file, to that the maximum benefit from all efforts can be applied to the investigation.

Rough Notes

Unless maintaining them is required by law, department regulation, or at the request of the prosecutor, it has always been my personal position that once the final report is typed, the rough notes used to generate the report should be destroyed. It has been my experience that once reports are written there is really no need for rough notes, other than for them to end up on the evening news or having them thrown in your face by a sharp defense attorney trying to make something out a completely insignificant inconsistency between your final report and your rough notes. Other than those two "benefits," I can't think of a reason to keep them once the final report is written. As long as this is always routinely done, or is a part of written policy, there is usually no problem in court, unless of course there is some legal requirement or policy to keep them.

Case Filing System in the Major Case

In addition to the use of computer-generated and stored paper files on the investigation, the use of portable filing boxes or cabinets should be considered. I personally prefer locking "banker-type" plastic filing boxes. In this manner all documents relating to the major case are kept in the same location, as opposed to having to hunt through several standard department "filing systems" to find what you need. Particularly in major case investigations, management should plan for the availability of these records for months & years later, and should anticipate a re-trial or appeal even if the suspect is found/pleads guilty.

In the major case, the typical filing system includes the following sections:

1. Activity Logs
2. Crime Scene Reports
3. Press Releases
4. Copies of All Evidence Reports
5. Photos
6. Autopsy Reports
7. Crime Lab/Medical Examiner Lab Reports
8. Statements/Confessions
9. Warrants
10. Case Reports

Periodic Case Review

Particularly in the major case investigation, it is critical that periodic review of the investigative effort take place. Unfortunately, this is often viewed as an undesirable and boring task which only applies when the case is closed, which is definitely not accurate. Although it may appear boring, this is a necessary management function, if it's not completed properly, disaster can happen. There have been many examples of lead connections missed and evidence or information gaps which were later discovered during a structured case review. Case review in the major case investigation must be viewed as an ongoing process, rather than a single event, that begins when the case is opened, and ends when the case is closed by whatever means. Periodic case review in the major case has the following benefits:

1. Ensures that the work is being done
2. Is a means of assuring accountability for the investigator's time
3. Ensures completeness of reporting
4. Keeps management abreast of the progress of the case
5. Can aid in the proper expenditure of your resources
6. Provides management the information to answer upper management or other inquiries

In order to be effective, it is imperative that an *experienced investigator* (usually the primary investigator, who is responsible for the written work product) conduct the review, as he or she will be much better equipped to recognize connections, unanswered questions, and so forth.

When to Review?

1. At set time periods–these are set by the person conducting the review, usually no less than monthly
2. When significant events occur
3. Prior to referral for prosecution or to another agency

It is also beneficial that the prosecutor assigned to the major case investigation (preferably assigned as the legal coordinator) periodically participates in case review to insure that legal requirements are being met and that procedural errors are not being committed which would be detrimental to the prosecution. In addition to making certain that the major case investigation is being properly conducted, having the prosecutor involved in the investigation and case review usually means that the matter will be handled much more expeditiously and be given priority by the prosecutor's office.

Investigative Summary Reporting

As mentioned when discussing the two basic types of investigative reports that are written, consideration should be given to completion of an investigative summary report to accompany the completed reports. Appendix 7 is a sample "Investigative Summary Template." Appendix 8 is a sample of a (Completed) "Investigative Summary."

The advantages of a summary report include the following:

1. Easier for prosecutors/referred agencies to get an immediate grasp of the facts
2. More organized and clearer
3. Insures completeness and attention to detail

Information in the major case investigation can come from a variety of sources, some which people would consider traditional, and some that are not. Chapter 7 will examine some of these sources, and how to best insure that the information being captured is properly analyzed and addressed.

CASE STUDY #4: MULTIPLE OFFENDER GANG MURDER

VICTIMOLOGY: Victim was a 19-year-old mixed race (extremely light complexion) female, adopted daughter of two extremely successful parents, both of whom had doctoral degrees. One parent was a school superintendent, the other was Chairperson of the Psychology Department at a local university.

MAJOR CASE CONSIDERATIONS: This was considered a major case due to the following elements:

- Extensive media coverage, once the identity of the victim's parents was known
- Heinous nature of the offense, which included beating, torture, and murder
- Involvement of both male and female high-ranking gang members
- Motive—jealously over victim's involvement with male gang members
- Multiple crime scenes and locations
- Time-line generation aspects to reconstruct a six-week time period

GEOGRAPHICS: The area in which the crime occurred is a gang-infested lower-middle class section of the city of Chicago. Although the majority of the residents are not involved in gang activity, there are a number of ranking gang leaders residing in and around the area which causes problems for all residents. Running through the neighborhood is a shipping canal that runs from Lake Michigan on the north to the Illinois River in Central Illinois on the south. There are several roadway and railroad bridges in the area.

SPECIFIC FACTS: on Sunday, April 26th, victim was found in a sanitary/ship canal which runs southwest through the city of Chicago into the southwestern suburbs and beyond. The victim was fully clothed, with her hands bound behind her back with elasticized cord, and her ankles bound together with green electrical wire. Approximately five feet of electrical wire trailed off the wire which bound her ankles. She appeared to have been in the water approxi-

mately two months, but this was difficult to determine as the water had
been extremely cold. Initial observation of the body indicated extensive trauma to both the back of the head and the face, which was
unrecognizable. Autopsy revealed that cause of death was drowning,
compounded by the blunt force trauma to the back of the head and
the face. Victim was identified through a driver's license found inside
her sock and later through fingerprints.

The area in which the body was found was industrial, the next pop-
ulated area (immediately to the northeast) was the aforementioned residential area. Between the location of the body and the neighborhood
which was later determined to have been the location that the body
entered the canal was a distance of over three miles, with numerous
bridges over the canal along the way. Each year, several (5 or more)
bodies are recovered from the canal.

IMMEDIATE ACTION TAKEN: In order to attempt to learn how
the victim ended up in the canal, which was approximately 60 miles
from where she lived, a thorough background investigation was conducted on the victim. It was learned that the victim was the child of a
mixed-race teenaged couple who gave her up for adoption immediately after birth. She was adopted at age 2 months by a couple who
would later become a Superintendent of Schools (Ph.D.), and the
Chairperson of the Psychology Department of a local university (also
a Ph.D.). The victim and her parents lived in a city approximately 60
miles from Chicago.

As she entered her teen years, victim began to get in minor criminal activity such as shoplifting. When her parents had her tested for
any mental/neurological problems, she was diagnosed as mildly schiz-
ophrenic. Treatment was sought by the parents, but the criminal activity and problems continued.

It was learned that the victim had not been seen by her family since
February 12, at which time she was spending time with friends on the
South side of Chicago. This necessitated the generation of a time line
so as to attempt to reconstruct the whereabouts and activities of the
victim for the period February 12–April 26, a span of ten weeks. The
victim's room at her home was searched, and documents such as
diaries and address books were recovered to assist in the background
and time line generation.

MAJOR DIFFICULTIES: The amount of time which had elapsed (ten weeks) from the time she was last seen to the time her body was found created difficulties for investigators. Although the friends with whom victim was staying when last seen by her parents provided a starting point. The names and addresses found in her diary and address books led to other neighborhoods and areas of Chicago. Investigative canvasses of those areas led ultimately to the neighborhood near the shipping canal. Following two weeks of investigation, it was determined that in mid-April the victim was seen by reliable sources in the neighborhood near the shipping canal. She was said to be staying at several houses in the area, with a variety of young males, most of whom were gang members, and none of whom wished to cooperate with police.

Once the victim was publicly identified and the status of her parents released, the media began extensive daily coverage, which caused even more reluctance on the part of residents to cooperate with police.

Based on the reluctance of the residents to cooperate, a determination was made to conduct a roundup of several males at a local strip mall on a Friday evening. It was felt that if enough of the young males were questioned regarding the last days of the victim that some leads might be developed and key suspects might surface. Unfortunately, this investigation was initiated the same week that the Los Angeles riots following the Rodney King verdict began, and racial tensions in Chicago were quite high. The plan for the roundup was scrapped, as it was felt that the level of tension and volatility of the time period might cause some issues in the area. Even without the roundup, however, solid suspects were developed through repeated investigative canvassing of the area. These suspects were gang members and included three males and four females.

When reconstructing the victim's last days, it was determined that the female gang members became jealous of the victim's involvement with male gang members. They lured the victim to a residence where she was tied to a chair, beaten and her hair was chopped off. The females then awaited the arrival of a female gang leader, who decided that a public beating and torture would teach the victim a lesson. The victim was then taken to a school yard and beaten, and later to a garage, where she was forced to sexually service a group of male gang members. The owner of the garage arrived on the scene and, while ignoring the victim's cries for help, told the female gang members that they needed to get the victim out of the garage immediately.

Three male gang members then became involved, fearing that the word would reach the police about the beating. They took the victim to a secluded railroad bridge over the shipping canal where they beat her with a concrete block while she was laying on the railroad siding (which accounted for the extensive trauma to the back of the head and face). They then tied her hands behind her back with elasticized cord, tied her ankles together with electrical wire, leaving enough wire trailing off to tie to a 100-pound sewer lid. They then threw the victim into the canal. Although severely beaten, the victim wasn't dead, and ultimately died from drowning.

Three female gang members and the three male gang members who had actually murdered the victim were arrested. The females were charged with the beating and unlawful restraint, and the males were charged with the murder.

LESSONS LEARNED:

1. Thorough investigative canvasses, utilizing proper personnel, can be absolutely crucial to the investigation. In this investigation, the repeated canvassing by a select group of investigators ultimately led to some reluctant residents to give us small bits of information that ultimately led to the development of suspects. Once investigative leads are developed in a certain area, flood the area with seasoned investigators until all leads are exhausted. Don't let up for a minute, keep up the pressure, as it seems that sometimes reluctant witnesses will come forward for no other reason than to get you to quit bothering them.

2. Conducting a thorough background on victims in unknown subject cases is crucial. In this investigation, the information gleaned from the victim's diary and address books led to several areas in which investigative canvassing could take place.

3. Assignment of an assistant prosecutor can be of real benefit to the major case investigation. In this investigation, there were three locations searched on the night of the arrests, the garage where the sexual assaults were to take place, the basement in which the victim was beaten, and the residence from which the rope and wire were obtained. The assistant prosecutor obtained the search and arrest warrants very quickly, which afforded

investigators the opportunity to stay on the street investigating.

4. Seeking out community leaders can be beneficial to the investigation. It is very true that even in the worst neighborhoods, there are decent people who will "do the right thing" if they are approached in a respectful manner. In this case, the brutality of the murder convinced some area residents to come forward and assist the police.

5. Don't fail to utilize specialists if they are available. In this case, the use of the "gang and nickname" data bases of the Chicago Police Department Gang Unit proved invaluable throughout the investigation.

CASE RESOLUTION: The three female offenders were given periodic imprisonment and probation for their part in the beating, in exchange for testifying against the males. The males received sentences of sixty and eighty years, and the third offender, who had been released from prison on an attempted murder sentence two weeks prior to this murder received life without the possibility of parole.

Chapter 7

SOURCES OF INFORMATION
AND VICTIM/WITNESS ISSUES

There are a variety of sources of information in the major case investigation, which include crime scene analysis, witness information, information from sources such as anonymous or confidential informants, and the use of "tip lines" or "hot lines."

"TIP LINES"

Many times someone with information is reluctant, for whatever reason, to openly assist police, and would rather do so anonymously via a special phone-in line which has been designated exclusively for receiving information regarding the major case investigation. If utilized properly, tip lines can be a very valuable mechanism for receiving information. While the best method of advertisement of the tip line is probably television, print media and radio should not be overlooked. This is particularly true with the proliferation of "talk radio" programs, which are always looking for topics to discuss. Major cases are very often discussed on these programs, and adding the tip line number to the conversation could be beneficial. This usually requires some contact with the radio program, but if it is made clear that the purpose of the contact is not to discuss the case, but rather to request the assistance of the public in collecting information regarding the case, this contact is usually not problematic. Many radio stations look at broadcasting this type of information to assist the police in their investigative efforts as somewhat of a public service announcement, and are usually eager to assist.

If a tip line is used, from the first time the number is advertised, however, there must be adequate personnel available to monitor the line. I once went to the facility being used as a command post for a major case investigation which was being commanded by a friend of mine. We talked for a while, and then prepared to leave the facility, when I noted that we were the last two in the building. I inquired as to who would monitor the "24-hour hot line" that had been advertised, and my friend said "Well, we didn't mean 24 hours literally, and besides, we have an answering machine." Not exactly the answer I was expecting.

Although it sounds rather simplistic, the persons assigned to monitor the hotline must not only be very familiar with the case, but should be trained interviewers as well, to be able to elicit information from reluctant callers. The use of light duty or even retired police officers is something that should be seriously considered, as they are trained to elicit information from reluctant people, they are also trained to properly document information received, and they are usually the type of people for whom security concerns do not apply. Regardless of who is used to man the tip line, the call takers should be provided with written instructions and fill-in type forms to facilitate their duties and aid in consistency. One excellent mechanism for capturing information gleaned during calls to tip lines is the use of an Intelligence Report. Appendix 8 is a sample of an "Intelligence Report."

Utilizing 911 dispatchers for monitoring tip lines is usually not the best method, for a couple of reasons. The Association of Public Safety Communications Officials (APCO) reports that the typical 911 call takes approximately 40 seconds (on average) to handle. Calls to call centers or tip lines during a major case take much longer. In addition, the fact that these dispatchers are probably required to not only handle calls to a tip line, but all of their emergency and non-emergency telephone and radio traffic simultaneously is really expecting too much for anyone. Throughout my career, I have had nothing but the highest regard and respect for dispatchers and telecommunicators, but in my opinion expecting them to perform their regular job duties and take on the additional responsibility of handling a tip line in a major case investigation would be asking too much. Call takers for major case operations will have an increased amount of anxiety associated with the case, and the already highly stressful job of the dispatcher would preclude any additional duties such as handling tip lines.

Ideally, the call center would be located in close proximity to the command post or Joint Operations Center, and it would be under the leadership of the major case management team, usually the Leads Coordinator. This allows for tighter connection between the call center and the leads/information management operation. This should ideally be a seamless operation, with information going from the call center to the leads intake desk quickly. Most tip lines include some type of caller ID or a similar mechanism on the line(s), and this should be strongly considered. Many emergency and even some non-emergency lines into police departments are taped, and the background "beeping" indicator that the calls are being monitored might frighten some callers off.

As with all leads, virtually all leads gleaned from hotlines, unless they are obviously provided in jest or by "mental subjects," *must* be followed up. Major case managers should be aware, however, that sometimes media personnel call in false leads to police tip lines in order to determine if they will actually be followed, and if you don't follow the lead, you run the risk of becoming the focus of an "expose" while the media conducts their own investigation. At other times, the media attempts to "direct" the investigation for their own benefit (or ratings) by digging up their own leads and providing them to the police. The problem with the media becoming involved in tip lines is that in their quest for ratings and sometimes "pizzazz," the media doesn't have to abide by the same rules of evidence or procedure that police do, and in the event they come up with something worthwhile while conducting their own "investigation," it may not be useful for us.

In the Beltway Sniper Task Force investigation, the call center was not located in the Joint Operations Center (Command Post). The call center expanded to over 100 phones at the height of the investigation. During the 23 days (October 2–24, 2002) of the investigation, calls averaged over 5,000 per day. On October 11th, however, 10,000 calls were received, and at some points about 1,000 calls per hour. During the course of the 23 days, over 100,000 calls came in that generated 16,000 investigative leads.

Although it started out with sworn personnel manning the hot lines, later secretaries, clerical workers, and FBI Agent trainees or civilian analysts took calls. Eventually, some retired FBI agents were assigned to take calls. As mentioned earlier, the use of law enforcement retirees should be considered, as they can handle stressful individuals and still obtain the necessary information from them.[1]

Some task forces have used private call-taking companies for lengthy cases, which although not ideal, might be something to consider, if, and only if, adequate protocols are developed for the employees taking the calls, and explicit instructions for how to handle "emergency" or "hot" calls which require immediate police action are provided. In a serial murder case in Baton Rouge, Louisiana, in 2002, police utilized a private call-taking company as part of their investigative effort. They felt that the company had the expertise, with a large number of trained and experienced call takers, as well as the equipment, with hundreds of telephones and digital recording equipment.

USE OF CONFIDENTIAL INFORMANTS
IN MAJOR CASE INVESTIGATIONS

The utilization of confidential informants, during a major case investigation is something that can be very beneficial to the investigative effort, and has been proven valuable on many cases. Many major organized crime investigations, such as those conducted against people like John Gotti, would probably not have been nearly as successful had it not been for the use of confidential informants, and confidential informants have also been extremely effective in major cases involving political corruption. Problems which can arise from the undisciplined utilization of confidential informants, however, can be major in scope and potential effects. The utilization of confidential informants has also been a source of embarrassment for many law enforcement agencies. The problems associated with the use of confidential informants during major case investigations are usually caused by one of the following:

1. **A lack of control over the activities of investigative personnel who are interacting with confidential informants.** Policies and procedures for investigators working with confidential informants should be carefully written, and adherence to those procedures and protocols should be absolutely mandatory.

---

1. G. R. Murphy and C. Wexler. Managing a Multijurisdictional Case. October 2004, Police Executive Research Forum (PERF) October 2004.

Disaster can occur, even with professional and dedicated investigators, if such policies and procedures are not in place and
enforced.

2. **A lack of adherence to controls over confidential informants themselves.** In the event that confidential informants are
not strictly controlled, the situations in which they place themselves, and by association the agencies which they are assisting,
can be very embarrassing. Instructions and parameters for confidential informants should be very clear and communicated to
them in writing.

3. **A desire to "make the big case" that clouds the judgment
of someone in a management position in a major case
investigation.** While it is true that solving the major case is a
primary goal for the major case management team, doing so in
a manner that results in the prosecution of the case being hampered is not a primary goal. The problems associated with confidential informants in major cases should not be ignored
because whoever is tasked with using the confidential informants
is too eager to "make the case at any and all costs." A prosecutable case is as important a primary goal as is the solution of
the case.

Based on the old (and very true) adage that "there's no such thing as
a good surprise," prior to using any confidential informant in a major
case investigation, the prosecutor should be made aware of their
involvement. Finding out that a confidential source was used in a
major case investigation is not something that the prosecutor should
hear about for the first time on the first day of the trial. The job of the
prosecutor is difficult enough without the people conducting the investigation making it more difficult.

Prior to paying any confidential informant for information in a
major case investigation, whether you believe there is a chance the
confidential informant will have to appear in court or not, the prosecutor must be notified. In the event that they are notified prior to such
payments, they can determine whether the payment should be made,
or in some cases, they can specify how it should be made. During a
particularly brutal multiple offender gang murder investigation, we
had received very credible information that the suspects and their
attorneys had learned the identities of our two key witnesses against

them. The attorneys were careful not to allow their clients to become involved in witness intimidation activities, but they did inform their clients that if these two witnesses were unable, for whatever reason, to testify that they would be in a much better position. The suspects then contacted some gang "enforcers" to pay the witnesses a visit, which resulted in our having to move both witnesses and their families from the area. This involved removing both witnesses from their jobs, which resulted in our paying for moving expenses, apartment rent and deposit, and subsistence payments. When the case came to trial the first question that the witnesses were asked related to the payment, and they were asked point-blank if it weren't true that they were being paid for their testimony in this case. The fact that the prosecutor knew the entire background of the threats, the moving of witnesses, and the payments made, precluded this matter from becoming an issue during the trial, and all three suspects were ultimately convicted.

USE OF REWARDS

Something that is as potentially volatile as the use of confidential informants in a major case investigation is the use of rewards for information. The use of rewards can be either good or bad, depending on the case. Rewards are used regularly in major cases, including cases involving international terrorism, and their use in major cases does not seem to have the negative stigma that it once carried. One of the main problems with rewards is the fact that they are being paid will definitely come up in court, and can sometimes successfully be used to attack the motivation and therefore the credibility of witnesses.

As with the use of confidential informants, it is essential that the major case managers make certain that the prosecutor is fully aware of any rewards for information which have been published, and any payments that have been made. This is particularly true if witnesses or confidential informants plan on making claim to any reward.

Having utilized rewards for information in several major case investigations, I would strongly recommend if you decide to utilize a reward, advertise the amount being offered the first time the reward is publicized. If you don't do this, you'll waste a lot of time negotiating with the countless people calling for the sole purpose of seeing what the amount being offered happens to be, and then claiming to have important information while they are bargaining for dollars.

If it is possible, utilize an existing system, such as "Crimestoppers" to handle the reward process. These folks are experts in the administrative considerations of rewards, they are extremely competent at eliciting information, and are also extremely easy to work with and accommodating. They work extremely well with law enforcement, and I have had a number of excellent and beneficial experiences with them. They don't require much, some general information regarding the investigation, and the amount of benefit that the (confidential) callers have provided to the investigation and/or prosecution. This is particularly true when dealing with multiple callers who provide pertinent information. The Crimestoppers program then has to determine how much reward the individual callers should receive.

While working on a joint task force investigating the robbery/murder of a gas station manager, the oil company that owned the station offered a sizable reward. During the investigation, we developed several witnesses. One witness was able to put the car belonging to one of the suspects at the scene shortly before the crime occurred. Another witness was with the offenders as they disposed of the weapon used, and then accompanied them past the scene while they described the crime. This particular witness was the son of an old confidential informant of mine, and of course the old informant wanted a piece of the reward for convincing his son to come forward and talk to us. In addition, the brother of this witness wanted a piece of the reward for having driven the witness to see us, explaining that en route the witness was having second thoughts about cooperating and that he had to be re-convinced by his brother to provide us with the information. So now we had four individual witnesses who were all clamoring for the reward money. We solved it by writing a memorandum which detailed the amount of assistance these four individuals had provided to the investigation and then leaving it up to the oil company to decide who received whatever.

FAMILY ISSUES IN MAJOR CASE INVESTIGATIONS

Particularly in cases involving the death of the victim, as soon as practical, an officer (other than the officer in charge or the primary investigator) should be assigned to act as liaison with the family. The continuity of having the same officer can be a source of comfort for the family and can aid in building rapport and trust with them. The selection of a suitable officer for this assignment is critical. The officer selected needs to be compassionate, tactful, and must be someone who can empathize with the family. The officer, on the other hand, needs to be able to switch gears and may have to keep his/her distance if necessary by withholding some information from the family that could be detrimental to the investigation.

Unfortunately the major case manager might be placed into the position of withholding information from the family liaison officer if they are getting too close to the family, for fear they might inadvertently leak something inappropriate to the family out of compassion or empathy for their plight. I found myself in this position on the investigation of a "road rage" incident that led to the death of two young college students. An extremely bright officer, with a background and advanced degree in psychology and counseling, was selected to function as family liaison during the investigation. After a while, it became apparent that the officer, motivated by nothing more than sympathy and sorrow for the family's situation, had provided them information on the investigation that should not have been disclosed. While I found the motives of the officer admirable, the damage was done and the officer had to be removed from the assignment and counseled.

The biggest questions the family of victims have usually relates to the last moments of their family member, particular in the case of violent crimes. My advice has always been to use your best judgment, be tactful and compassionate, and try to truly empathize with their loss. I have been involved in many situations where I knew the victim had truly suffered at the end, and had looked the grieving family in the eye and lied to them, telling them instead that the death was very quick. I believed in those situations that perhaps the truth would have done more harm than good, and I didn't want their last memory of their loved one to include visions of them writhing in agony. While this might not have been the best approach, this is a very personal call to make.

Many times the families of victims are encouraged by media to go on camera in a "plea" for assistance with the major case investigation. Although the police cannot "order" the family not to grant interviews with the media, I feel it is appropriate that both sides must be addressed regarding camera appearances. They should be told although their appearance might generate some investigative leads, every dysfunctional person may come forth in the viewing area to bother, harass, and hurt them. There have been many occasions where family members of victims have been subjected to late-night harassing phone calls and other disturbing behavior after appearing on camera. Another aspect of family members appearing on camera is that when the prosecutor's office becomes involved in the investigation, some of the comments of the family could have a negative bearing on the prosecution.

Another difficult situation to deal with regarding family members in a major case investigation is that sometimes the family will have an "expert" providing them information on how the investigation should be conducted. It has been my experience that these experts sometimes have rather dubious backgrounds for someone who is giving advice on a criminal investigation. These experts sometimes advise family members that their personal method of investigation would be different (and usually better) than what the police are currently doing, which might not coincide with the manner in which your investigation is being conducted. The difficulty with this is that it can cause the family to begin funneling "leads" of their own, usually provided by the expert as the expert attempts to direct your investigation. I have observed situations in which this type of problem has placed the family at serious odds with the police.

It is my experience that the major concerns of most family members be kept abreast of major developments in the investigation, rather than hear about them through the media. In most cases, this is something which can be done to accommodate the family members without hampering or damaging the investigation. Once again, placing one's self in their situation can explain some of their feelings and requests.

Another issue that can cause animosity with family members of victims or violent crimes, particularly in cases where the subject is unknown, is the background of the victim can be a crucial element of the investigation, and must be thoroughly researched. Gathering the victim's background, however, can cause bitterness with family and friends of the victim, as they might perceive an attempt is being made by the police to somehow "dirty up" the victim, making them appear somehow responsible for whatever befell them. These problems can be alleviated if investigators take the time to explain to family members that looking into the victim's background can, and probably will, benefit the investigation. When searching the personal property of victims, be as compassionate and professional as possible with the family, and try not to have them present.

It is imperative that when dealing with a missing person, make certain to have dental records, fingerprints, etc., *on hand*, rather than merely *available*, as this will allow for quicker identification in the event a body is recovered, which might afford the family the opportunity to end the "not knowing" stage and move into the grief process.

WITNESS ISSUES

In addition to problems associated with family members, there are a host of problems associated with witnesses in a major case investigation. In addition to the usual problems associated with your witnesses being arrested and/or leaving the area, in a major case there are other inherent problems. Witnesses sometimes become "caught up in their own importance" to the case, and begin asking for things that you cannot give. They begin to make demands that you cannot and should not grant, and sometimes they seem to make their assistance to police and prosecutors somehow "contingent" on your meeting these demands.

Another issue with witnesses if their identity becomes known, is there will be hordes of media descending on them for "exclusive" interviews. Sometimes witnesses become engrossed in their "15 minutes of fame," and grant interviews. In the event this transpires, (particularly if they are paid for these interviews) you can imagine the negative impact that this will have on the prosecution.

If you perceive the witness to have the potential for becoming "difficult to handle," it is prudent to get their testimony somehow "locked in," by some type of sworn statement or testimony. Many jurisdictions utilize the Grand Jury process in this situation, to confirm and solidify the testimony of difficult or recalcitrant witnesses. The Grand Jury appearance can sometimes dissuade or preclude the witness from changing their minds, or their testimony, later, as in most cases it could result in perjury charges for the witness.

When handling witnesses, spend as much time as possible to make them happy, but don't become their servants, who carry out their least desire lest you lose their testimony. Make things as convenient as possible for them, with transportation to court, and so forth, and as much as possible explain exactly what's going on every step of the way, particularly during the prosecution phase.

In the event you suspect your witnesses have become the target of threats and/or retaliation, do not hesitate to provide them with adequate protection. These witnesses are your responsibility, and the ramifications of a witness in a major case investigation incurring harm or worse can have a chilling effect on other potential witnesses in this or future cases.

While conducting an investigation into a particularly heinous murder case and after having moved our witnesses and their families several times for their safety, we were provided intelligence information that associates of the defendants planned to utilize explosives and automatic weapons to storm the court facility in an effort to either kill the witnesses or rescue their comrades. Considering the gang affiliations and brutality of our offenders, we planned and conducted an extensive protective services detail on our witnesses, and enhanced security of the entire court facility throughout the trial. Fortunately, nothing happened, but we would have been derelict in out duties had we not taken the necessary steps.

Although sources of information can cause a number of headaches for the major casem anager, the failure to manage personnel effectively can also result in a number of serious problems, most of which can be avoided. These problems and methods to avoid them will be discussed in the next chapter.

Chapter 8

PERSONNEL MANAGEMENT

There are a number of significant challenges related to personnel in the management of major cases. While most of these challenges impact everyone involved in the major case investigation, without doubt the greatest impact of these challenges is toward management personnel, particularly the major case manager. These challenges include: (1) acquisition of an adequate number of personnel; (2) selection of those personnel (including management personnel) based on their specialized skills or expertise; (3) allocation of personnel, and interaction with stakeholders; (4) to include media and political entities.

PERSONNEL ACQUISITION AND ALLOCATION

Perhaps the most difficult thing for major case managers to remember is although their case is extremely important, and in fact might be the most important matter ever investigated by the agency or agencies involved, there is a finite number of personnel that they will be able to acquire to address the major case investigation. The fact is there will always be "routine" cases happening which will require investigation, even while the bulk of the agency's efforts are directed at the major case. There will be need to have a number of personnel available for these routine cases, which are anything but routine to the victims. It would be very difficult, if not impossible, to explain to the owner of the liquor store (just robbed for the third time this year) that his investigation will have to be "put on the back burner," as all available resources are being directed at the major case and he'll have to wait.

Regardless of the type of major case being investigated, to arbitrarily devote all investigative personnel to the major case, to the exclusion of everything else, will cause a great deal of anger and consternation among the citizens. This will in turn lead to complaints sent to elected officials, and ultimately those complaints, anger, and consternation will find its way back to the police department through those elected officials.

With regard to a single agency major case investigation, personnel resources from other units within the organization may have to be temporarily assigned to the major case investigation. This can cause animosity or conflict on a variety of levels: animosity or conflict between the major case managers and command personnel of other units which are losing their personnel to the major case effort, and animosity or conflict on the part of some of the investigative personnel being taken from their "home units" to be added to the major case investigation.

In the matter of major case managers and command personnel from other units which are being stripped of personnel to fulfill manpower needs of the major case, the command personnel from these units may begin to feel that the importance of the work of their unit has suddenly become "second-rate." They may feel the work being performed by their unit is not nearly as important as they thought it was, and this feeling might cause the perception their personnel are being considered as mere "filler" for the major case. In addition, the personnel actually being taken from units to work on the major case are often irritated because they are removed from their own caseload, which will, to some extent, suffer by their absence. Having to put aside work that one considers important and worthwhile can (understandably) cause some resentment. If that resentment carries over and projects itself into the manner in which they approach their duties on the major case investigation the major case might suffer.

Another element in major case management that can be a source of conflict is the fact major case investigations usually result in a considerable budgetary expenditure. This is the same budget that contains the financial resources for the entire agency, and when the commander of one unit sees their own budgeted resources being transferred to the management of the major case, it can cause resentment. But it can go much further than that, in that police department budgets are parts of a larger overall municipal, county, or state budget, which funds expenditures by all departments—police, fire, public works, and so forth. The police department is allocated a portion of that overall budget, which in effect is their "slice of the pie." Each department within the municipality, county, or state is expected to live within their budget by practicing "fiscal responsibility," and not exceed their allocated amount. As mentioned earlier, one major case can destroy the payroll and overtime budget for many agencies, and when the police department's overtime funds are gone, it is sometimes necessary to draw funds from the overtime account of say, Public Works or the Fire Department. As conscientious and professional "team players," as most fire chiefs or public works superintendents are, when they see their budgets being gobbled up by one major case they have a tendency to become irritated. The plans they had for equipment, training, or personnel expenditures are not possible, and sometimes the animosity this generates is manifested in a negative way in the relationships that exist between department heads. Multiple agency major case investigations are not by any means immune from these issues. Major case managers must be very cognizant of the fact they will oftentimes have to "make do" with the personnel and other resources assigned from outside agencies without having had the opportunity to actually select the personnel or resources.

With these potential problems in mind, the major case manager must determine how much manpower they will need which must be decided at the onset of the major case investigation. Regardless of how many people they think are needed, they have to make certain a "major case posture" is assumed early on. It is essential that the major case manager does not underestimate the complexity or difficulty of with whatever they are faced.

The major case manager must focus their attention on the fact that *they are involved in a complex, multifaceted investigation.* By maintaining this as their focus, they can prevent themselves from underestimating required resources and responses on a number of levels. Assuming a major case posture is essential, and if they do not take this posture and underestimate what they need with regard to personnel or other resources, their investigative efforts will certainly suffer.

Adopting a major case posture early in an investigation will also help to insure that key personnel are involved from the onset, and that an effective command structure and adequate resources can be allocated. By using a planning document such as the Major Case Management Planning Checklist described in Chapter 3, the major case manager will focus attention on the various necessary components of the major case team. They will be less likely to overlook a necessary function or component.

If an error is made with regard to personnel acquisition, I would strongly recommend the major case manager err on the side of safety, in other words if you think you need ten additional personnel, ask for twenty. You probably won't get twenty, but if you get fifteen you're still ahead of the game. Having an adequate number or more than enough personnel on a major case investigation is quite a bit easier than not having enough and having to scramble for additional personnel later. I've always felt that having extra personnel on a major case investigation is a lot like carrying a gun off-duty—I'd rather have the gun and not need it, than to need it and not have it. I'd rather have too many personnel and have to send some home because they weren't needed than not have enough personnel and need them.

Having adequate personnel on hand allows for effective delegation of duties, as outlined in Chapter 4. An investigative unit that I commanded received a call from a very small (and very poor) suburban police department requesting assistance in searching for missing child. The child was about 8 years old, and had not arrived home from school on time. The area in which the child lived was an extremely poor community, with a great deal of drug and gang-related crime. In addition, there were more than a few child molesters residing in the area. Approximately fifteen uniformed state troopers and investigators converged on the town at their police station. The police station consisted of one small office that was part of a two-car garage. There were too many people to fit into the "station," so we set up our temporary command post on the hood of a squad car parked at the entrance to the building. We began our operation by getting as much information as we could on the missing child and spread our maps out, starting to divide up the community for a grid-type search. We had someone else making copies of the girl's photo to pass out to our personnel. When we were ready to begin the search, the chief of police addressed the group. As he concluded, he asked for questions, and one of the officers noted that the little girl was reportedly wearing a "blue jacket" and asked approximately what shade of blue the jacket was, light blue, dark blue, and so forth. The chief thought for a minute, looked up and said "About the same shade of blue as the little girl walking down the tracks over there," pointing to a girl walking down the tracks. Needless to say, it was the little girl who was missing. The good news was that we had many more people than we needed at that point, as the child was no longer missing. The bad news was that the little girl had been sexually assaulted while on her way from home and had escaped from the person who molested her and walked down the tracks toward home. We had more than enough personnel on hand and were able to quickly identify and arrest the offender, but since that incident I have always tried to err on the side of safety and have more personnel than needed for a variety of situations, whether they related to major or smaller cases.

The time period immediately following police notification of a crime is critical, and command personnel who don't initially request and assign adequate personnel will be subject to extensive criticism later. You only get one chance to do this right—at the beginning of the case.

There seems to be a natural tendency of police officers (especially Chiefs) not to appear as "alarmists." Nobody wants to be "the little boy who cried wolf," and make a bigger deal out of something than it is. This type of thinking when it relates to major cases must be avoided, and I have to believe that it would be better to be teased for "over-reacting" than to be chided for "underreacting" by not taking your situation seriously enough. Excess personnel can always be sent home, and as mentioned, it is more difficult to request more personnel when you're short-handed. It will be problematic if extra personnel is added at a later date. This creates the additional burden of bringing the personnel up-to-date before they can begin working. Depending on how fast the investigation has progressed, they may never acquire the same speed as the personnel who have been on the case from the beginning.

One method of adding to personnel without unduly burdening other investigative units is to utilize uniformed patrol personnel. Regardless of whether they have investigative training or expertise, this should not be overlooked. Uniformed personnel can perform a variety of necessary duties during a major case investigation, which otherwise would necessitate the assignment of investigators. Chances are, there aren't enough investigators to go around, and utilizing investigators for assignments that do not require investigative expertise is not satisfactory management. The actual duties which uniformed personnel and other non-investigative personnel can use will be discussed later in this chapter.

There is another very important consideration when it comes to personnel, and this is: in the event that unsuitable and/or disruptive personnel are assigned to a major case, the major case manager should have the absolute authority to send them back to their home assignment or agency at his or her discretion with no questions asked. This unsuitability might be due to unfavorable attitude, poor interpersonal skills, lack of expertise, deficiencies at report-writing, interviewing, or a host of other reasons. The fact is, if they aren't working out, dismiss them and move on with the case. Unsuitable personnel in a major case can act as a "cancer" in the investigation, and negatively impact the work and morale of the rest of the major case investigative team. This cannot and should not be tolerated by major case managers.

I had a situation in which I was asked to command a large task force that had been formed to address a child murder case. There were investigators from approximately eight different local, county, state, and Federal agencies, and the case was moving along well. The personnel assigned went through no screening at all, they were simply assigned by their agencies to assist on the case, and the overwhelming majority of them were outstanding. There was one officer assigned, however, who began to make life difficult the day he got there. This officer, a politically involved fellow who was the nephew of a local political official, (which was how he got his job in the first place) had been to a few training schools but had never worked on anything close to a major case. Approximately a week into the investigation canvasses of several areas were taking place and he was assigned to one of the canvassing teams. He came back to the command post early one afternoon, caught me alone, and began to regale me with the number of training schools that he had attended. He then got right to the point, complaining that with his background didn't I think he should be assigned something more important than "merely canvassing for leads." I stopped for a minute and thought about the veteran investigators and even some FBI Special Agents who were at that moment assigned the same canvassing duties (who were immanently more qualified than this knucklehead), and who never complained about their assignments. I told him that it appeared to me that he thought that he was much too well-trained to be "wasting his time" on canvassing and he quickly agreed. I told him how sorry I was that I had wasted such a talent as his on a mundane assignment and asked for his lead sheet back, which detailed the areas that he was to cover on the canvass team. He gave the lead sheet back to me and I told him to get his notebook out and get ready to write down his next assignment. When he got the notebook ready and his pen in his hand I told him "Get the hell out of here, you are no longer assigned to this case. And tell your chief I'll call and explain why I sent you home when I have time." I turned around, walked away, and got back to work, feeling better, I must admit. What an idiot! I often wonder what explanation he did give to his chief and to his uncle and political mentor when he returned to his department, because I never did get a call asking why I sent him home.

SPAN OF CONTROL OVER INVESTIGATORS

Span of control is usually defined as the optimum number of personnel that can effectively be supervised by one supervisor. Most texts used in "Police Supervision 101" recommend a span of control for patrol officers of 8–10 officers per supervisor. While this might be a suitable span of control for patrol personnel, I feel that it is excessive for investigators. This is not to say that the work being accomplished by patrol officers is any easier, I do think that it is usually not as complex as that being done by investigators, particularly investigators assigned to a major case investigation.

Something else about span of control that I have always found to be true is that there is an inverse correlation between span of control and the complexity of the work being accomplished. In other words, the span of control over personnel performing less complex functions can be larger than it could be over personnel performing more complex tasks. As an example, I don't feel that supervisors over very complex investigative work such as computer or financial crimes would be capable of supervising as many investigators as someone over a burglary unit. I'm not saying that burglary is simple, and I'm certainly not saying that burglary investigations aren't important, but I don't think that most routine burglary investigations are usually as complex as computer or financial crimes.

I have always felt when supervising investigators that a span of control of 5–7 investigators is more realistic. I feel this smaller group or people performing more complex duties can lead to better supervision, more accurate accountability, and a better review of accomplishments.

In many major case investigations, personnel are divided into teams, and the supervisors of those teams of investigators will themselves have to perform investigative duties while simultaneously supervising the work of others. The fact that these team leaders are performing investigative duties in addition to supervising others will necessitate a smaller span of control for them, and I feel that 5–7 is adequate.

SELECTION OF PERSONNEL

While Chapter 4 discussed how to organize the major case investigative effort and mentioned duties and requirements for a variety of positions, until now the strategies for actually selecting those personnel have not beem examined. Perhaps the most important personnel selections to be made are for the major case manager/case manager and the investigators themselves.

MAJOR CASE MANAGER

The selection of the major case manager is critical to the success of the investigative efforts. The leadership that will be exercised by the person in this position is going to set the stage for the efforts of all subordinate personnel. This is not the position for someone who is being "tested" or "groomed" for higher command. This is not the position for someone to be placed in solely on political considerations. I have seen both of these things occur with disastrous results. In the case of a pre-planned and established task force, the commander is usually selected by the advisory council or policy board, and sometimes is selected on a rotating schedule. Many task forces rotate command on a two or three-year basis among member agencies, to increase that amount of "ownership" of the individual agencies which make up the task force and to provide the appearance of fairness by giving each agency a chance to lead the task force. The person in this position must have *proven ability* to manage complex multifaceted investigations, and not just "good potential." The road to hell, I have always believed, is paved with unrealized potential and unfulfilled good intentions.

This assignment is vastly different from leading an agency, and there are many highly proficient command personnel and even chiefs, who, although extremely talented at running a unit or agency, might not be as effective managing a major case. In addition, very few law enforcement executives have received training in leading a task force or major case effort. When considering what type of person would be best suited to manage a major case investigation, one should first consider what actual duties are entailed. There are a multitude of duties involved in managing a major case investigation.

In the case of a multiagency approach, the major case manager must be able to effectively balance the needs of individual agencies with those of the entire task force or major case investigative team. Each agency involved in a multiagency effort has its own needs and its own organizational culture. The effective major case manager is astute enough to recognize the different cultures and needs and manage the overall effort with those things in mind. I was involved in a case that demonstrates exactly the ideas of an agency's needs and culture.

Following a violent home invasion with shots fired at the victims in an extremely affluent community, the state police unit that I commanded was called for assistance. Upon arrival we were briefed by the detective commander and the chief and started to proceed with assignment of leads. One of the first leads to be covered was the interview of an elderly woman who lived down the street from the victims. This elderly woman had been clearing snow from her car when she was accosted by two armed gunmen running from the scene of the home invasion. They knocked her down and stole her car. Our investigators and the detectives from the agency were to conduct her interview as well as a canvass of the neighborhood. About an hour later, the detective commander and I were standing near the communications center when a call came in from a resident with a complaint. The dispatcher turned to me and asked if one of our investigators was driving a blue Buick, to which I replied that yes, one of them was, and asked if perhaps they were blocking someone's driveway. The dispatcher informed me that the resident didn't have a blocked driveway, but they wanted the vehicle moved immediately from the front of their home because they felt it was unsightly to their neighborhood. As I rushed to get the phone to tell the resident my personal opinion of their request, the detective commander ran in front of me, telling me that he'd handle it. I couldn't believe that this (obviously) wealthy resident would be more concerned about an older car being parked in front of their house than they were of the home invasion and assault of one of their neighbors. The detective commander took it all in stride, and explained that calls such as this were routine from the residents in that community. He further explained that the police department in his community didn't usually park in front of resident's homes when contacting them, but rather on the side and the officers routinely went to the back door. Not having had much experience working in affluent communities, this was somewhat of an "organizational culture shock for me," but the police department and its personnel took it as a routine way to do business in that community.

In the case of a single-agency approach, the major case manager must be able to maintain focus over the investigation while not engaging in competition with the rest of the agency. When discussing acquisition and allocation of personnel, the point was made that hard feelings or conflict could occur between units of an agency. While this is true, the major case manager must be able to keep his or her focus in spite of these conflicts. The major case manager must also be able to distinguish between executive and operational responsibilities. This person is just that, a manager, who can no more be knocking on doors or interviewing suspects than a chief of police can be out issuing parking tickets. This is definitely not the assignment for the individual who has to be out on the street all the time, or someone who has to be involved in each and every aspect of each and every investigation. The hard feelings which result from this type of overinvolvement during normal everyday routine investigations are exacerbated greatly during the major case. Detectives get irritated when this occurs, because their roles are being modified. The boss isn't supposed to do their jobs for them, and it (understandably) irritates them a great deal when it occurs.

The major case manager needs to remain focused on all priorities, sometimes emphasizing certain priorities over others to meet changing demands and conditions, but the real challenge is to balance competing priorities while continuing to provide effective leadership. As previously mentioned, the major case manager must be able to make order out of chaos, and more than that, they must be able to focus on the "big picture," not getting bogged down in individual issues. The major case manager must also remember that taking full control may not be possible. To be effective they must be able to delegate appropriately to competent personnel. Having a competent deputy major case manager can assist greatly, if the major case manager really knows how and when to delegate.

In a multiagency operation, the major case manager must balance the needs of the entire investigation with the obligations of participating local law enforcement executives to be responsive to their own citizens and elected officials. The major case manager should not expect participating agency personnel to keep their supervisory personnel appraised of the progress of the investigation, instead the major case manager should personally maintain regular liaison with them. Law enforcement executives from participating agencies are often inundated with demands for news about the case from their own elected officials, and they have a responsibility to keep those officials informed. If these communications channels are not open, it could be perceived that participating agency executives are not receiving enough information. In the case of major crimes task forces, a mechanism to keep the policy board or advisory council appraised of the progress of the investigation is usually included in the intergovernmental agreement, memorandum of understanding, by-laws, or policy and procedures. In addition, it is a good practice that prior to any major events in the investigation, such as arrests, execution of search warrants, or anything that might be considered "newsworthy," the major case manager arranges for these participating agency executives to be thoroughly briefed. This will allow them (if appropriate) to provide a little "advance notice" to their own elected officials that something is going to come out in the media.

Anyone selected as the major case manager of a multiagency major case investigation needs to realize that in addition to the extreme stress and criticism coming at them from outside the investigative effort, that there are also elements within the effort that can be a cause of consternation for them, which include:

1. **Participating agency command personnel discussing the direction, speed, and flow of the investigation with the media.** This can create some real difficulties due to the possibility that they might inadvertently release something that shouldn't be released. The fact is that in a major case, particularly a

very high profile major case, participating agency command may get a little bit envious of the major case manager getting their "15 minutes of fame" with the media, and want to get their own notoriety.

2. **Participating agency command personnel conducting numerous unwarranted (and usually unwanted) visits to the command post.** This can be disruptive as it can cause their personnel assigned to the investigation to either stop or at least put their own work on pause because "their boss is here."

During a particularly high profile murder investigation my own boss, the director of my agency, called to inform me that he was planning to visit the command post the next day. He must have detected some concern in my voice and asked if this would create any difficulties for me. I appreciated the opportunity for input, and told him if he did show up, it would definitely cause difficulties since the media, which were camped out nearby, would descend on him, and that at least our agency, if not all of the personnel would probably put their investigative efforts "on pause" while he was at the command post, both of which would be disruptive to our investigative efforts. He said he understood and would cancel the visit. I truly appreciated his understanding and told him so, after which I breathed a big sigh of relief.

3. **Favored personnel being placed on task forces, who might not be the most talented/dedicated.** This can be problematic, because as explained earlier, this is not the place for the next "rising star" who might not have the skills or background to participate in a major case investigation.

4. **Participating agency command allowing their own personnel to circumvent the major case manager and the major case chain of command.** This is extremely irritating, and the best way to avoid it is to have all participating agency command personnel, at the onset of the major case investigation, made clearly aware of the chain of command that has been established. They should be provided a copy of the chain of command, and it should be clearly explained to them that the personnel whom they graciously assigned to the major case will be held to that chain of command for the duration of their assignment.

Following the successful conclusion of the "Beltway Sniper Task Force" in Montgomery County, Maryland in 2002, the members of the Task Force were polled and asked what they thought the leader of such an effort needed to be able to do. They responded that the leader must be able to effectively:

- Think in terms of "we"
- Be receptive to involving other agencies
- Be open to new ideas
- Put the goal of solving the case first
- Publicly recognize the good job people are doing
- Let competent people do their jobs
- Shield the workforce from external pressures and distractions, allowing them to focus on the investigation
- Remain calm under pressure, even have a sense of humor under stress.

And their number one response: **does not micromanage**.

Considering that this input came from a group of law enforcement professionals assigned to one of the most high profile and noteworthy investigations in U.S. history, I think it would be a sound idea for the major case manager of any major case to at least attempt to meet these standards.

INVESTIGATIVE PERSONNEL SELECTION

There is no question the selection of the best possible personnel can either make or break the investigative effort, and that appropriate personnel are absolutely critical to the success of the major case investigation. In many cases, the major case manager, when attempting to acquire enough personnel to successfully address the major case investigation, will simply have to settle for the investigative personnel that he or she is given, with no selection opportunities available. If given the opportunity to select investigative personnel, however, the major case manager must realize that the desire for the most experienced and competent personnel for the major case effort must be tempered with the fact that an agency's most talented personnel are usually the busiest, and often the least likely to be commissioned to assignments other than their own investigations that are already being conducted.

Actual selection procedures for major cases or for major crimes task forces vary in sophistication, from simple interviews to the completion of various psychological tests/interviews, which is usually restricted to long-term permanent or semi-permanent task forces. If given the opportunity to select investigative personnel for the major case, those making the selection should consider the following:

- **Objective data found in personnel records, such as attendance, absenteeism, complaints, and awards.** This usually provides an accurate representation of their daily work behavior
- **Subjective data found in supervisory performance evaluations.** Examines traits such as: motivation, stability, street knowledge, persistence, intelligence, judgment, teamwork, reliability, and dedication.

In addition to these considerations, investigative personnel selected to be participants in a major case investigation also need to be:

1. **Comfortable working long-range investigations, with a lengthy attention span.** This is not the assignment for the investigator who has to constantly move from case to case due to boredom. Major case investigations are more like long-term narcotics conspiracy cases than they are the typical "make a buy-kick a door in" cases, and it has been my experience that personnel who enjoy doing the longer term cases are sometimes more suitable for major case investigations.

2. **Available for open-ended long-term commitment.** Free from school/secondary employment commitments—although I truly admire officers who return to school for degrees or advanced degrees as well as those who work secondary employment to provide for their families, in this situation the major case must come first. Advising potential personnel of this fact prior to their selection is essential.

3. **Adaptable to working extremely long hours with little time off.** This can present a problem with personnel covered by collective bargaining agreements on occasion, when a small number of extremely contract-conscious individuals insist on

regular breaks and are more concerned with overtime than they are with the major case effort.

4. **Willing to sacrifice their free/family time when on an extended investigation.** Major cases are open-ended operations, with sometimes "no end in sight." This can cause investigators to miss family events or extracurricular activities.

5. **Possess excellent verbal and written skills.** If they don't have these, you probably don't really want them assigned to the major case investigation.

6. **Up to date on the latest evidentiary techniques and legal matters.** You won't have time to train them, they need to know these things coming into the major case.

7. **They must *want to be involved* in the major case effort.** This is very similar to undercover work, only those police officers who really want to do it will be successful. Personnel assigned to a major case investigation who don't want to be there can cause irreparable problems for the entire investigative effort and should be avoided if at all possible. As was previously mentioned, however, regardless of how talented these personnel are, there must be a provision for the major case manager to be able to return personnel to their parent agency or unit in the event that they're found to be unsuitable.

There are several uses for non-investigative personnel, such as patrol officers, some of which have been mentioned previously, but if patrol officers are going to be used, even if it merely consists of asking them to collect street level information and developing intelligence, there are some things that should be considered:

1. Keep them apprised of what's going on, as much as practical and possible, taking into account security issues. You do not want to negatively impact a major case to avoid hurting a patrol officer's feelings by withholding information from them, but sometimes that's a risk you have to take.

2. If you are going to expect them to gather information pertinent to the major case, however, we must provide them with a consistent and standardized data collection and reporting system. A simple "Intelligence Report" (shown in Appendix 9) document can be disseminated and used for collecting intelligence infor-

mation that can then be merged into the information and leads management system in place.

3. It is imperative that you provide feedback to patrol personnel about information that they submit. Without this feedback they may see their efforts as unappreciated and could cease to seek, collect, and submit information. Although media leaks are a concern, denying even basic information to the officer that supplied the information can lead to a reluctance to supply any additional information. Keep in mind, however, that security of the investigative effort must be the major concern, and sometimes the feedback that patrol officers receive might not be immediate. In any event, however, they should be acknowledged for their input and thanked for their efforts.

There are several other duties which are part of a major case investigation that can and should be planned, conducted, and in some cases supervised by non-investigative personnel. These can include:

- Large scale searches or investigative canvassing,
- Crime scene preservation,
- Overt surveillance activities such as roadblocks to question large numbers of motorists.
- Coordinating the efforts of volunteers who are conducting searches, flyer distributors, etc.

The major case manager might also consider the use of light duty or even retired police officers for jobs like copying, filing and other clerical duties (if a sufficient number of clerical personnel are not available). Security of command post facilities will be something that police officers understand immediately, but not most volunteers. Although the use of volunteers in the major case investigation can be extremely beneficial, having an officer, not necessarily an investigator, assigned to coordinate and supervise the efforts of those volunteers is a sound idea. Volunteers might be useful for transportation of task force personnel or others involved in the major case who might be traveling distances, arranging for lodging, or food service, or other non-police duties.

During the "Green River Murders" investigation in Washington state in the 1980s, it was later determined that Gary Leon Ridgway, one of the most notorious and prolific serial killers in U.S. history, had volunteered and actually assisted police searching for his own victims. In 2003, Ridgway pled guilty to the murders of 48 counts of murder, although he says that he actually killed 90 or more women, most of whom were prostitutes. It is not unheard of for the perpetrator to come back as a volunteer to determine how much the police know, learn the operations and methods of the police, or to somehow get a thrill from being that close to the investigation that he or she initiated.

STRATEGIC BRIEFINGS

One of the most important mechanisms for insuring that personnel assigned to a major case investigation are kept apprised of the progress of the case, as well as a mechanism to assign duties and review leads and other information, is the strategic briefing. Of all the strategic briefings that will be conducted in the major case investigation, there is none that is more important than the initial briefing. The initial briefing for personnel will act to set the stage for later operations, and should be carefully planned. It is at this briefing that the major case manager is given the opportunity to demonstrate both their leadership style and their personal outlook toward this investigation for the first time. In the event this is a multiagency effort, command personnel or (preferably) the chief executives from all contributing agencies should be at the initial briefing to demonstrate a "show of unity" for the operation.

In one of my assignments as commander of a state police district, we were requested to assist a municipal police department in a murder investigation. This was a very old community, having been founded in the mid 1800s as a farming community that had grown immensely. This was, however, the first murder that anyone could remember occurring in this community. As we met for the initial briefing, the chief of the department that requested assistance stood to say a few words, thanking us for the assistance. He then stated that "if we solve this case, it will be due to a joint effort." Up to that point I hadn't planned to say anything, after all, we had a very experienced squad supervisor and an equally experienced lieutenant that would direct the investigation, but the chief's comments concerned me. I did stand up to speak and told the assembled investigators that there was no "if" involved in us solving this case, and that I was absolutely infuriated that someone would come into their community and murder a woman in her own home. I went on to say that we were going to catch the person who did this, and that nobody was going to rest until we did. The initial briefing of a violent, heinous crime is not the time to give the people charged with the investigation the idea that "we'll possibly be successful." Can you imagine a coach of any athletic team taking the attitude and telling their players that we'll "try really hard and hope for the best" in the locker room before the big game?

It is at briefings like this that the procedures for the investigation will be provided to the Investigators, and they must be very carefully explained if you want the personnel assigned to be in compliance with them. These procedures will include:

Initial Briefing Topics

1. **Leads and information management.** Explain the information and leads management program, and provide examples of any forms or flowcharts that would augment the explanation. Explain how leads are processed, documented, and assigned.
2. **Paper flow of reports and time requirements for finished reports.** If these time requirements are not provided, you can plan on getting reports in late. If the personnel are not advised of the proper flow of paper, bottlenecks and lost documents will occur.
3. **Report writing format.** As mentioned earlier, the easiest method in a multi-agency operation is to allow personnel to utilize their own forms and formats when writing reports.
4. **Briefing schedule.** Most major case investigations have at least two briefings a day, and sometimes more if necessary. Briefings are usually held in the morning, at which overnight activities are discussed and leads are assigned, and in the afternoon or evening to discuss completed leads and plan for tomorrow's activity. It should be stated that personnel are expected to attend briefings to be kept abreast of the progress of the investigation and so that the minute details of the investigation can be discussed. In the event that investigators are on an interview or otherwise unable to attend the briefing, they should notify their chain of command. In the event that shifts of investigators are

working the investigation, enough overlap of time will be necessary for briefings, and will have to be built into the briefing schedule.

5. **Administrative/logistical concerns.** Personnel need to know where to gas up their squad cars, get batteries for cameras and flashlights, etc. They also need to know how to turn in requisitions for equipment, bills to be reimbursed, and also how to turn in their overtime slips and other personnel reports.

6. **Security of information.** The critical need for security at the command post and with regard to information must be carefully discussed, to avoid later issues.

7. **Dealings with media.** I think that a discussion of the duties of the Media Liaison is warranted. Personnel should be advised that the media liaison is the only person who is authorized to speak to the media, and that they should refer any media inquiries to the media liaison.

8. **Appropriate demeanor around the command post.** It may sound petty, but personnel need to be reminded that their Mothers don't work at the command post, so they should clean up after themselves, and also that the command post is not somewhere to meet friends or family members or a place to hang out when off-duty.

9. **Staffing and organizational breakdown and the chain of command of the operation.** Personnel should be provided with a copy of the table of organization of the major case investigative team, showing the names of persons filling functional components. These personnel should all be present at the initial strategic briefing so that all participants can see who they are and meet them. The chain of command should also be clearly explained.

In addition, three things ***must* be stressed as being *completely non-negotiable:***

- Adherence to the chain of command
- Organized management of leads
- Proper media strategies

It is also imperative to state during the initial briefing that **no inde-**

pendent investigative activity will be permitted, and that all information gleaned by investigative personnel will be turned over to the leads coordinator for assignment. Make it very clear that this doesn't preclude investigators from following leads logically to the next step, but it does not allow "independent investigations," in which investigative efforts are being conducted by personnel who circumvent the proper lead management format. If this is allowed to occur, it will lead to confusion, duplication of efforts, and can negatively impact the investigative effort.

TEAMING OR PARTNERING OF INVESTIGATORS

Another aspect of major case management involves teaming up or partnering investigators. I feel strongly that this should be the decision of the major case management, and not left to the individual investigators. This can be somewhat sticky, in that certain people get used to working together and don't appreciate changes to that. On the other hand, in a major case investigation with a limited number of talented personnel, it is the responsibility of the major case manager to see to it that personnel are used to the best advantage of the investigative effort. Having the two best interviewers work together, for example, might not be the best use of their talents. Teaming the best interviewers with less experienced personnel might get more bang for the buck and share the talents of these experienced personnel. Partnering senior personnel with less experienced personnel is also sometimes beneficial. When considering the partnering of investigators, one should take into account the following:

- Specialized expertise or skills of investigators
- Major case investigative experience of investigators
- Knowledge of geographic areas involved in the investigation
- Knowledge of specific crime types or patterns
- Knowledge of criminal groups and their operations

The biggest difficulty with regard to ascertaining expertise and talent is that if you're dealing only with personnel from your own agency, you already know their skills and areas of strength. When dealing with personnel from outside agencies, however, this assessment might not be possible. Sometimes making discrete inquiries of parent agencies of personnel assigned might provide information on their level of experience, which can assist greatly in determining their assignment. Sometimes, however, the only way that you learn their talents, strengths, and weaknesses is by observing them in action.

Matching Abilities to Assignments

Matching abilities to assignments is something that case managers do on a daily basis, but this issue can take on much more serious ramifications during a major case investigation. If possible, of course, personnel assignments should be based on individual personnel skills. The difficulty in the major case that often arises, however, is that there are sometimes a limited number of personnel with specific skills. In these situations, it might be necessary, albeit undesirable, to assign personnel out of their particular area of expertise. Assignments within the major case investigation should take into consideration, if possible, the following:

- Aptitude of the investigator
- Complexity of the assignment
- Specialized training
- Special interests of the investigator

TEAM APPROACH IN MULTIPLE INCIDENT INVESTIGATIONS

When dealing with multiple incidents (of an unknown number or a single suspect) it may be helpful to treat each incident as a separate investigation, and assign an investigative **team** to handle each incident. This allows the personnel assigned as the team for that incident to become intimately familiar with all aspects of that incident and the associated victim(s), without getting bogged down mentally with the entire case.

Information will be passed along during regularly scheduled briefings from all teams, which will keep all investigators up-to-date on all cases, but still allowing them to focus on their team's assignment. It is ideal in a multiagency situation that the team consists of individuals from different agencies "paired" with each other. Not only will this effectively spread the wealth that each individual agency brings to the investigation, it is an effective way for establishing "esprit di corps" among the members of the major case investigation. Obviously, the major case manager must remain well versed and up-to-date on all teams' activities, in order to maintain an overall picture of the progress of all investigations.

It is absolutely critical, and often not addressed, that at every briefing the major case manager or their designee must ask all personnel "Is there anything we're overlooking, or something we haven't examined?" *all personnel,* regardless of experience, agency, or status, must be encouraged to voice their opinions. Giving input, suggestions, or theories, is often difficult for newer personnel or those who have little or no experience with major investigations, due to their fear of embarrassment. Those new or inexperienced personnel, however, might just be the person to come up with the suggestion, comment, or approach which could be extremely valuable to the investigative effort. I think it is certainly worth asking the question at every strategic briefing, as otherwise that input might not be received for whatever reason.

MAJOR CASE PERSONNEL SUPERVISION

In most major case investigations, if the initial goals and procedures of the investigation have been passed along to the investigators, supervision should not be any more difficult than normal. The seemingly inherent difficulty with major case investigations, however, is that personnel have a tendency to do one of two things:

- **Overwork themselves to the point of fatigue.** This is usually due to their professionalism and dedication to the investigation, but if this is allowed to go on unchecked, it will lead to judgmental errors and slipshod work, due to fatigue and stress. Occasionally, personnel will need to be ordered to take time off. This applies to supervisory personnel, and managers must force themselves to take time off and away from the investigation. Time off means just that . . . not sitting in a bar discussing the case with the guys, but time away from the case.
- **Get caught up in the notoriety of a high-profile investigation.** It is very easy for investigators and management personnel

to allow the instant notoriety often associated with major cases to begin to cloud their judgment. In addition, it seems that media personnel have an uncanny ability to bring out the absolute worst in otherwise professional, serious minded law enforcement personnel. There have been many instances in which off-handed comments to media personnel have wound up in print or on the evening news. Off-handed comments to the public can cause some harm as well, which is especially true if the community in which the crime occurs has been severely affected by the crime. I have found that periodic reality checks with personnel are often a good idea, and can keep cops from going off the deep end and getting caught up in the glitz and glitter of the media interest in the major case.

AVOIDING A PREMATURE SHUTDOWN

Oftentimes, when an arrest is made, or when a firm suspect is identified, investigators have a tendency to sit back, breathe a sigh of relief, and want to go on to the next investigation This is particularly true if there is overwhelming evidence of the subject's guilt. In a major case scenario, however, this can be very detrimental to the case, as much important work remains to be completed after the arrest, such as matters relating to firming up the case in preparation for prosecution.

Caution must also be exercised that security of information and leaks to the media do not occur once an arrest has been made, as some officers have a tendency to let their guard down, and this seems to be the time when many damaging leaks occur. The time period after the arrest is best spent tying up "loose ends" and making certain that all reports, etc., are finalized. This can also be the time when some witnesses might come forward, as their fear of the subjects might lessen.

MAINTAINING FOCUS OF PERSONNEL

In many major cases, there is a difficulty in maintaining the enthusiasm of personnel assigned after the initial thrust of the investigation wears off, with its accompanying excitement. This is particularly true when the investigation reaches a point where incoming leads diminish and it seems that little or no progress is being made. It is at these times that personnel are most likely to become discouraged and lose focus on their efforts. One method of maintaining focus, particularly in the case of violent crimes, is to personalize the investigation, by humanizing the victim(s). When investigators see the victims as people, rather than merely statistics or nameless victims, they may tend to maintain their edge and focus longer.

There are various methods to humanize victims in a major case:

- Investigators should refer to victims by name where possible, of course there is a case number affixed to every major case investigation, but that number is not that person, and using the victim's name can help maintain focus on what they're really doing.
- Investigators should be provided with background information on victims and their families if possible. If they can continue to see victims as human beings with families, people who have been probably permanently impacted by the crimes which are being investigated, they are more likely to maintain their focus, regardless of frustration or discouragement.
- Consideration should be given to displaying photographs of the victim(s) in an appropriate area of the command post. This will be a constant reminder to the personnel involved of exactly what they're doing there, and how important their efforts truly are.
- It might even be appropriate sometimes to provide each investigator with a photograph of the victim(s), not only for identification purposes during interviews, but also for them to carry with them as a reminder of the purpose for their efforts.

In major case investigations not involving violent acts, emphasizing the damage being done by the offender(s) can act in the same manner as personalizing or humanizing the victim(s). Perhaps the most personal example that I've ever experienced with regard to humanizing a victim occurred during a child murder investigation. This investigation involved a large task force comprised of local, county, state, and federal investigators, and we utilized a command post at a municipal police department. In order to help the investigators maintain focus on the reason for our efforts, I arranged for a photo of the victim to be provided to each of the investigators assigned to the task force. I then had the same photograph enlarged to approximately 18″ by 30″ and had one copy placed at the front of the command post and one copy placed on the doorway going outside. The goal was to have that little girl be the first thing these investigators saw when they entered the command post and the last thing they saw when they hit the street. The non-verbalized message was for them to look at this beautiful little face and then tell me why they don't want to go back out there. Look at this little girl and tell me how tired you are, or that you missed your kid's little league game, or that you're frustrated. I didn't just give those investigators, all good men and women, a photograph of that little girl to carry, I was trying to give them a piece of that little girl to carry around with them. Although this particular case happened many years ago, I know some of those investigators who were assigned to that case, some of whom are now chiefs, and who still have those pictures in their offices. Of course, I still have mine among my personal papers.

About a week into the investigation, we found her decomposed body in a nearby community. When I arrived at the command post the next day, an officer was taking down the photos and some other items off the wall. I asked him who had given him permission to remove the items and he told me that his chief had become so upset when he walked in and saw the items that he ordered them removed. I reminded the officer that it was I, not his chief, who was in command of the task force, and asked him to please put the items back up, which he did.

When I walked into the chief's office to tell him that I had countermanded his order, I found him crying at his desk. Apparently the pressure and stress of the investigation, combined with the discovery of the body, was too much for this good man, who was a father himself. I explained I had ordered the items to be put back up on the wall because although I was extremely upset myself, *nobody* was going to lose sight of why we were there or what we were doing, and it was my opinion that sometimes on a major case we need to be clearly reminded exactly what it is we're doing.

I've always believed that cops are the finest people that God ever put on this earth, and if you keep them focused they will do some incredible things. The person in charge of the major case is the one with the responsibility to keep them focused. It's not easy, but then if it were easy *anybody* could manage a major case, which we know is not true. In addition to personnel issues that arise during the major case investigation, there are administrative and logistical considerations that are also very important. These will be discussed in the next chapter.

CASE STUDY #5: MASS CHILD MOLESTATION

VICTIMOLOGY: The total list of this offender's victims will probably never be known, but hundreds were revealed and dozens were identified. As with most pedophiles, this offender had victims of preference, in this case young boys, prepubescent, ranging in age from approximately 7 to age 14.

GEOGRAPHICS: Victims were identified from states throughout the Midwest. Many of the offenses occurred at a boarding school for boys in Wisconsin, and many others occurred at a year-round school with a camping and Indian lore curriculum in rural Kentucky. In addition to these locations, offenses also occurred in the various states from which the offender obtained his victims.

SPECIFIC FACTS: The offender began molesting boys in the early 1960s in his home State of Tennessee, he had picked up two young boys and convinced them that sitting naked on a block of ice and then being anally raped with a broomstick was "the manner in which young Indian boys proved their manhood." He was caught and sentenced to ten years in prison. This Indian lore theme would continue throughout his history of sexual abuse of children. Following the completion of his sentence, the offender left Tennessee and moved to the State of Wisconsin, where he was employed as the Dean of Cadets at an all boys military boarding school. The principal and owner of the school was also a pedophile.

The offender worked at the school for a period of 19 years, during which time he and the principal molested hundreds, if not thousands, of students. As with many pedophile offenders, however, his desire for new victims was virtually insatiable, and after a number of years as Dean of Cadets the offender opened and ran an Indian lore camp for boys in rural Kentucky during the summer months.

A few years after the offender opened the camp, the boys military school came under police investigation by the state of Wisconsin, and as soon as indictments for the offender and the principal had been secured the principal committed suicide. The offender, for whatever reason, was permitted to leave the State of Wisconsin without being charged.

The next summer the offender sought and obtained licensing by the

Board of Education for his Indian lore camp to became a year-round school, with a camping and school curriculum. The offender had a slide/movie presentation and brochures professionally prepared which he used to recruit victims and their parents. The presentation and brochure depicted the camp/school as a wholesome place, and the offender gave presentations at churches, schools, park districts, and for community groups.

A few years later, the offender was contacted by police in a Chicago suburb while parked in a van behind a discount store at 2 am. In his van, the offender had a 10-year-old boy, from a nearby suburb. The offender was able to produce a permission slip signed by the the parents of the young boy, allowing their son to be with the offender for the summer. The officer on the stop, however, didn't think that the offender's story sounded right and decided to search the van anyway. The subsequent search of the van resulted in the recovery of thousands of photos of young boys in sexually suggestive poses, some of which depicted the boys engaging in sex acts with the offender. The offender was taken into custody, but quickly released.

IMMEDIATE ACTION TAKEN: It was quickly determined by the Prosecutor's Office that the search of the van was illegal, and therefore the photos and other evidence inadmissible, but at least the offender's activities had come to the attention of the police. The investigation began with a very thorough and in-depth background check on the offender, beginning with his initial arrest in the 1960s. Once his background was established, contacts were made with all of the States in which he had resided, and a task force was established. The task force consisted of child sexual molestation investigators from two states, in an effort to identify as many victims as possible, and a series of task force meetings were held to determine the most appropriate investigative strategies.

Along with the photos recovered in the offender's van were several brochures depicting the camping and Indian lore curriculum at his school. It was determined that several of the photos depicted acts which had taken place at the school. The state police in Kentucky accompanied the Kentucky Board of Education to the school for an inspection visit, which resulted in the recovery of several hundred photos depicting child molestation, many of which featured the offender engaged in acts with children. The offender was arrested and jailed for Possession and Manufacture of Child Pornography while the investigation continued. The offender was later charged with sexual assault of two boys, aged 13 and 12, at his camp.

MAJOR DIFFICULTIES: Through research it was determined that the various states had widely varying provisions in their statutes of limitations regarding child molestation. Efforts were made to research the various provisions to get the best possible prosecution of the offender. All records of the military school had been destroyed, which meant that offenders from that location could not be contacted. As with several other similar cases, there were victims and their parents who came to the offender's defense, attempting to coerce other victims not to cooperate with police. Several of the victims' parents had no desire to assist the police, and several openly refused to allow their sons to participate in the investigation.

Contact was made with a child molestation victims/survivors group, and they were brought into the investigation as a resource for dealing with both victims and their parents. This proved to be very beneficial, particularly when dealing with adult victims who had been molested as children. The victims/survivors group had a great deal of experience in interacting with these victims, which assisted in the investigation.

LESSONS LEARNED:

1. Perpetrators of this type of crime, particularly pedophiles, are incredibly prolific, and care must be taken to leave no stone unturned in searching for additional victims.
2. Oftentimes, the sheer numbers of victims identified will preclude the offender from wanting to go to trial, thereby sparing the victims from having to testify, which points toward the need to do thorough backgrounds and identify as many victims as possible.
3. In the event that other jurisdictions are involved in offenses, bring them into the investigation as soon as possible. The addition of the Kentucky State Police in this investigation assisted greatly, particularly due to their connections with the Board of Education.
4. In the event that specialty groups/resources are available and

willing to assist you, don't ignore them just because they're not law enforcement personnel. After proper and thorough screening, they may be very beneficial to the investigation.

5. In cases of mass molestation, don't overlook those victims who may be beyond the statute of limitations, as their testimony in aggravation (following a conviction) can be of benefit. In the case of this offender, several victims of past sexual assaults, some as long as twenty years earlier, were prepared to testify.

CASE RESOLUTION: The offender was convicted on all five counts of Aggravated Criminal Sexual Abuse by a jury in Illinois after a somewhat bizarre three-week trial in which he acted as his own attorney. The 59-year-old offender received a sentence of sixty years in prison. Following his sentencing in Illinois, he was tried in Kentucky and received another forty-year sentence. He has since died in prison.

Chapter 9

ADMINISTRATIVE AND
LOGISTICAL CONSIDERATIONS

In addition to the myriad of responsibilities that the major case manager will face with regard to actually managing the investigative effort, there are many responsibilities that relate to the support of that effort. Included in those responsibilities are the selection and establishment of a suitable command post, clerical considerations, supplies, evidence handling, and all aspects of security for the operation.

COMMAND POST FACILITIES

The location selected to serve as the command post or Joint Operations Center (JOC) must be carefully considered, as once the command post is established it can become very cumbersome to move at a later date. Selecting the most suitable facility therefore, is an important administrative and logistical element of the major case investigation. Moving a command post or JOC after it has been up and running could negatively impact public confidence by sending the message that the law enforcement agencies managing the major case investigation is less than competent. In addition, valuable investigative time is wasted in moving the command post or JOC, and from a practical standpoint, moving a command post is logistically difficult, in that communications equipment, phones, etc. have to be re-installed at the new site.

Similar to the well-known mantra of real estate people the world over, the three most important things to consider when considering a command post are location, location, and location. Especially in a multiagency effort, a centrally-located command post can enhance communications and save time that would otherwise be spent in transporting information or personnel to multiple locations. Although there are multiagency situations in which individual agencies can (and in some cases should) investigate their own offenses, the need for a single command post to direct the overall investigative effort in most cases is essential for coordinated efforts. When selecting a location to be used as a command post, the following items should be considered:

1. **Location.** Should be convenient to the major geographic areas which encompass the crime scene and the area under investigation. This will save travel time for all personnel, particularly the investigators assigned to the major case investigation.

2. **Suitability.** Should be suitable for long-term use and comfortable enough for the personnel assigned. There is no way of knowing how long a major case investigation will take, and as was discussed earlier, planning for the long term makes much more sense than anticipating a quick resolution of the investigation. When arranging for a location to be used as a command post, beware of for as long as you need it or other handshake-type agreements. These agreements can sometimes become problematic, particularly if the owner of the location needs to have the location back, for whatever reason, before the major case investigation is concluded.

   I am aware of a double murder investigation in a small community where the major case manager sought out the local VFW manager to see about utilizing their facility as a command post. This was due to the fact that the law enforcement agencies involved in the investigation did not have a suitable facility. The local VFW was centrally located, and large enough for the major case effort. As would be expected from an organization such as the VFW, they were more than happy to assist law enforcement, the handshake agreement was made, and the command post was set up and established. Approximately a week later, the VFW manager came to the command post to inquire as to when they were going to be done with their investigation, because a dance had been scheduled months earlier for the upcoming Saturday night. Needless to say, this was problematic.

3. **Convenience.** The location must provide adequate space for operational and administrative personnel and equipment, as

well as adequate washroom facilities and parking. The parking area should be a secure area, and of adequate size for the personnel assigned to the investigation, as well as any assisting agency personnel and command.

The location should also have some type of food service nearby, so that personnel assigned can either go out for meals or the food could be delivered to the command post. Regarding food for personnel, there are pros and cons for having food delivered or to having the personnel use nearby restaurants. If you're going to cater in, keep the food out of the main command post, which keeps work areas cleaner and also makes breaks to stop for meals more likely. The downside of catering food in is that personnel do need a breather every so often, and relaxation during meals can be a welcome break in the action. On the other hand, if they are all eating at the same location they're always in touch and are probably talking about the case. The downside of using nearby restaurants is the time spent traveling and eating can become excessive, and security of discussions in a restaurant is not always the best. Investigators seem to have a habit of discussing case work at some inappropriate places.

4. **Security.** The command post must be secure from compromise by non-involved personnel, especially media personnel eager for an "exclusive," or by the criminal element. Some type of alarm systems and a requirement to display identification or the use of sign in/out logs might be appropriate, depending on the situation, and in most cases worth considering. Prior to selection of a suitable location for a command post, the person tasked with making the selection should conduct a security survey of the facility and surrounding area to assess the ease in which unauthorized persons or the press could enter. The command post should not be located in a facility used for normal resident walk-in business, and controls at parking areas may be necessary. Obviously, there must be some way to limit access to only those individuals who are required to be at the command post.

COMMAND POST AND DATA SECURITY

In addition to the command post itself, however, the security of the data in a major case investigation is also critical. Considering the fact that many very sensitive investigations are based on allegations, not established facts, points directly to the need that the information contained in those allegations must be protected. Lives and careers can be ruined by information leaks regarding untrue allegations, and once the court of public opinion has ruled, the reputation of the person harmed is usually not recoverable. Security of documents and data can also have an extremely harmful impact on the prosecution of the case, and security systems need to be designed with that in mind as well. Perhaps the best method for maintaining security of facilities, documents, and data in a major case investigation is to utilize the military model for security. Although the military has, in recent history, had classified documents and facilities compromised with much accompanying negative publicity, in most or possibly all of those cases the compromise resulted because of some type of human error which violated the security policy. The military model of security is based on three independent principles: Clearance, Access, and Need to Know.

- **Clearance.** Refers to the level of security which the person possesses. During the commissioned service portion of my military career as a Naval Intelligence Officer, I held a Top Secret (TS)-SCI (Sensitive Compartmentalized Information) security clearance. Top Secret is a more stringent clearance, which is granted as the result of a Special Background Investigation (SBI). Top Secret clearances generally afford one access to data that affects national security, counterterrorism/counterintelligence, or other highly sensitive data. There are far fewer individuals with Top Secret clearances than Secret clearances. A Top Secret clearance can take as long as three years to obtain, and it must be renewed every five years. Sensitive Compartmented Information (SCI) clearances are assigned only after one has been through the rigors of a background investigation and a special adjudication process for evaluating the investigation. SCI access, however, is assigned only in compartments. These compartments are necessarily separated from each other organizationally, so an individual with access to one compartment will not necessarily have access to another. Sounds like quite a complicated process, and believe me, it is, but with good reason.
- **The concept of clearance.** Relates to the major case investiga-

tion in this manner: if a patrol officer, not involved in the major case investigation, were to request to examine data or documents relating to the investigation, they would (and should) be denied. In fact, some investigative personnel who were not assigned to the major case investigation would (and should) also be denied. The simple fact that someone is a law enforcement officer and is trustworthy does necessarily not constitute a clearance for them to have the ability to view and examine documents or data in a major case.

- **Access.** Refers to physical access to the data, facility, equipment, or information being protected. At one of my last military assignments at the Joint Analysis Center (Intelligence) in Molesworth, England, physical access to the data on which I worked consisted of a rather complicated process. When I drove onto the base, I was required to display one set of identification documents to the gate security personnel (who were manning .50 caliber machine guns behind sand-bagged emplacements). Once onto the base, I parked and then entered a maze of barbed wire and concrete bunker surrounding a security office, where I showed another document, and then was able to approach the building in which I worked. Another ID check by a guard inside the building, combination locks on the office door and on the safe, a password on the computer, and I could begin the day's work. Another complicated process, but important, considering the sensitivity of the information on which I was working.

  Although it is highly unlikely that any major case investigative effort would feel the need to go to such extreme lengths for security, the use of appropriate measures to limit physical access to facilities, data, or documents needs to be implemented. Things like keyed locks or some type of mechanism like card readers or scanners, combination locks on safes, computer passwords, and a requirement that computers be either shut down or "logged off" when not in use are not excessive, and should be considered.

- **Need to Know.** Refers to whether or not the person seeking access to the data or information being protected actually *needs to know* what it contains. A person might have the proper security clearance and be permitted physical access but might still lack the need to know, and should therefore be denied the opportunity to examine the data or information. This is similar to clearance when it relates to law enforcement personnel, but suffice to say that only those investigative personnel actually *assigned* to the major case investigation should be permitted to examine data or documents relating to the investigation.

- **Adaptable.** Part of planning for the long term as it relates to command posts means that the command post must be adaptable enough for additional personnel, furniture, and communications and other equipment which might be needed later.

- **Suitable interview rooms.** There are pros and cons of conducting investigative interviews at or near the command post. On the positive side, people are being interviewed in a secure and controlled environment. On the negative side, the media is probably camped outside of your command post, and might get the opportunity to see and film whoever it is you are bringing to the command post. In some cases you may be interviewing someone whose identity you don't want revealed.

  I learned this one the hard way through one of many mistakes I've committed. While working on a major case as part of a task force, we had what we felt were suitable interview rooms located in the same building as the command post. We had picked up a recently-released sex offender and planned to interview him in one of the rooms. Even though the investigators bringing the man to the location took the back-alley route and brought him into the building through a different door around the block, the man somehow appeared on the evening news. He had nothing whatsoever to do with the case, and was merely being interviewed because of his status. The fact that he was a recently released convicted sex offender notwithstanding, he shouldn't have appeared on the news as he was not in any way connected to this case.

- **Adequate space for personnel briefings.** When discussing the importance of strategic briefings in Chapter 8, the importance of those briefings was explained. The command post facility must have adequate space for those briefings, as well as for investigators, command personnel, and support/administrative personnel to perform their functions. Having people sitting on top of each other in extremely crowded conditions does not provide an atmosphere conducive to doing good work. It is strongly recommended that press briefings not be conducted at the command post, as holding them there can be very disruptive, which will be discussed in Chapter 11.

When the federal government agrees to assist local, county, or state law enforcement agencies in the investigation of a major case, they are more than willing to set up the command post, which they call a Joint Operations Center (JOC). The FBI Critical Incident Response Group (CIRG) and the ATF Critical Incident Management Response Team (CIMRT) established the JOC used during the Beltway Sniper Task Force, and they did a superb job. They set up a 5,000 square foot JOC on three levels in just over 24 hours. The FBI had agreed to pay for building rental, furniture, and all equipment, including projection screens, phones, and other office equipment. There are certain requirements for a Federal JOC, which include:

- 5,000 sq. ft. minimum facility
- Agencies requesting assistance should have one primary and several secondary sites available
- Agencies are encouraged to think "out of the box" regarding site selection
- There should be adequate pace to allow all participants to be visible to each other, but the site should also include a number of rooms for private meetings.

When setting up seating in a command post, I feel that a "U-shaped" seating arrangement, with a table at the open end of the "U" that contains the major case manager, primary investigator, and leads coordinator, and whatever other management personnel that need to be there for briefing works best. This configuration encourages everyone to provide input into the discussion, particularly at strategic briefings when the person conducting the briefings asks for input or different directions for the case to go, as discussed in Chapter 8. This type of configuration makes it more likely that the newly assigned person who has a great idea and who might not otherwise feel comfortable enough to voice that idea will do so.

Mobile Command Posts

Some agencies have access to mobile command posts, which are usually some type of a "Winnebago" vehicle, or a towed trailer of some sort. While some of these mobile command posts are extremely elaborate, with top-shelf furnishings, they are usually only suitable for short-term command post use when used for a major case investigation. I wouldn't want to use one for more than a week or so. Although the mobility of these vehicles can be a plus, as case management requirements occur, they are usually not suitable for extended long-term use. If they are used, however, they must contain appropriate space, communications equipment, and other necessary equipment such as: fax machines, phones, and television equipment.

Communications

The communications between personnel assigned to the major case investigation can be a problem, particularly in multiagency operations. In established task forces, the issue of communications channels and intra-operable radios and other communications equipment have been addressed. In situations where a group of agencies band together to address a major case investigation with no intention of staying together when the case is concluded, these issues have probably not been addressed, and can become problematic. It is essential that some type of common communications, such as common radio frequencies or programmed mobile phones be acquired, and if possible these devices should utilize some type of anti-scanner technology. While many states have common emergency channels for radio communications as part of the National Law Enforcement Telecommunication System (NLETS), these are usually not suitable for major case or non-emergency use. Hard-line telephone communications can cause additional problems, therefore the decision to have installation of additional lines must be made as soon as possible. Additional phone lines are like additional investigators, it's better to have too many and not need them, than to not have enough and need them. The use of mobile phones is common, but in some areas, particularly rural areas, they are of limited use due to wireless coverage issues.

Specialized Equipment

The use of specialized equipment or specially trained personnel should not be disregarded due to the difficulty associated with obtaining the equipment or the personnel. If the equipment is necessary to conduct the investigation, regardless of the difficulty, it's better to at least attempt to obtain it than to be criticized later for not having tried. Good preplanning and a thorough knowledge of available resources can make equipment or personnel acquisition much easier. If at a loss regarding a specific type of equipment, contact chiefs of police associations or other police organizations which may have knowledge of or access to equipment.

It has been my personal experience that specially trained personnel, such as underwater search and recovery personnel, pilots, K-9 handlers, etc. look forward to opportunities to practice their specialties, and appreciate being called upon to assist in major case investigations. In addition, some non-law enforcement clubs and special interest groups also appreciate assisting in things like large-area ground searches (metal detector, mounted posse units, etc.) or for other duties such as flyer distribution.

Clerical Considerations

Adequate clerical personnel are absolutely necessary in the major case investigation, so that the routing and flow of paper does not become bogged down. Without adequate clerical support, the time lag between completed interviews and completed reports can become tremendous. Even if investigators are typing or word processing their own reports, clerical personnel will be needed to index and search reports for lead connections, etc., otherwise the reports are not usable for intelligence purposes. Reports can also contain material which is necessary for further lead development, which is often needed, and without adequate clerical personnel these leads might be overlooked.

Clerical personnel utilized for major cases should ideally be experienced personnel, so that they possess a familiarity with police reporting systems, and are familiar with police reports and police jargon. In the event that the use of "temp" personnel is being considered, rather than utilize temporary clerical personnel for assignment to the major case investigation, these should be used as backfill for more mundane duties at the law enforcement agency, with the agency's experienced clerical staff diverted to the major case effort. The use of experienced clerical personnel on the major case is beneficial with regard to administrative assignments, such as timekeeping, vouchers, and travel claims. The use of experienced personnel also eliminates the need for concern regarding the security of the investigative reports. There have been major case investigations where clerical personnel and others have been offered money for "leaking" photos and other documents to the media, and by using experienced and trustworthy clerical personnel for the major case the concern for leaks is usually diminished.

ADDITIONAL LOGISTICAL AND ADMINISTRATIVE CONSIDERATIONS

These are often overlooked as not being crucial to the investigation, but in reality are as crucial to the investigation as are adequate personnel, and they include:

- **Lodging.** Commuting long distances wastes time, increases fatigue, and decreases motivation of personnel. If at all possible, investigative personnel should be lodged near the command post in suitable motels. Having all investigative personnel lodged in the same place can also add to the feeling of "esprit d' corps," as they will interact more frequently. If cost-saving is a concern, as it usually is, consider doubling up in rooms to save money, also check out government, long-term, or corporate rates. Most motels are reasonable and will make accommodations for major case investigations if approached properly.
- **Timekeeping.** Although matters such as overtime, timekeeping, and the expenditure of official funds are not often considered important concerns of the major case supervisor, they must be taken into consideration. This can present serious problems later such as non-documentation for expenditures on witnesses or confidential informant payments. Another issue regarding timekeeping is that if it is not kept up-to-date, serious problems for personal timekeeping records will result, as well as the possibility of union contract violations and the resulting grievances.
- **Supplies.** Whenever possible, in a multiagency operation personnel should be requested to obtain their personal supplies from their parent agency. Don't assume, however, that all personnel will comply, and a supply of notebooks, pens, flashlight batteries, etc. need to be acquired.
- **Office equipment.** In the event that the command post is set up off-site, that is not located in a police facility, office equipment

might have to be rented for the duration of the major case investigation. Equipment such as copy machines, printers, and fax machines will be absolutely necessary. In some cases, even if the command post is set up in a police facility, office equipment is rented for fear that the constant use of the equipment major case personnel could disrupt the agency's normal operations. In the event that office equipment like copiers, printers, and faxes are rented, spend the extra money and get the "industrial strength" model, as these will be in constant use. I can remember standing next to a "bargain basement" combination copier/fax/printer (and possible microwave oven) during a major case, waiting (not so patiently) for 50 copies of an investigative canvass document to print out for distribution to personnel involved in the canvass. I could have probably drawn the 50 copies by hand myself faster than this device was printing them out. Needless to say, at that point I wished we'd have spent a little more money for the more powerful model.

Photographic Needs

In most cases, crime scene technicians will be responsible for photography and related processing during the major case investigation, however occasionally last minute photo requests often come up, such as enlargements of digital photos, photos of victim for investigative personnel, and so forth. In some emergencies, the use of commercial developers might be your only option, however, the security of the developing is a major concern. The photos themselves will often be considered evidentiary items, and must be safeguarded against unauthorized copying, or against selling or otherwise providing photos to the media/defense attorneys. Most commercial developers utilize totally automated equipment, and you should consider having an officer stand by the processor while the film or digital media is being made into prints made for added security.

Evidence Handling

Do not let your major case suffer irreparable harm due to chain of custody or other evidentiary issues. I would recommend that you use the "keep it simple but separate" method of evidence handling for the major case investigation. It is strongly recommended the crime scene/

evidence coordinator handle and process all evidence, as this will address chain of custody issues and aid consistency and thoroughness. The procedures regarding chain of custody, proper documentation, and so forth must be carefully explained to all investigators at the initial strategic briefing, as many, particularly in multiagency operations, may be unfamiliar with procedures of another agency. This is another good reason for assigning all evidence handling/processing duties to the same person.

For agencies that use bound ledger-type books in which to log evidence by hand, it might be worth considering the establishment of a separate evidence log for the major case itself, rather than using the evidence log that is used for all other items of evidence in the storage facility. This can save time in court later, as the documentation and logging of all evidence related to the major case investigation will be contained in one location, and you will avoid paralyzing your existing evidence system when taking your everyday evidence log to court on the major case.

There seems to be a natural inclination to interpret the term "major case" as referring to homicide cases exclusively. This is not true, as there are a number of very major case investigations that do not involve homicide investigations, and these cases have their own inherent problems and issues, which will be discussed in the next chapter.

CASE STUDY #6: OFFICER-INVOLVED SHOOTING

VICTIMOLOGY: The offender was a 20-year-old black male gang member who resided on the West side of Chicago. He had an extensive criminal history, including robbery and weapons offenses. At the time of the incident, he was wanted on a warrant charging armed robbery.

MAJOR CASE CONSIDERATIONS: This was considered a "major case" due to the following elements:

- Officer-involved shooting resulting in the death of an offender
- Extensive media coverage
- Political involvement of local elected officials

GEOGRAPHICS: The neighborhood in which the incident occurred is a gang-infested area of Chicago, consisting of single family and multiunit apartments.

SPECIFIC FACTS: While part of a multiagency Fugitive Investigation Strike Team (FIST), two officers went to the rear door of the offender's apartment in an effort to locate him. One of the officers observed the offender running through the apartment and ran around to the front of the building to radio for assistance. The officer then observed the offender running out of the house and down the street. The officer radioed for assistance and also instructed a neighbor to call 911. The chase entered a vacant lot, a struggle ensued, and the offender attempted to turn the officer's weapon toward the officer. The weapon discharged, nearly striking the officer. The officer was then able to turn the weapon toward the offender and the weapon discharged again, striking the offender in the head, killing him instantly.

IMMEDIATE ACTION TAKEN: The officer involved in the incident was removed from the scene, and a crime scene established. It was determined that the Violent Crimes Unit of the Chicago Police Department, and not the state police (parent agency of the involved officer) would handle the investigation to provide an element of objectivity to the investigation. An extensive investigative canvass of the immediate neighborhood and surrounding area was initiated. In addition, a thorough background investigation on the offender was initiated. As part of the investigation, written statements were taken from the officer involved in the shooting and his partner. The Prosecutor's Office sent a supervisor to review the incident. Several local political figures arrived on the scene, "demanding" information from the both police commanders. The local media arrived, and requested statements from police command personnel involved in the investigation, which was denied by command personnel from the Chicago police and the state police.

MAJOR DIFFICULTIES: There was extensive media and political interest from the onset, and media personnel involved went to great lengths to "scoop" each other. Upon refusal of the agencies involved in the investigation of the incident to speak to the media, they began to utilize other methods to gain information. This included an anti-police reporter interviewing fellow gang members of the deceased offender. These interviews included the gang members re-enacting the "execution" of their friend. Scenes of these re-enactments were shown on the afternoon and evening news programs.

LESSONS LEARNED:

1. Some type of press statement or news conference should be held as soon as possible, and if the incident looks justified, you should make a statement that preliminary investigation has not revealed any wrongdoing. In the event that the incident appears initially to involve violations of policy or the law, indicate that the investigation is ongoing.
2. The media will be clamoring for information regarding the victim, and if it is something that could be released to the media without harming the investigation or any subsequent prosecution. Make certain that you have the information on the victim available.
3. The background investigation and investigative canvass can never be too thorough. In this case, the investigative canvass revealed an elderly woman who spent all day looking out her window. The woman had observed the entire incident, and her testimony at the civil case repudiated the testimony of the gang members who were friends of the victim.

4. In the event that the media begins to "play dirty" and unfair, take an aggressive approach when dealing with them. Once the re-enactments of the execution were aired, any comments to that particularly reporter immediately ceased.

CASE RESOLUTION: The incident resulted in a civil suit, filed by the family of the decedent. The suit began, and halfway through the suit, prior to the matter going to the jury, it was settled for a relatively small amount of money.

Chapter 10

NON-HOMICIDE MAJOR CASE OBSTACLES

At the beginning of this book the idea of "relativity" when defining what is and what is not a major case was discussed. In some communities with little or no serious crime, an armed robbery might be considered a major case, while in other areas some murders might not reach the level of a major case, it's all relative. Some people, when they hear the term major case, think exclusively of homicides, which is not always true. Many other types of crimes can rise to the level of a major case. With that in mind, there are a number of obstacles and issues inherent in non-homicide major case investigations which should be considered. I have personally had most of these obstacles occur in non-homicide major cases in which I was involved, and the best way for someone to avoid these obstacles and issues is to know that they can happen.

MAJOR FINANCIAL CRIMES

Perhaps the biggest obstacle that some agencies encounter when addressing major financial crime is that there sometimes seems to be a reluctance to bring non-police personnel into these investigations. This can occur even when the non-police personnel are more qualified than personnel conducting the investigation, but their assistance is not considered based solely on the fact that they are non-police. People like bank auditors, credit card investigators, the National Insurance Crime Bureau (formerly known as the National Auto Theft Bureau), and other organizations can be extremely beneficial in these investigations, and to "blow them off" because they're not police is ludicrous.

The term used by sociologists when referring to a situation in which groups maintain distinctions between themselves and others is "boundary maintenance," and when it is practiced by law enforcement personnel it can be very dangerous.

Imagine a group of concentric circles—the center circle represents local (municipal) law enforcement, the next ring outward is county law enforcement, the next ring outward is state law enforcement, and the final ring is federal law enforcement. Boundary maintenance occurs when the smaller ring refuses to work with some or all of the larger rings. When a municipal agency refuses to cooperate with county, state, or federal agencies during a major case investigation, in an effort to maintain their own little kingdom, they are in effect lessening their chances of a successful conclusion. This type of boundary maintenance is dangerous and needs to be avoided in all cases, but particularly in financial crimes investigations.

In a similar manner, when confronted with a major financial crime investigation, the agency which does not possess the expertise and then refuses to seek or accept that expertise is only hurting itself. Not really, however, because they're also hurting the victims by not aggressively attempting to solve the crime. These types of investigations can and do involve specialized accounting, computer, and analytical skills which most police investigators do not possess. Another problem with financial crimes is manpower allocation, which is much more difficult to estimate than in the typical violent crime investigation.

Due to the nature of these financial offenses and the ability of offenders and their associates to rapidly destroy/alter critical evidence, timing can sometimes become a crucial element in these investigations, and adequate manpower to address multiple leads in a timely manner can be important. Another problem inherent with financial crimes is that modern financial criminals tend to utilize computers in their criminal acts on a regular basis, and the improper handling of computer evidence can spell disaster for many investigations.

In cases involving financial type crimes and fraud schemes, the preservation of evidence, Chain of Custody of documentary evidence, and its subsequent presentation in court can "make or break the case," and many police investigators are not equipped to address these issues. In addition to non-traditional financial analysis techniques, however, several standard investigative procedures, such a surveillance, interviewing, and so forth, are also used, and it might be a good idea to utilize non-financial crimes personnel for these functions, saving the "financial crimes experts" to utilize their own specialty.

Several states have access to "financial crimes investigative associations" or other networks made up of experts in this area, who might be able to provide guidance regarding the number of personnel needed to adequately address the types of leads which require follow-up investigation in these types of crimes. Another source of investigative assistance could be local banking institutions, which routinely have these types of investigative analysts on their corporate staffs. Other sources might be the FBI, HIDTA units, or Secret Service, due to their involvement in stolen/forged government checks and subsequent interaction with the banking industry. Part of major case prior planning should be to identify these experts now, rather than to wait for the major case to occur and then scramble for their assistance.

MASS CHILD MOLESTATION INVESTIGATIONS

Large scale or mass child sexual molestations can be among the most difficult non-homicide cases to address, due to the introduction of a number of non-criminal elements:

1. **Public Involvement.** Particularly if the alleged offender is prominent in the community, there are often elements of the public which will intentionally (or unintentionally) hamper your investigation. Unfortunately, this is usually based on their (often misguided) belief that the alleged offender "couldn't possibly have done this." A unit which I commanded worked an investigation on a very popular leader in a youth scouting program, and when it became public that we were looking at this individual as a suspect in the molestations of several members of the program, we actually had parents marching back and forth in front of the police department in something of a silent protest that we were investigating this "outstanding young man."
2. **Uncooperative Victims/Parents.** This can hamper your investigation even if it does not involve prominent offenders. Parents are sometimes reluctant to allow their (victim) children to participate in your investigation, for a number of valid reasons, such

as a desire to not traumatize their child any further, a desire to avoid publicity and the ensuing embarrassment to themselves, their family, and particularly their child.

While I fully realize that it is our job as police to convince these parents to assist us in our efforts to make cases on these molesters by having their children cooperate with us, as a parent myself, I can understand why they would often be reluctant to do so. There have been a number of molestation cases in which I've been involved that parents have flatly refused to allow their children to cooperate with our investigation, and in some cases I could really sympathize with their plight. In other situations, however, I could not, and rather than sympathize with them, I resented their lack of cooperation. While investigating a series of molestations being committed by this co-owner of a very large and very successful auto dealership, we learned that a co-owner of the dealership (without the knowledge of his business partner) would have his mechanics and car hikers pick up young (12–14-year-old) girls and bring them to the dealership. Once at the dealership, the molester would take the girls into his private office which featured a hot tub, bar, and fold-out bed. It was there where the molestations occurred. While focusing on one victim, the parents of the victim suddenly ceased cooperation with us and wouldn't allow their daughter to talk with us. I was advised by the investigator assigned to the case that shortly after their cooperation ceased that he had seen both parents of the young girl driving new cars which (coincidentally I'm sure) both bore dealer stickers of the dealership.

3. **Uncooperative School Officials.** Particularly if the offense(s) occurred on school property or somehow involved school functions or personnel, schools can often be uncooperative. The potential liability issue can become paramount to school officials, and may hamper their cooperation. It should also be remembered that most school board officials are elected, which can introduce another element (politics) into your investigation.

   While no school wants to be associated with a child molestation investigation, one would think that the protection of the children would trump any concerns about liability, but sadly this doesn't always happen.

   There are many ways that school officials can hamper your

investigation. Your access to children can be hampered by school officials, which might make interviewing much more difficult, and schools sometimes attempt to address these issues in a non-criminal manner, which can have later implications on your criminal case if you do ultimately make a prosecutable case. While a chief of police, I was contacted by a school superintendent and told about a molestation that had occurred on a school bus returning children from a school-sponsored field trip. The offender, a 14-year-old male, had fondled a 12-year-old female while she slept, and when the victim woke up the hand of the 14-year-old was up her skirt. The superintendent, who held a Ph.D. and was truly a very professional educator and administrator, was asking for advice on handling the parents of the victim. I was shocked when I learned that this incident had occurred over a week ago and that the school had addressed the issue by suspending the offender. Of course, I immediately met with the superintendent and informed him that this was a criminal act and that we should have been notified immediately. That was the last time that a situation like that occurred in that district, as they realized the criminal nature of such activity.

In order to have effective relationships with school officials to preclude them wanting to handle something that should rightly be referred to the police, it is important for good liaisons with your school officials to be established and maintained. Besides school officials, however, having liaisons with child advocates such as support groups and/or medical personnel who specialize in pediatric medicine can be critical, and the time to initiate these liaisons is not the first day of your mass molestation investigation. These liaisons should be established and maintained long before the major case occurs.

4. **Uncooperative Civic/Social/Religious Organizations.** Particularly in cases which involve adult volunteers or even employees, organizations which provide civic/social/religious/ youth services can seriously hamper your investigation in a number of ways, to include denying your access to victims or possible victims through official or unofficial means, actually conspiring to not cooperate with your investigation, or denying access to suspects through legal means, such as obtaining organizational attorneys for them. Unfortunately, I am personally

familiar with all of these strategies. In addition, sometimes organizations conduct their own investigation, which they will then publicize. Unfortunately, these are not investigative organizations, and the investigations that they conduct are not suitable for such incidents. The concern for diminished liability can oftentimes cloud the judgment of even the most legitimate organization. While our unit was conducting the investigation of a child counselor who was employed by a religious organization I was asked by the investigator assigned to accompany him to a meeting with one of the ranking members of the organization. This individual with whom we met was not only a member of the clergy, he was also an attorney, and provided not only spiritual but legal services for the organization. At the first meeting I explained that it was not our intent in any way to create embarrassment for the religious organization, and that both the investigator and myself were in fact active members of that particular denomination. I explained that we needed the list of this counselor's clients, so that we could determine the extent of the counselor's offenses and so that we could locate as many victims as possible for the subsequent prosecution. This clergy/attorney turned to the individual who was in charge of counseling programs and told him to get us the list of names immediately. We thanked him and left.

After about two weeks, we had still not received the list, and the investigator assigned came to me to voice his concern. I called to make an appointment with the same clergy/attorney and was told that he was very busy and couldn't see me for at least two months. It is amazing to me how quickly someone's calendar clears when they think that a marked squad car might be parked in front of their headquarters for as long as it takes for them to cooperate. We ultimately got the appointment for the next day, but when we arrived not only was the clergy/attorney and the person in charge of counseling programs present, but there were also two attorneys from one of the most prestigious law firms in the city. The clergy/attorney asked me the reason for the meeting, and I told him that we had not yet received the promised list of clients. One of the attorneys began to answer and I told the clergy/attorney that I wasn't there to speak to his attorney. The clergy/attorney looked me right in the eye and informed me that they had conducted their own investigation and that the allegations were unfounded, so therefore we would not be receiving any list of clients. I told the clergy/attorney that as a member of that particular religious denomination I was appalled. He again repeated that the allegations were false and that the meeting was over. As I have thought back on that situation over the years, I find it easy to imagine why that particular religious denomination has paid out millions, if not billions of dollars to victims of child molestation committed by their current and former employees.

There are some other problem areas inherent in mass child molestation investigations, which include:

- There is a real difficulty in estimating the amount of manpower needed, particularly if the number of victims or potential victims is large.
- There is a real difficulty in logistically pursuing the investigation, due to lack of suitable interview space, lack of personnel trained in specialized interviewing, and the inability of local medical/psychological personnel to address large groups of victims.
- Logistical difficulties, such as funding for travel, particularly if the offender has resided/worked in several areas, can also cause problems. This is often a result of the prolific nature of these offenders, and their ability to move and "re-invent" themselves when suspicions start to surround their activities.
- Although there have been vast improvements in consistency of charges for these types of crimes, varying prosecutorial differences sometimes make it necessary for Investigators working multi-jurisdictional investigations to "shop for the best deal" from different jurisdictions. Fortunately, however, this is becoming less of a problem.
- Due to the titillating nature of the offenses, the media will naturally begin a "feeding frenzy" when they become aware of your mass child molestation investigation, which can also hamper your investigation. I am aware of an agency that investigated allegations that widespread molestations were taking place at a day-care center in their community. Rather than request outside assistance, this department initiated their own investigation. They did not

have a suitable facility, and when the parents and potential victims arrived at the police station, they were surrounded in the parking lot and nearby streets by media representatives, who did what media representatives do. Due to the lack of suitable interviewing rooms, some of the parents and potential victims had to wait together, which I'm sure didn't enhance the investigative efforts.

- Child molesters themselves seem to have an uncanny ability to make the investigation of their offenses extremely frustrating. Many child molesters (some of whom are clinically referred to as pedophiles) are not only very manipulative, some are extremely intelligent, and they use their intelligence and manipulative abilities to coax victims and their families into refusing to cooperate with investigations. In addition, I have personally observed what appears to be something of a pattern of conduct from child molesters once they are confronted with their offenses, and this pattern has occurred enough times to make it worth mentioning. Once confronted, the child molester often responds as follows:

1. Makes very angry denials, such as "How dare you accuse me of something like this," complete with feigned anger and the accompanying histrionics.
2. Threatens retaliation and/or law suits toward anyone involved in the investigation.
3. Condemns their condemners–I actually heard a child molester, when referring to his victim, say that "if only she hadn't dressed so sexy none of this would have happened" (the victim was an 11-year-old girl and the offender was in his 40s).
4. Pleas of guilty, even though they "didn't really do anything," as they are merely pleading guilty to spare the children (their victims), who they love dearly, the trauma of having to go to court.
5. The final ploy of "I'm sick and I need help"–this one is really hard to argue.

The time to address many of these issues related to liaisons is not the first day of the mass child molestation major case investigation, the time to address them is right now. Stop and assess the number and level of your liaisons with school, medical, psychological, support group, religious, and logistical personnel, and if you don't have those liaisons, establish them. If you do have them, good for you, now work on maintaining and strengthening them.

MAJOR PROPERTY CRIMES INVESTIGATIONS

Although not often considered major cases by most investigators, large-scale property crimes investigation, such as "sting projects," extensive theft, fencing, or burglary investigations, or other large-scale property crimes investigations can also come with their own inherent problems. The problems inherent in large scale property crimes investigations can have a dramatic impact on the successful prosecution of your case. Many of these problems involve the recovery/handling/ storage/retrieval/return of evidence. One of the biggest problems in major property crimes cases is properly recovering and processing only those items of evidentiary value, which is often difficult as many investigators usually take the "we'll collect it all just in case" attitude. This can lead to problems with regard to storage as well as keeping track of all of the various items of evidence, particularly if some of the items cannot be identified as stolen and must be returned to someone. In many cases, some of the recovered items may not be identifiable, and may have to be returned to the suspect, which makes it more critical for record keeping to be exact. I am aware of several situations in property crimes investigations where expensive items could not be identified and were misplaced during processing, which led to lawsuits and in some cases disciplinary action for investigators. Bar coding systems for evidence processing can be of major benefit in these situations, as all items, no matter how numerous, can be quickly identified, tagged, and a proper record of their existence and whereabouts can be properly maintained.

MAJOR NARCOTICS INVESTIGATIONS

The problems inherent in major narcotics investigations include their own difficulties, such as the supervision of undercover personnel and extensive officer safety issues. Supervision of undercover personnel, particularly during major narcotics investigations, is among the most challenging of supervisory duties. This is due to the fact that nature of undercover work dictates that a great deal of autonomy is necessary for the undercover officer to function. In addition, while initiative and creativity are an integral part of the undercover officer's duties, problems often begin when undercover officers exceed the boundaries of this autonomy, and engage in excessive creativity and initiative.

Working undercover puts one at the absolute center of attention, and can be a rather intoxicating experience, particularly for the newer investigator. In addition, it is often necessary that the undercover officer call the shots when operating on the street, and herein sometimes lies the problem. In order to effectively and safely call the shots, a great deal of discipline is necessary, and without this discipline, the inherent danger of any undercover operation is increased dramatically. In addition to undercover officers themselves making these investigations difficult, some investigative supervisors themselves get caught up in what narcotics officers sometimes refer to as "Kilo Fever," in which large seizures of either narcotics or cash are the ultimate goal. This type of thinking can lead to poor judgment and faulty decision-making from supervisors. Some investigative supervisors don't want to appear as if they are stifling their undercover officers, nor do they want to appear as overly cautious to their personnel, and so as not to appear so they allow their personnel to take absolutely unnecessary risks.

One method to preclude this from occurring is to insist on an investigative/operational plan when supervising undercover officers. Many times the plan must not only be discussed, it must actually be rehearsed with the undercover officer prior to the operation. Decisions must be made ahead of time as to how much latitude will be afforded the undercover officer, particularly if it involves any deviations from the plan. An example would be how many times the undercover officer will be permitted to move locations after the initial meeting with suspects. The basic plan, however, must be strictly adhered to under any circumstances, it's much better to call off an operation than to attend a funeral. In the event that the undercover officer repeatedly demonstrates that he/she cannot operate according to the plan, they should not be allowed to work undercover and might need to be replaced.

Supervising undercover personnel during long-term undercover projects will sometimes also involve managing any personal conflicts which might arise, due to the stress and length of many undercover projects. I supervised an 18-month undercover project that started out with two good friends working undercover together and culminated with the same two people despising each other, and sometimes arguing in front of suspects. One of the suspects, after being arrested, mentioned how "convincing the arguments were" between the two undercover officers. Little did he know that they weren't acting.

OFFICER-INVOLVED SHOOTING INVESTIGATIONS

While I realize that individual agencies and different states have their own protocol for investigating situations in which officers use deadly force, I think that these situations can definitely be classified as major cases and wanted to mention a few pitfalls for the person managing these investigations. Whenever a police officer uses deadly force on a citizen, there are elements of the public that will immediately be critical, assuming that the action taken was not justified. This unfortunately seems much truer today than it was when I began my career 35 years ago. There are also elements within the police department that will take the exact opposite approach and immediately assume that the action was justified. Both of these approaches can be dangerous.

Having been involved in situations in which officers utilized deadly force, both as a supervisor of the officer involved as well as the person investigating the incident, it has always been my belief that the physical and mental well-being of the officer needs to be of primary concern, regardless of the circumstances. Whatever actually happened will ultimately come to light, but right at the onset of the post-incident investigation the officer's well-being needs to be considered. Allowing the officer to remain on the scene while the initial steps of the investigation take place is not a sound idea. If the officer remains on scene several things will occur, none of which are good. Some fellow officers, in an effort to be supportive, will approach the officer to tell them what a great job they did, while other officers, also trying to be supportive, will be offering legal advice. Having the involved officer on scene also makes it much more difficult and uncomfortable for the personnel working the investigation of the incident, whether they are crime scene investigators or the investigators assigned to the follow-up investigation. The officer should be removed (not allowed to drive) from the scene. This is for his/her own benefit, as well as for the benefit of the personnel conducting the initial crime scene investigation. In the event that a fellow officer who is a friend is available, he or she can remove the affected officer. It must be made very clear to this officer that their assignment is not to interview the involved officer about the incident, but strictly to provide transportation. In the event that more than one officer is involved, they should be separated. This is not in any way based upon the assumption that they will "concoct a story," but is a good practice because it can preclude later legal challenges and also because separating witnesses in any major incident/offense is good sound investigative procedure.

Arrangements should be made to notify the officer's next of kin of the incident as soon as possible, so that they don't learn of it second-hand or through the media. I learned this one the hard way when an officer was involved in a pursuit which ended in a crash and shoot-out. Fortunately, the officer was not injured in the crash or the shoot-out. Upon arrival at the scene, I was so busy that I neglected to assign someone to contact the wife of the officer involved. The officer's wife, who was at work, got a call from a neighbor who had seen the incident on TV and had recognized the officer's car number (which was painted on the top of the squad car) from having seen it parked next door. The officer's wife, fearful that her husband was injured, drove quickly to the scene, getting involved in an accident on her way. When she arrived at the scene it was the first time I stopped to think about calling her, and the fallout was not pretty.

Once the officer is removed, a determination needs to be made exactly who will conduct the investigation. There are different schools of thought on this, whether to conduct your own investigation or to request that another agency conduct it. Many large police departments conduct their own shooting investigations, while smaller agencies often have someone else conduct them. There are some inherent problems in conducting your own investigation, however, and they should be considered:

1. If the use of deadly force is ruled justified, an element of the public will assume a cover-up has taken place.
2. If the use of deadly force is ruled unjustified, an element of the PD will assume that the officer is being made out to be a scape-

goat in order to keep the public happy and to diminish liability.

A possible solution to this dilemma would be to request that an outside agency conduct the investigation, and this appearance of impartiality and outside review might be the best method. There are some other considerations regarding the investigation of officer-involved deadly force incidents:

Crime Scene and Neighborhood Canvass

Although these are critical in any case, the criticality of investigative canvasses becomes even more important in the officer-involved shooting. Rather than give way to the urge to hurry out and get this element of the investigation completed, stop and think it through. The personnel selected need to be aware of the importance of locating witnesses (if any) to the incident, and the importance of gaining their cooperation with the investigation. In the event that witnesses are located and it is believe that they are fabricating their recollections in an effort to cast the officer(s) involved in a negative light, the information needs to be documented exactly as they provide it. The time to re-examine their stories and refute any untruths is for the follow-up phase when your investigation has uncovered more information with which to work. By allowing these witnesses to provide fabricated information initially, you improve your chances to impeach any later testimony. In addition, witnesses who appear uncooperative or who appear to be fabricating their recollections need to have their background thoroughly checked to determine if they have some type of a motive for their non-cooperation and/or fabrications.

As with any major case, you can assume that you will be second-guessed and critiqued by the media, the family of the victim, talk radio, and so on. The critical element of this type of an investigation is that it provides an appearance that the investigation is being conducted with the following things in mind:

- **Impartiality.** Nobody is coming into this investigation with any preconceived notions about what occurred, and the investigation will go wherever the leads take it.
- **Objectivity.** The facts are the facts, and will not be clouded by a desire to either clear or convict the officer involved.

- **Thoroughness.** There will be no stone left unturned in this investigation, with the only ultimate goal being the truth.

It is also important the police department give the appearance that in the event the action was not appropriate, the matter will be handled in strict accordance with applicable laws.

Additional Supervisory Responsibilities

There are additional responsibilities for supervisors of officers involved in deadly force incidents, both for the officer involved and for their co-workers, which include:

1. Arrange for the insertion of a critical incident management team into the work unit as this can be very beneficial, not only for officers involved, but for dispatch personnel who handled the incident on the radio or clerical staff who work with and are close to the officers involved.
2. As much as possible, candidly and openly discuss the incident with personnel rather than allow the "rumor mill" to generate gossip and half-truths, and as much as possible address personnel with as many of the facts as you are able.
3. Afford those personnel directly involved in the incident with individualized access to counseling or other peer support programs.

Officer-involved shooting investigations routinely generate a great deal of media attention, and effectively dealing with the media during major case investigations can be very difficult. In the next chapter we will examine some strategies for dealing with the media during the major case investigation.

CASE STUDY #7: MASS CHILD MOLESTATION

VICTIMOLOGY: The total list of victims of this offender will probably never be known, but several victims in Illinois were revealed. As with most pedophiles, the offender had "victims of preference," in his case young boys, prepubescent, ranging in age from approximately 11 to age 13.

GEOGRAPHICS: The areas in which these offenses took place were all very upscale suburban communities. The victims, however, came from less affluent areas, and some came from single parent homes.

SPECIFIC FACTS: This offender was originally from the Houston, Texas area, where he had established a program called "Kids in Faded Jeans," which was a "counseling" program for "at risk" pre-teen youth, mainly young boys. Following the receipt of allegations of improprieties with some children who attended his program for counseling, the police became involved. The offender was never prosecuted, however, due to a combination of lack of victim cooperation and community support. He was advised by police in Texas, however, that he should "vacate the state" as soon as possible. As with many pedophiles, when their activities come to light and become public, they move from the area and begin to "re-invent" themselves. This offender moved to the State of Illinois, and sought out church groups, youth organizations, and community groups, offering to work with young people, even on a volunteer basis. The offender claimed to be several things which would appeal to young people and adults alike, including his claims that he was a:

- Former prisoner of war from the Vietnam War
- Medal of honor recipient
- Martial arts expert
- Computer expert and teacher

Due to the difficulty for programs to obtain volunteers, none of these claims were ever investigated or verified. In fact, one of the local churches, which had been using the services of the offender, provided him with an apartment, rent free, on their property in exchange for him teaching his classes.

The offender marched in the Memorial Day and other parades wearing military fatigues and bedecked with full-scale replica of the Medal of Honor around his neck and several ribbons mounted on his chest, to include the Silver Star, Bronze Star, and Purple Heart, plus several campaign and overseas ribbons. Many of the investigators involved in the case were themselves military veterans, and the offender wearing these ribbons and purporting himself to be a former prisoner of war was considered tantamount to sacrilege in their eyes.

The offender was offering training in martial arts to prepare these children in the event that they were approached by someone intent on sexually molesting them. The son of a suburban police detective approached his father and asked for permission to join the offender's "self-defense" class, which was being offered for free through a local church group. The father, having just completed a training program in pedophiles and how to recognize their activities, began looking into the offender and his background. When the subject's background became questionable, although no official criminal record existed, the detective contacted the Child Sexual Exploitation Unit of the State Police and an investigation was initiated.

IMMEDIATE ACTION TAKEN: The investigation began with a thorough background check on the offender, which included his military service record. The military records revealed that although he had served in the Air Force, he had never been assigned overseas or in combat, and that he was discharged due to "psychological reasons." Once this information was established, contacts were made with all of the areas in which he had resided. An investigative task force was established, which included investigators from all of the suburban areas in which the offender had established programs.

The detective who initiated the investigation learned that his son had a close friend who had been spending a great deal of time with the offender. The detective began talking to the mother of his son's friend and learned that the child was becoming more dependent on the offender and distant from his mother. The mother, who had been totally supportive of the offender, was now becoming somewhat disillusioned with him. She offered to allow her son to be interviewed quietly, so as not to alert the offender. It was learned during the interview that the child had been molested some years earlier by a friend of his mother, and that he had been recently repeatedly molested by the offender, as had several of his friends. All of the boys were reportedly fearful of the offender, who described himself to them as a ticking time bomb, based on his days as a POW and they and their families would be harmed if they reported the molestation. It became apparent that traditional investigative methods were not likely to be successful, and an investigative plan, utilizing a "non-traditional" approach, might work with this offender, based on his incredible ego.

It was determined that the child who had been interviewed would try and convince the offender that his "uncle," with whom he had also been having sexual relations, had made child pornographic movies of the two of them together. The child was to tell the offender that the uncle might like to film a movie featuring he and the offender engaging in sexual activity. Playing on the ego of the offender, an introduction was arranged for the offender to meet with the uncle, who was actually an undercover officer. Through the skill of the undercover officer and the limitless ego of the offender, the introduction was successful. The offender agreed to make a pornographic film with the child and the uncle.

A suite at an upscale hotel was rented, and professional camera gear was brought to the suite along with a camera man (another undercover officer). The offender brought the child to the room, and also brought a duffel bag of sexual toys and paraphernalia to use during the movie filming, and the trap was set. Once the child was safely out of the room, the offender was arrested.

MAJOR DIFFICULTIES: On paper, this offender appeared to be a pillar of the community, freely giving of his time to protect children and teach them life skills. It was felt, and later confirmed, that many parents in this type of investigation will support the offender and not allow their children to cooperate with the investigation, unless there is overwhelming proof of the offender's culpability. Following the arrest of the offender, as the investigation continued, many of the victims' parents openly refused to assist the police, and some began an anti-police campaign with the local media outlets. In addition, many flatly refused to allow their sons to participate in any way in the investigation. The churches, park districts, and some community groups with which the offender worked even began talking about mounting a legal defense fund for him. Rather than drag on this nonsense, we decided to show a small amount of our hand to a selected group of officials.

With the permission of the prosecutor's office, we had a private screening of the video made in the hotel room with the minister of the church who had provided the offender with the apartment, a community leader who had befriended the offender, and a park district official. That evening plans for the legal defense fund were trashed and some parents allowed their children to be interviewed as part of the investigation.

LESSONS LEARNED:

1. Don't get locked into traditional investigative methods, use your imagination, and if you think that there may be another way to approach an offender which would not irreparably harm your case, consider it.

2. Plan on encountering community opposition to prosecution sometimes, and occasionally seeking out the cooperation of community leaders might be beneficial in cases where support for the offender is interfering with the investigation. In addition, have an aggressive media plan in action to counter support for the offender. In this case we made strategic leaks to selected members of the media that they might want to check with the authorities in Houston, Texas, and some other places where the offender had resided.

3. Oftentimes, the sheer numbers of victims identified will preclude the offender from wanting to go to trial. In this case, as with many offenders of this type, when confronted with the amount of evidence against him, to include several victims and the videotape of his activity in the hotel suite, the offender pled guilty.

4. In the event that other jurisdictions are involved in offenses, bring them into the investigation as soon as possible. By doing this, no stone will be left unturned and the combined investigative efforts will be beneficial.

Chapter 11

MAJOR CASE MEDIA STRATEGIES

GENERAL INFORMATION

This is not a book on media relations for police, but when one considers the amount of media coverage of most major case investigations, I thought it prudent to at least mention some concerns and considerations with regard to interacting with the media while managing a major case. There are a number of great books and training programs dealing with media relations, and I would urge any major case manager to seriously consider training in this area for themselves as well as their media coordinator. Included in training offerings of which I'm familiar is the program offered by Rick Rosenthal of RAR Communications, which is among the best media training I've ever seen. Mr. Rosenthal is a former news anchor for a very large station, and the information that he provides in his classes will better prepare any major case manager for the rigors of dealing with the media.

While police frequently criticize the media for focusing on the negative aspects of their work, police critics frequently claim the media overlooks many police mistakes that they should be exposing to the public. In reality, the attitude of the media towards the police is really somewhat ambivalent. Although news stories about heroic cops are rare, the entertainment side of the media frequently glamorizes our profession, making it appear more exciting than we know it to really be. Those of us in the law enforcement profession need to admit that deviant acts committed by cops are news stories, as they involve persons in positions of authority who have violated the public trust.

The relationship between the news media and the police is very complex, and is more symbiotic than antagonistic, as we police serve

192

as major news sources, and sometimes the only news source. If this is true, and I believe it to be true, to constantly upset the police by reporting negatively on police activities is not in the best interest of maintaining the police as willing news sources.

In recent years we have seen something of a new trend in journalism that is very adversarial in its approach, and particularly adversarial to police. This new breed of journalists are often more interested in angles than answers, more concerned with being social missionaries than journalists, and often never let the facts get in the way of a good story. Fortunately, this type of media person seems to be in the minority, as most media representatives are very professional.

We need to keep in mind that in a free society, the media fulfills a need, and that for the most part, the media personnel are simply doing their jobs. The major case manager can expect bias, but should demand fairness from the media. Establishing a good working relationship with the media is something which is best handled on a daily basis, not the first day of the major case investigation. I remember going to Poland on behalf of the U.S. Department of State to work with Polish National Police in the aftermath of an off-duty officer-involved shooting that had caused a great deal of negative media reaction. While myself and the two other American police commanders on the trip were being briefed by the Polish National Police command, they explained in somewhat astonished tones that the "media had lied to the people and not told the truth about what happened." Of course the two Americans and I looked at each other thinking "OK, so what's your point" in response to the statement. We then realized that at that time Poland was experiencing its first truly free and democratic form of government and free press, which is why they were surprised.

INTERVIEWS DURING THE MAJOR CASE INVESTIGATION

Some police decide that if there is any chance that the media will report in a negative manner what it is they're doing that they are better off simply saying "no comment" and leaving it at that. Unfortunately, during the major case investigation this is not really an option. During the major case investigation, we need to communicate a great deal to the public, so that they know the matter is being professionally handled.

We do interviews with the media based on what we perceive to be our own communication objectives, which need to be publicized. If we don't provide the media with something that we would like publicized, I can guarantee you that they will publicize their own objectives, which could be contrary to yours. During a major case investigation into an officer-involved shooting I decided that we weren't going to release anything to the media in time for any of the afternoon or early evening news programs. As I watched the news coverage on the after-noon news of the media filming gang-banger friends of the decedent "reenacting the murder of their comrade by the police," I realized that by not saying anything I had put the media into the position of having to fill the air time with something. I further realized that the communications objectives they decided to fill the air time with were diametrically opposed to our objectives. Painful lesson, but very well learned. Having some type of communications objectives ahead of time is the key to success in any interview, regardless of the topic. Police should not let their interviews with the media become "question driven," where they are on the defensive, trying to come up with answers to the media's questions. Instead, interviews should be driven by the message that the police wish to get publicized. If you know what you want your message to be and are professional and consistent and brief in your delivery of that message, you have properly interacted with the media.

In any major case investigation, the first day is vital with regard to the media, and the first few hours are critical, as the stage will be set with regard to two very important elements of your media plan:

- Your rapport with the media
- The perceptions made about you and your efforts by the public

In Chapter 4 when discussing the various functional components of the major case investigative effort, the position of media coordinator was discussed at length. The media coordinator is responsible for see-ing to it that the message of the major case management team is devel-oped and presented, whether this is a single-agency or multiagency investigative effort. The media coordinator ideally should be someone who has a thorough knowledge of media policies and procedures, and a great deal of experience with preparation of press releases and preparation and delivery of press briefings and interviews. The media coordinator must be capable of developing and maintaining ongoing positive relationships with media personnel, particularly during very stressful and difficult times when there is not much news to report. The media coordinator must be able to prepare and conduct regularly scheduled press briefings at designated locations as well as writing and disseminating press releases. Major case managers who try to assume responsibility for working with the media while managing the investigation will learn quickly that trying to do both functions doesn't usually work, and it will detract from the effective leadership of the investigative effort.

There are certain types of information which should not be released, unless of course you have a written policy or procedure or are operating under a state law that mandates releasing the following types of information:

1. **Names of minors arrested or taken into custody.** In most states, unless the minor is being charged as an adult for a very serious crime, their identity is protected from release.
2. **Observations about a defendant's character.** Your observations about a defendant's character usually are based in opinion only and have no real bearing on the case.
3. **Statements, admissions, confessions, alibis.** Attributable to a defendant, or refusal or failure of the defendant to make a statement. I don't see how releasing this information will benefit your investigation, and it will come out in court anyway, which is the proper forum.
4. **Reference to evidentiary matters.** Including fingerprints, polygraph exams, ballistics tests, lab results, or refusal of the defendant to submit to any test or examination. This too, will come out in court later, and why take a chance on making the job of the prosecutor any more difficult than it is by releasing something that you shouldn't.
5. **Reference to any investigative procedures.** Including surveillance techniques, operational specifics of covert activities or other information which may compromise current or future investigative activities. During a multi-kilo drug transaction I had an officer under my command shot and seriously injured. Imagine my surprise the next day when I read a detailed account of the fact that the room had been equipped with sever-

al listening devices and cameras, disguised as clock radios, garbage cans, etc. Although this information had no real bearing on the case against the individuals who had shot our officer, the information could have had a deadly impact on the next under-cover drug transaction in which this type of equipment was used.

6. **Statements concerning the identity, testimony, or credibility of prospective witnesses.** Although this seems pretty obvious, I've seen police mentioning enough information about witnesses that the offender can easily deduce their identity. Once their identity is known, not only are they sometimes in danger, but they are also going to be subjected to requests for media interviews or otherwise compromised. These compromises of witnesses can render them ineffective or "tainted" for any resulting prosecution in which their testimony would be needed.

7. **Statements relating to evidence or arguments in the case.** Anything of this nature should be left up to the prosecutor to release if they choose to do so.

8. **Opinions relating to guilt or the possibility of a plea to the offense charged or to a lesser offense.** If the defendant's attorney isn't smart enough to figure out that they should plead their client to a lesser charge, why should we make the suggestion to them?

9. **Information concerning a defendant's prior criminal record.** Even in the case of a conviction that is usually public record, without the prior approval of the prosecutor.

10. **Don't ever commit yourselves to a time or "deadline" for the solution of the case.** Every time I hear a law enforcement official say something to the tune of "arrests are imminent" I cringe. Statements on when the case will be solved usually do nothing but come back to haunt you if the case isn't solve by the date you "predicted."

SCHEDULED PRESS BRIEFINGS

These are usually advisable for the following reasons:

1. If regularly scheduled briefings are not held, media representatives may begin taking other measures to obtain information. I

have seen media representatives going through dumpsters at night looking for discarded notes or reports, and I've also seen them following investigators around and then trying to interview people to whom the investigators just spoke. According to participants in the Beltway Sniper Task Force, the media was caught:

- Listening through walls and ceilings
- Using cameras to look through third floor command post windows
- Paying citizens for access to private property for better camera angles into crime scenes

2. Regularly scheduled briefings allow the media coordinator or other designee to build up a rapport with media representatives. They can also be used as an opportunity to set ground rules for future encounters on this or other cases.
3. If scheduled press briefings are held, the public will be left with the impression that the matter is being handled, thereby instilling confidence in their minds. Scheduled press briefings can also be used as a mechanism to notify the public of specific concerns that might affect them and which police want released.
4. Regularly scheduled briefings allow the investigation to gain exposure which can aid in development of leads, particularly if tip lines are utilized. They can even allow the major case investigative team to communicate with the offender(s), if desired.

Location and Frequency

In a long-term investigation, identify one permanent site for scheduled press briefings, and make certain that it is separate from the investigative effort so as not to be distracting to personnel assigned to the investigation. Typically scheduled press briefings should follow a schedule that roughly coincides with the times of the newscasts. This is a courtesy that is usually extended to accommodate the media to file their stories at an opportune time. My good friend, Rick Rosenthal of RAR Communications, Inc. a former news anchor and probably the most outstanding media trainer I've ever encountered, teaches that police spokespersons should "feed the animals at the same time each day, or they'll start rooting through the garbage." What he means is that regularly scheduled press briefings will provide information to the media and help dissuade them from digging up their own information to put on the air or in print.

UNSCHEDULED PRESS BRIEFINGS AT EMERGENCIES

While it might sound obvious to avoid unscheduled press briefings during emergency situations, there are situations in which you might not be able to avoid them. If you cannot avoid a press briefing due to circumstances, you need to get your emotions in check before opening your mouth. Even if you only have a few minutes to formulate a plan of what you need to say and the message you want to deliver, come up with a plan and discuss it with someone prior to saying anything. If you think about it, emergency situations can be an opportunity to get your message across in a dramatic manner, if you're willing to seize the initiative. While you're trying to make yourself some notes of pertinent information, the simple act of sitting down and writing them out can help to calm you down and make you think things out first. While assigned as commander of a multiagency drug enforcement task force, one of our undercover officers was seriously wounded in a shoot-out with a drug offender during a drug transaction at a motel. Upon my arrival at the scene I was besieged by about a dozen reporters, from print, radio, and TV entities, and they wanted something to put on the air immediately. I asked for about ten minutes and promised I'd have something to say when I came back. I went into the motel to check on our other personnel, and after speaking with them I sat on the hotel bed and made some notes on the notepad from the bedside table. I ran some ideas for a press briefing past a police commander who was also on scene and he gave me some suggestions for other things to add. When I was comfortable that I did indeed have a message to give to the media I went out and held an impromptu press briefing, which went very well. The message that the police commander and I had developed was that although this operation was very well-planned and well-staffed, that there is an inherent danger in this type of work and you can't eliminate all of the danger, no matter how hard you plan. The briefing went very well, and I was able to leave and rush to the hospital to be with our officer.

Utilizing Programs Such as America's Most Wanted

Particularly in high-profile major cases, there may be an occasion to utilize a program such as *America's Most Wanted* or similar programs to get information out to the public which could publicize your efforts and might aid in lead development. This type of exposure can be very beneficial, and some of these programs have an excellent track record for generating leads and locating fugitives. You do need to remember, however, that this is TV, and sometimes the facts get set aside for a better camera shot, or more dramatic plots or scenes. If you do decide to use one of these programs, try to stand your ground when it comes to the facts, but keep in mind that sensationalism sells, and if it comes down to the sensational or the true, they'll probably go with the sensational. We were involved in a kidnapping case in which a sheriff's deputy was kidnapped from a southern state and driven to the Midwest where she was released. When the show aired I was surprised at the amount of "poetic license" that was infused into the program, but it ultimately resulted in the capture of the offenders in the northwest United States, so at least it was effective.

MEDIA RULES FOR SURVIVAL

I'll close this chapter with what I have always considered some media "rules for survival." While I admittedly haven't always followed these and have made mistakes by not doing so, they are worth sharing so that you don't repeat the mistakes I've made.

- You do have the right to remain silent. You have no legal, moral, or social obligation to talk with a reporter you have reason to believe is out to get you.
- There's really no such thing as "off the record." They can call it background or whatever, but if you say something it may be quoted or misquoted. You must remember that there are no rules here, including violating one's confidence, which some media reps seem to do with impunity. If you do plan to go "off the record," make certain that it is with a reporter you can trust.
- Cover your flank. If they can't get to the major case manager, they'll settle for anyone as a news source, including your investi-

gators, clerks, or other support personnel. Remember these people can't afford any "dead air time" or blank newspaper space, so they will come up with the information from somebody. Making your media plan and rules perfectly clear at the initial strategic briefing can probably preclude many of the leaks or unauthorized comments to the media that would otherwise occur.

• Professionalism works. The media is often looking for controversy and confrontation, and if you give it to them it will escalate, you can count on that. By maintaining a professional demeanor and only making well-thought professional comments you can defuse a number of otherwise volatile media situations.

• Never accept the media's terminology if it's incorrect. It is an old media trick to attempt to put their words in your mouth, so that the idiotic statements that are made can be attributed to you. If you don't agree with the terminology that they are using, correct them if they're wrong. A unit which I commanded was asked to investigate a very high-profile incident of the possible suicide of a young man in a local police department lockup while he was being held on a DUI charge. The media was becoming insistent on some type of a statement. Although the personnel under my command were investigating the in-custody death, it was the responsibility of the local police department to handle the media. The chief (former) of this department didn't have much experience in addressing the media and asked me for any pointers I might be able to provide. He and I sat down and came up with a press release, which stated that the state police would be conducting the investigation of this incident as a non-involved party, and would report the findings to the prosecutor's office. I suggested that the chief walk into the room where dozens of print, radio, and television media were waiting, hand out the press release, and politely refuse to answer any questions as this was an ongoing investigation which was being conducted by another agency. He walked into the room and before he could even start talking a reporter shouted at him "chief, how long was the victim in custody before he was killed?" to which the chief replied "About an hour and a half." I was absolutely astounded at what the chief had just done. He had allowed the media to portray the young man as a "victim," and had indirectly stated that this young man had been "killed" while in police custody. Needless to say, the rest of the press briefing didn't go any better, with reporters shouting questions at the now frantic chief, with him trying to explain that what he said was not really what he meant. Unfortunately, it all went downhill from there, with the members of the police department holding a "vote of no confidence" on the chief about three months later, which ultimately led to his being replaced.

- Media are excellent at using your vanity against you. The media are excellent seducers, and they can get police to say any number of things that they want to hear by simply playing on their vanity. I find it a little far-fetched to think that every drop-dead gorgeous news reporter, male or female, graduated number one in their journalism school, and would surmise that at least in a few cases their appearance might have had something to do with them getting hired. The fact that they are so attractive has probably caused more than one police official to say something really stupid as they weren't concentrating on what they were saying, but rather on the appearance of the person asking the questions. In addition, don't think for a minute that you can beat them at their own game. This is what they do, and they do it very well. Don't exaggerate, as it can come back to haunt you. Instead of exaggerating, it is sometimes best to use generalities, which are a little vaguer. For example "several" is much easier to defend if confronted than "hundreds" might be.

  The media can also target the vanity of police by using confrontational tactics, knowing that cops as a profession are extremely competitive and usually won't back down from a challenge. When we go to a bar fight and identify the main culprit, we usually tell him or her that they will be leaving with us. For anyone foolhardy enough to respond that they're "not going anywhere with us," we usually are successful in convincing them otherwise. When the media decides to use confrontation to test our vanity, however, this is probably the one challenge from which you should back down as this is one battle that you can't win.

- Set ground rules for the media. When conducting press briefings, let the media know ahead of time what you can't discuss, and don't discuss it. Of course, they'll ask anyway, which gives you the opportunity to re-state your position by stating "As I've already indicated earlier, I can't discuss that." This also gives you a reason, if they persist in questioning you about things you've already established that you can't discuss, to ignore the questions of the reporter who can't follow instructions and instead answer the questions of some other media representative.

- Listen to the questions and only answer the questions. Just like we're taught to testify in court, don't answer until you've actually listened to the question, and once you've answered the question, stop. It is possible, sometimes, to turn the question around by rephrasing it to suit your needs. For example, if you're asked if someone is a suspect and you haven't decided if they are or aren't yet, and answer such as "If you're asking if that person has been ruled out as a suspect, the answer is no." You didn't say that they were a suspect, and didn't say that they weren't.

  Don't ever answer "what-ifs" or any hypothetical questions, and state clearly that you won't entertain any such questions. Keep you answers short, sweet, and to the point, and only answer the questions. Don't open the session up to additional questions, unless you can anticipate what those questions might be and they would be part of the message that you want to present. If you know that you're going to be interviewed on a major case, have your message ready and rehearse the answers to what you assume will be the main questions beforehand with someone who will be constructively critical of your answers. If there are questions that you know will have a bearing on later prosecution, run your answers past the prosecutor so as not to hamper their later efforts. If the prosecutor asks you to avoid certain answers, then avoid them.

- Don't ever lie, argue, or lose your temper with the media. If you don't know the answer to a question, say so. If you're "almost sure" that you know the answer, take the safe route and say that you don't know. Don't ever allow yourself to be led into an argument with the media, as was mentioned earlier, you can't win. They always have the last word, and remember that if you lose your temper, you lose big time.

- Don't use police jargon. Real cops know that none of us actually use police jargon when conversing with each other, that type of thing is reserved for police reports or for rookie cops for their first month on the job. After about the first month, their field training officer will turn to them and tell them to "knock it off, we don't really talk like that." The use of police jargon when talking to the media, makes it sound like we're trying to "put a spin" on our answers, similar to what politicians do every day. When the public hears us trying to spin answers, I feel that it makes us sound both phony and evasive, which is probably not the message that we want to present during the major case investigation or at any other time.

As with any other facet of major case management, pre-planned efforts usually have a much better chance of success. In addition, once the major case investigation is concluded, the after action critique can provide a wealth of valuable information. Both of these topics will be discussed in the next chapter.

CASE STUDY #8: MULTIPLE OFFICER-INVOLVED SHOOTING

VICTIMOLOGY: White Male, 52 years old, 25-year police officer, assigned as a Sergeant with a suburban police department

MAJOR CASE CONSIDERATIONS: This was considered a "major case" due to the following elements:

- The victim's status as a veteran police officer
- The fact that the victim was killed by other police officers
- The involvement of two police agencies
- Extensive media coverage

GEOGRAPHICS: The area in which the incident took place is a gang, drug, and prostitution-infested neighborhood, in a suburb that is very economically depressed. The police has had a number of scandals throughout its history.

SPECIFIC FACTS: The newly appointed chief of police of the suburb had been appointed with a promise to "clean up" the prostitution, gangs, and narcotics trafficking that plagued the city. He contacted a county law enforcement agency and asked that tactical Officers be assigned to address these issues. Due to security concerns and a past history of leaks with regard to this type of police activity, the chief was the only person aware of the county agency's participation. Five tactical officers from the county agency were assigned to the operation, and they proceeded to the area in three separate vehicles. These tactical officers were, for the most part, very inexperienced in this type of operation.

At approximately 3:00 a.m., the tactical officers observed a vehicle enter the area and park near an intersection. The vehicle was occupied by a middle-aged white male on the driver's side and a younger black woman on the passenger side. The Tactical Officers decided to approach the vehicle and pulled their three cars up to the intersection in a "felony stop" configuration, which blocked the suspect vehicle's route of escape. One of the tactical officers approached the driver's side while the other four fanned out along the front and passenger side of the vehicle. The tactical officer on the driver's side of the vehicle informed his fellow officers that he observed a handgun on the seat in front of the driver, which put all officers in a heightened state of alert. The driver then allegedly picked up the handgun, pointed it at the tactical officer standing on the driver's side of the vehicle, then allegedly moving the handgun across the inside of the vehicle until the gun was pointing at the passenger side of the vehicle. At that point the four tactical officers on the passenger side of the vehicle opened fire on the driver. The black female in the passenger's seat ducked down onto the floor in front of the passenger's seat, where she remained until the shooting stopped. No rounds were fired from inside the vehicle. The victim (driver), who was shot multiple times, died instantly on the scene.

IMMEDIATE ACTION TAKEN: A request was made for the state police to conduct the investigation, and to report directly to the prosecutor's office "Public Integrity Unit," which was responsible for handling officer-involved deadly force incidents. The state police responded with a command officer, a crime scene investigator, and a squad of investigators and initiated the investigation.

MAJOR DIFFICULTIES: While the preliminary investigation was taking place, both the county agency whose officers had done the shooting and the victim's department were on scene. The concern for conflict, and possibly even violence, between the two agencies was a real concern, particularly because both departments were clamoring to become involved in the investigation, including internal affairs for both agencies. It was made clear by the prosecutor's office that neither department would be involved in the investigation.

Prior to the arrival of the state police, evidence technicians from the county agency had arrived on scene and began taking photographs and making measurements. They were removed from the scene and told that the crime scene personnel from the state police would be handling the scene. Neither department trusted each other, however both agencies (somewhat begrudgingly) trusted the state police to conduct an impartial investigation of the incident. The agencies involved refused to talk to one another, or to talk to the state police if anyone from the other agency was present. This created communications issues in that the agencies had to be both interviewed and briefed separately.

Unfortunately, all of the tactical officers involved in the shooting had left the scene together when it was discovered that one of the tactical officers had been hit in the foot and had very minor injuries from a small piece of jacketing from one of the many rounds fired. While the wounded officer was being treated, all of the involved officers were together, unsupervised, at a local hospital. Due to the status of the victim and the fact that a police officer had been shot and killed by other police officers, a media circus ensued, with all TV, radio, and print media on scene. Scheduled press briefings were held for the first three days of the investigation.

LESSONS LEARNED:

1. Don't allow evidence or crime scene technicians from an agency to begin processing a scene unless you are absolutely certain that you are going to stick with them as the sole entity working the scene. Trying to get evidence technicians to come into and work a scene after another agency has already begun processing can be extremely problematic. In this case, after the county agency's evidence personnel began photographs and measurements, the state police crime scene personnel were very reluctant to have any involvement in the processing.

2. Make certain that officers involved in this type of a situation are separated prior to obtaining statements. This is not to infer in any way that officers are not trustworthy enough not to compare recollections of an incident, it is simply sound investigative practice that separation of witnesses take place. Due to the fact that these officers were not separated, all personnel in the emergency room and anyone who had come into contact with the group of officers had to be interviewed, which took a great deal of time.

3. Make certain that all "preliminary" work done before your arrival is fully reported. In this case, there had been some preliminary interviews conducted, and as was mentioned the scene processing had begun. It is imperative that all of this preliminary work be thoroughly documented, and that the agency responsible for the investigation must be provided with this documentation.

4. Keep outside agency command personnel appraised of progress, but at your pace. In this case, due to the animosity between the agencies, keeping them apprised of the progress of the investi-

gation was done separately. Even though both agencies were clamoring for continuous updates, it was explained that they would be given updates and briefings when it was convenient for the command responsible for the investigation.

CASE RESOLUTION: The family of the victim mounted a law suit against the chief of the department as well as against the county agency whose officers had shot the victim. The case never went to court and was settled for "an undisclosed" sum very quickly.

Chapter 12

LIAISONS, PRE-PLANNING,
AFTER ACTION CRITIQUES

MAJOR CASE LIAISONS

One of the best ways to increase your chances that your next major case investigation will be successful is to make certain that your prior planning for that investigation is thorough. That prior planning includes a number of liaisons with people and organizations that can insure that your major case goes much smoother. As with any other prior planning, the time to get these liaisons started is now, not the first day of your major case investigation. Most of these liaisons and relationships are not forged by a written policy or "dictate from headquarters," they are normally forged over a lunch or a cup of coffee. Once they are formed, they need to be maintained through communication on matters of mutual interest through a bond of friendship and mutual respect for each other. These liaisons include:

- **Prosecutors' offices.** There should be an ongoing liaison between law enforcement agencies and prosecutors prior to the major case investigation, so the major case investigation will merely be an extension of that relationship. Almost anyone in a law enforcement investigative management position should already have some type of personal relationship with their local prosecutor, and these relationships will be extremely useful during the major case investigation. In established major case task forces, these relationships are developed during the task force planning stage, and are maintained throughout the life of the task force. Many task forces have assistant prosecutors assigned as members of the task force, which can be extremely beneficial when the major case occurs.

- **Departments of corrections/probation/parole.** Although these agencies may not be used in every major case investigation, these agencies will often be needed, and the liaisons should be established well ahead of time. It has been my experience that having these liaisons ahead of time can save you a great deal of time and frustration when you need information very quickly during a major case investigation. You don't want to be in a position where you're waiting for return phone calls regarding records checks or information on prisoners, probationers, or parolees, particular if you need that information now. I have had a number of good friends over the years in positions with corrections, probation, and parole, and they have not only been an extremely valuable resource during major case investigations, but during routine investigations as well, and I have found them to be the type of people who are willing to extend themselves to provide assistance whenever its requested.
- **Medical examiner or coroner's offices.** These folks can be a source of investigative leads and a great deal of information, and obtaining that information from someone who you actually know is much easier than from someone you've never met and who is in essence just a "voice on a phone" rather than a personal acquaintance. When discussing functional positions in Chapter 4, the position of crime scene/evidence coordinator was examined, and this is the person who should have the best liaisons with medical examiner or coroner's offices. In the event that specific tests, and so forth are being requested, it sometimes is beneficial to have the person in this position handle the liaison with coroner or medical examiner's staff, as there seems to be more of an affinity between the two positions, possibly due to similar jobs.
- **Community organizations.** Oftentimes, particularly when a case is emotional, such as a missing or murdered child, there are elements within the community who may express a desire to help with the investigation in various ways. Having liaisons with some of these groups ahead of time can provide the major case manager with a valuable resource when the need arises, and if these liaisons are already established it will make obtaining these resources much easier. In the event that there are things that

members of these community groups can do, such as passing out flyers or getting involved in large area searches, they probably won't present a problem, as long as their efforts are properly supervised. As was pointed out earlier, you must still maintain security of information, however, as perpetrators of crimes sometimes later become "volunteers," to find out what you've got, such as in the case of the "Green River Killer," Gary Leon Ridgway, who "assisted" the police in Washington to search for the bodies of his own victims.

Some of the community groups which might be beneficial during the major case investigation can include:

Scouting Programs/Youth Groups. Can provide search personnel, handout flyers, etc.

Victim Advocacy Groups. Can provide safe havens, transportation, counseling

School Liaisons. Useful when large numbers of school children must be interviewed

Mental Health Facilities. Can provide mental health professionals for immediate counseling and/or advice

Church Groups. Sometimes helpful in getting neighborhood residents to assist you

PRIOR PLANNING

In addition to establishing and maintaining effective liaisons, a great deal of prior planning is necessary for major case investigations, and this should not be overlooked. As was pointed out earlier, there is no "schedule" for when the next major case will occur, so the prior planning for these incidents should begin as soon as possible. Some of the things that should be considered when planning for involvement in a major case investigation would include:

- **Communications personnel.** The time to set up liaisons with phone company representatives, or other telecommunications personnel, is *not* the day that the investigation begins, but rather well before the incident occurs. Being able to pick up a phone and get immediate service is a great deal more efficient than going through several channels at the communications carrier and perhaps not getting it done at all. While commanding a multiagency major case task force, on the first day of the task force I was asked by the chief of the local police department in whose jurisdiction the crime had occurred what type of equipment or resources I needed to proceed. I told him that I needed about a dozen phone lines dropped into the command post as soon as possible, thinking that it might take a week or more to get the phone lines. Imagine my surprise the next morning when I arrived at about 6:30 a.m. and observed a huge phone company truck and four phone company employees installing the lines. I had asked for a dozen and had received eighteen. I found that the reason for the "personalized service" was that the chief was personal friends and a golfing buddy of a vice president for the phone company who happened to live in his community. Good prior planning and good liaisons work.

- **Command post facilities.** Not every agency is fortunate enough to have a facility with suitable space to use for a command post in the event a major case investigator occurs. Agencies that do not have such a facility available should start planning for a suitable site now, as you can never know when you'll need it. When planning for a suitable facility, don't limit yourself to governmental buildings or police department buildings, but rather consider any suitable facility which might be available. Once you locate a suitable facility, meet with the owner of the facility and discuss the potential use of their facility as a command post for a major case investigation sometime in the future should the need arise. Even for agencies that have suitable facilities such as training or meeting rooms, keep in mind that if the meeting or training room is being utilized for a week-long training class that your use of that meeting or training room for a command post might just get "trumped," so you need to consider alternate facilities.
- **Maintaining records of available specialized equipment.** You never really know what type of specialized equipment might be needed for a major case investigation, but sound prior planning dictates that you make a list of every type of equipment that you can imagine that might need and how best to obtain that equipment if it is needed. This is similar to any other prior plan-

ning, in that sometimes you need a piece of equipment, such as a helicopter with a Forward-Looking Infrared Radar (FLIR) to search for a missing person, and being able to pick up a phone and get one is much better than trying to find one in the yellow pages of the phone book.

• **Maintaining records of available specialized personnel.** Similar to specialized equipment, records should be maintained on the specialized personnel who would be available to assist in a major case investigation. There are a number of specialties that not all police agencies have on staff, such as polygraph examiners, graphologists, psychologists, and others who could be useful in a major case investigation. Determining as best you can what some of these specialties might be and how best to obtain them is something to consider when conducting prior planning. In addition to maintaining these records, however, establishing and maintaining liaisons with these specialists can go a long way to promote a spirit of cooperation, necessary when their particular talents are needed.

• **Determining training needs of assigned personnel.** The time to identify training deficiencies of assigned personnel is not the first day of the major case investigation, but rather during that individual's regular assignments. Addressing these training deficiencies or providing refresher training for personnel can save time, embarrassment, and increase efficiency and effectiveness when those personnel are called upon to "gear up" for a major case investigation.

AFTER ACTION CRITIQUES

When a tactical unit is going on a high-risk operation, such as a search warrant execution, they do a great deal of prior planning, to minimize the risks to personnel and offenders and to maximize the effectiveness of the operation. Upon completion of these operations, these units conduct an "after-action critique" of the operation. In a very similar manner, when a major case investigation is concluded, it is essential that an after-action critique is conducted. The critique should be conducted so that both positive and negative aspects of the investigation are brought to the attention of the agencies involved for utilization in future investigations. As with any critique, all personnel involved in the investigation should attend, and they all must be strongly encouraged to provide open and uncontrolled input into the process. It has been my experience that "holding back on their input" is usually not something that you have to worry about with tactical or special operations personnel, or most cops for that matter. Open and uncontrolled input must be encouraged as sometimes people holding back their true feelings might cause the people conducting the critique to miss something that could greatly improve the next major case investigation. Rather than to allow the after-action critique to become a "gripe session" or get into "personality assassination," I would strongly recommend that a format be developed and adhered to which adequately covers all aspects of the investigation, to avoid wasting time on non-specific issues. Appendix 10 is a sample "Major Case After Action Critique."

Critiques are worthless if they are completed and placed on a shelf, however, and once completed the critique should be forwarded to the command of contributing agencies for review, and for whatever necessary action needs to be taken. In this manner, the critique will benefit future investigative efforts by pointing out areas of needed improvement which are then addressed. There are a number of items which should be critiqued, which include:

Organization of the Investigative Effort

- Was an adequate chain of command established in a timely manner?
- Was the chain of command understood and followed by personnel assigned?
- Was a comprehensive organizational structure developed and communicated to personnel?
- Were the various components and functions of the organizational structure clearly defined and implemented?
- Were the various assignments among investigative personnel clearly defined and implemented?
- Was there an effective level of cooperation among participating agencies?
- Was a formal prearranged agreement in place?
- Was the agreement adequate to suit the needs of the investigation?

- Was administrative communication among participating agencies adequate?
- Was their adequate legal assistance provided?
- Were the investigative techniques utilized effective?
- Were there any investigative techniques not utilized that should be considered for future major cases?

Management of the Information Systems

- Was the mechanism used for information and leads management adequate?
- Was the leads management system used to its full potential?
- If a non-computerized leads management system was used, was it adequate for investigative needs?
- Were strategic briefings held on a regular schedule?
- Did strategic briefings accurately reflect management of the investigative effort?
- Were all personnel adequately briefed as to the progress of the investigation?
- Were all personnel provided an adequate opportunity for input during strategic briefings?

Security (all phases) of Command Post and Information

- Was the security system that was utilized adequate?
- Was command post security compromised in any way?
- If compromised, were problem areas addressed sufficiently?
- Was information security compromised in any way?
- If compromised, were problem areas addressed sufficiently?
- Are security improvements needed for future major cases?

Resource Acquisition/Allocation (Personnel)

- Were there adequate personnel assigned to the investigation?
- Were the personnel assigned adequately skill for participation?
- Were there any problems with individuals assigned?
- If problems existed, were they adequately addressed?
- Were any training needs identified among assigned personnel?
- Were adequate clerical personnel available?

- Were clerical personnel suitable for investigative assignments?
- Were any specialized personnel needed/utilized?
- Have records been made of personnel assigned, specialty personnel, and clerical personnel for future major cases?

Resource Acquisition/Allocation (Equipment)

- Was there an adequate amount of administrative equipment available?
- Was any specialized equipment needed/utilized?
- Was there specialized equipment needed that was not available?
- Were technical personnel available for specialized equipment operation/maintenance?
- Have procedures been put into place to insure equipment needs are in place for the next major case?
- Have records been made of equipment sources for future major cases?
- Was adequate communications equipment available?
- Have records been made of communications equipment sources for the next major case?

Resource Acquisition/Allocation (Finances)

- Were adequate financial resources available?
- Were those financial resources used in an effective manner?
- Have additional funding sources been explored/identified?

Laboratory/Crime Scene/Evidence

- Was an assignment made for crime scene/evidence duties?
- Was the person assigned effective in this position?
- Were laboratory and crime scene requests/reports processed in a timely manner?
- Was the evidence handling/processing/storage system used adequate?

Non-Law Enforcement Resources

- Were any non-law enforcement groups/resources needed/utilized?

- If utilized, were they suitable?
- Were unsuitable groups or individuals adequately addressed?
- Were records established regarding these groups/resources for use in future major cases?

Personnel Support and Logistics

- Was the command post facility adequate and secure?
- Were personnel support facilities adequate?
- If utilized, were lodging arrangements for personnel adequate?
- Were any personnel needs that arose appropriately addressed?
- Were relief assignments made in a timely manner?
- Were meal services available for investigative personnel?
- Were records made of potential command post locations?

Media Management

- Was an effective media coordinator immediately assigned?
- Was the developed media strategy adequate?
- Was the scheduling of press briefings adequately addressed?
- Were press releases completed in a timely and thorough manner?
- Were media inquiries adequately addressed?
- Were there any unauthorized leaks of pertinent information?
- Were there any other security concerns relating to the media?

In addition, some questions need to be considered, such as: if one aspect of this major case investigation could be improved to have made this major case investigation operate more smoothly, what would it have been, and how could it have been successfully addressed or improved? If there were problems noted during the major case investigation, were mechanisms put into place to apply the organizational structure and other successful components to future major cases? As a concluding element of the after-action critique, I would try to determine the overall greatest strength and overall greatest weakness of this effort, so as to correct and avoid the greatest weakness and learn from and repeat the greatest strength.

CONCLUSION

I believe that the professional management of major case investigations is among the most difficult of managerial duties, and that it is full of sacrifices, pitfalls, and obstacles. I sincerely hope that some of the material in this book will provide some ideas, techniques, and strategies to assist you in competently and professionally managing your next major case investigation.

Teaching all over the country affords me the opportunity to meet a great number of cops. Many of these are investigators and/or investigative managers, and I have always been impressed with their desire to learn and improve. I have also been impressed with their dedication to our profession and to their assignments and duties. I am very appreciative of what they have taught me. I have learned something valuable from each class I have conducted. I have also walked away having made many new friends, for which I am very grateful. I always end my classes with an overhead slide that contains what I believe has always been and will hopefully continue to be my basic philosophy toward our profession.

We should never forget that those of us privileged enough to be in the law enforcement are truly doing God's work:

- *We get the privilege of protecting those who need protection.*
- *We get the privilege to stand up for what is right and good in society.*
- *We occasionally get the privilege to right some of life's wrongs.*

APPENDICES

APPENDIX 1

INTERGOVERNMENTAL AGREEMENT
_____ MAJOR CRIMES TASK FORCE

The undersigned Public Agencies, charged with the duty of enforcing the law and investigating heinous and complex violent crimes, recognize that the most effective means to accomplish that duty is through the combination of resources and the joint exercise of their respective authorities; each of them do now enter into this Inter-Agency Agreement to conduct joint investigations involving major violent crimes which necessitate substantial commitments of resources for prolonged periods of time. The purpose of this Agreement is to provide the citizens of Northwest Indiana with the most effective Law Enforcement skills and protection against those who engage in actions detrimental to the safety of the public.

In consideration of the terms herein set forth and the mutual covenants and obligations of the parties hereto; it is hereby agreed by the undersigned Member Agencies of the _____ Major Crimes Task Force, (hereinafter called "Member Agencies") including the following participating police departments:

List of Member Agencies Here

I. **Parties:**

The _____ Major Crimes Task Force (Task Force) shall consist of the member Agencies who have signed this agreement.

In the event that additional Agencies request to participate in the Task Force, their acceptance will be contingent upon the majority vote of the Task Force Board of Directors and payment of all fees applicable at the time.

II. **Purpose:**

The purpose of the _____ Major Crimes Task Force is to provide comprehensive investigative services to Member Agencies of the Task

Force including but not limited to those cases outlined in the "Case Acceptance Guidelines" when requested to do so by the Chief of Police of Member Agencies or their designee, with the approval of the Board of Directors.

The Task Force agrees to provide comprehensive investigative services to Member Agencies in accepted cases upon request of the Chief of Police or the designee of the Police Department of the local jurisdiction in which the crime occurred. The member agencies agree that the Chief of Police or their designee shall contact the Task Force Commander at the onset of the discovery of an offense which they which they feel qualifies for Task Force services.

The Task Force Commander shall confer with the requesting agency and the Assistant Task Force Commander to determine if the case shall be accepted for investigation by the Task Force.

The following guidelines will be used to determine case acceptance:

CASE ACCEPTANCE GUIDELINES

A real or suspected violent crime such as:

1. **Homicide**
2. **Non-Parental Kidnapping**
3. **Serial Arson, Rape, Sexual Assault**
4. **Police Involved Shooting/Deadly Force/In-custody Deaths**
5. **Other exceptionally heinous offenses**

III. **AUTHORITY:**

Each member Agency agrees to assume liability for its respective personnel assigned to the Task Force, as well as for vehicles and equipment assigned to the Task Force. Each participating Member Agency assumes responsibility for members of its police force acting pursuant to this agreement, both as to indemnification of said police officers as provided for by the Indiana statutes and as to personal benefits to said police officers, all to the same extent as they are protected, insured, indemnified and otherwise provided for by the Statutes of the State of Indiana and the ordinances of the participating municipalities when acting solely within their own corporate limits.

IV. **BOARD OF DIRECTORS:**

The Board of Directors shall consist of the Chief Executives of participating agencies or their designees.

The Board of Directors may establish an advisory board to assist and guide them in their duties and responsibilities. The advisory board will be comprised of as many members and organizations as determined by the Board of Directors, but advisory board members shall not be permitted to vote on board issues.

Simple majority of Board of Directors shall constitute a quorum for voting purposes. Each Board member shall have one (1) vote. For a vote to be registered, the Board member must be present during the vote.

The Board's responsibility shall include, but not be limited to:

- Determine all major policies and procedures of the Task Force
- Establish financial controls
- Make decisions on problems
- Make final decisions on when the Task Force will be activated and deactivated (pursuant to discussion with the Task Force Commander)
- Review Task Force activities and manpower once activated
- Meet bi-monthly during the first year of operation and then quarterly to discuss Task Force issues, problems, manpower, activities, etc.
- Determine who will hold the position of Task Force Commander
- Determine training needs

The Board of Directors may determine further By-Laws for governing the Task Force which shall not be inconsistent with this agreement.

V.   COSTS/EXPENSES:

The Requesting Agency agrees to pay for costs of investigations of crimes occurring within the Requesting Agency's jurisdiction incurred by members of the Task Force when the Chief of Police or their designee has requested the investigation, excluding the salaries, wages, benefits, and ordinary travel costs.

The Requesting Agency shall pay for extraordinary travel and investigative expenses of officers of other Member Agencies if the expenses have been determined to be necessary for the investigation by the Task Force Commander and Requesting Agency Chief.

Each Member Agency shall be responsible for the cost of training their designated Task Force personnel to meet requirements as established by the Board of Directors

Each member Agency will be responsible for a one-time initial membership fee to be used for Task Force equipment and supplies. This fee shall be $_____ per Member Agency.

The Board of Directors may vote to increase or decrease this fee but in no event shall any increase exceed 10% of the initial fee in any calendar year.

If the Board of Directors determines that the initial fee should be increased above $_____ plus 10% in any calendar year, the Board shall submit their request for additional funds in writing to each Member Agency who must approve the increase by a three-fourths (3/4) majority vote of all Member Agencies.

The Board of Directors may vote to asses each Member Agency an annual upkeep fee to cover the costs and expenses for supplies and equipment. This fee shall not exceed 10% of the current initial fee two times in any calendar year, except if approved by a three fourths (3/4) vote of all Member Agencies.

VI.   LIABILITIES/INSURANCE:

Each agency will accept liability to the extent required by the Worker's Compensation Act for personal injuries occurring to its officers while engaged in Task Force activities.

Member Agencies will furnish their assigned officers with a suitable vehicle and will bear sole responsibility for the costs of maintaining and insuring said vehicle. Member Agencies will also furnish their assigned officers with a cell phone or pager, firearm, and handcuffs.

Each Member Agency agrees to assume liability for its respective personnel, vehicles and equipment assigned to the Task Force. Each participating Member Agency assumes responsibility for members of its police force acting pursuant to this agreement as to indemnification of said police officers.

VII.   TASK FORCE PERSONNEL:

Each Member Agency agrees to designate a minimum of one Investigator who will be assigned to the Task Force. All Task Force Members shall report to the Task Force Commander.

All decisions on operational issues shall be decided by the Task Force Commander with the advice of the Chief of Police of the originating agency requesting the Task Force.

A Chief of Police of any Member Agency may volunteer to assign an additional Investigator from his agency to the Task Force. The selection and assignment of officers for the Task Force shall be determined by the Task Force Commanders according to experience and training of proposed

Member designees.

The Member Agencies agree that they shall make any of their Task Force investigators assigned to the Task Force available for investigations and training as needed by the Task Force.

It is agreed that each officer participating as a member of the Task Force shall be bound by the policies and procedures of his or her own Member Agency in addition to any policies and procedures of the Task Force.

VIII. ADMINISTRATIVE/OPERATIONAL PROCEDURES:

The Member agencies agree that the investigation of crimes within the Member Agencies' jurisdiction that have been accepted by the Task Force Commander and the Board of Directors shall be conducted according to the procedures of the Administrative/Operational Procedures as written.

IX. ASSET FORFEITURE ON TASK FORCE CASES:

Any assets seized or forfeited as a result of a Task Force investigation shall be distributed and used according to existing State Law. However, any participating Member Agency agrees to designate fifty (50) per cent of any such distribution as Task Force Training and Expense funds to be used according to guidelines determined by the Board of Directors.

X. MISCONDUCT:

1. Misconduct by any member of the Task Force shall include the following:

   a. Violation of Task Force policies and/or rules or procedures.
   b. Conduct which may tend to reflect unfavorably upon any of the parties of this agreement.

2. In exigent circumstances, the Task Force Commander has the authority to remove any Task Force member and return them to their agency. As soon as possible after removal of the Task Force member, the Task Force Commander shall contact the Chief of the member's agency and explain the reasons for the removal.

3. Upon receipt of a complaint from a law enforcement agency, a Prosecutor's office, or any other credible source alleging misconduct by a Task Force member, the Task Force Commander shall discuss the allegations with the Chief of the Investigator's Member Agency. The Board of Directors, after conferring with the Chief of the Investigator's Member Agency, shall decide whether the allegation/infraction should be investigated by the Member Agency or the Task Force. The Member Agency shall

have the sole authority/responsibility to administer discipline in matters of misconduct unless a criminal complaint is verified, then the information will be forwarded to the Prosecutor's office .

XI. **TERMINATION/MODIFICATION OF AGREEMENT:**

This agreement shall be in full force and effect between all Member Agencies who have signed this agreement until such time that the allocation of the aforementioned resources are no longer possible or an alternate funding source is determined. A Member Agency may withdraw from the Agreement at any time by written notice by the Chief of Police or command level designee of the Member Agency to the remaining Board of Directors.

The undersigned representative(s) of the _____
Task Force hereby agree to the above terms and conditions of this Intergovernmental Agreement:

Signed:_____Date_____

Signed:_____Date_____

APPENDIX 2

BY-LAWS OF THE
_____ MAJOR CRIMES TASK FORCE

ARTICLE I - NAME AND PURPOSE

SECTION 1: This organization shall be known as the

_____ MAJOR CRIMES TASK FORCE

SECTION 2: Planning for the unexpected is basic to law enforcement's pre-paredness and effectiveness. It is recognized that the sharing of resources and personnel enhances the capabilities of local law enforcement agencies. It is the purpose of the _____ Major Crimes Task Force to coordinate these cooper-ative efforts toward a common goal pursuant to the underlying intergovernmental agreement.

ARTICLE II - AUTHORITY

The _____ Major Crimes Task Force is established pursuant to the Intergovernmental Agreement as adopted by the participating agencies (hereafter Agreement).

ARTICLE III - MEMBERSHIP

SECTION 1: The members of the _____ Major Crimes Task Force are:

LIST NAMES OF TASK FORCE MEMBER AGENCIES HERE

SECTION 2: Other agencies may become members of the _____ Major Crimes Task Force upon adoption of the "Agreement" by the corporate authorities of the agency and approval by a two-thirds vote of the Board of Directors and pay-ment of any membership or assessment fees required of subsequent members,

Major Case Management

along with providing an investigator(s) who is recommended by the Task Force Commander and approved by the Board of Directors.

SECTION 3: Members who fail to meet any obligations, including but not limited to providing an officer or payment of membership or assessment fees in accordance with the Agreement or with these By-Laws, may be suspended or expelled from membership by a majority vote of the Board of Directors.

ARTICLE IV - BOARD OF DIRECTORS

SECTION 1: The Board of Directors shall consist of _____ representatives from the Member Agencies of the Task Force. The Directors shall represent the following agencies:

LIST NAMES OF TASK FORCE MEMBER AGENCIES HERE

The Executive Board will consist of members of the Board of Directors, and will assume the positions of Chairman, Vice-Chairman, Secretary, and Treasurer.

The Board of Directors may establish an Advisory Board to assist and guide them in their duties and responsibilities. The Advisory Board need not be affiliated with member agencies, and will be comprised of as many members and organizations as determined by the Board of Directors, but Advisory Board members shall not be permitted to vote on board issues.

SECTION 2: The Board of Directors shall establish or approve an Operating Plan that is not inconsistent with these By-Laws and the "Agreement." The Operating Plan shall provide procedures for requesting, rendering and receiving aid under the Agreement. The Board's responsibilities shall also include, but not limited to: determine all major policies and procedures of the Task Force, establish financial control, make final decisions on problems, make final decisions on activations and deactivations, review Task Force activities and staffing once activated, determine who will hold the position as Task Force Commanders and Assistant Commanders, and determine training needs.

SECTION 3: The Board of Directors shall have the authority to take appropriate action to accomplish the purpose of the _____ Major Crimes Task Force.

ARTICLE V - MEETINGS

SECTION 1: The Board of Directors shall meet every other month for the first year of the _____ Major Crimes Task Force existence and then at least quarterly thereafter at a time and place determined by the Board of

Directors. Special meetings may be called by one-third (1/3) of the members of the Board of Directors.

SECTION 2: A simple majority of the Board of Directors shall constitute a quorum for meeting and voting purposes. Board members must be present to vote.

SECTION 3: The current edition of Roberts Rules of Order shall govern meetings in all cases in which they are applicable and not inconsistent with these By-Laws.

ARTICLE VI - DUTIES OF OFFICERS

SECTION 1 - CHAIRMAN: Set dates, time and place, and agenda for Board meetings. Contact Board of Directors when Task Force is activated. The Chairman may call other meetings for resolving emergencies or when otherwise needed, and shall designate that an audit/inventory to be completed on financial records and equipment each fiscal year as determined by the Board of Directors.

SECTION 2 - VICE-CHAIRMAN: When the Chairman is absent, serves as next in command. Assist the Chairman as requested and conducts meetings when Chairman in unavailable.

SECTION 3 - SECRETARY: Keep accurate records of all Board meetings, document all activations, record all training and is responsible for all correspondence.

SECTION 4 - TREASURER: Keep accurate records of all Task Force funds, pay bills, and prepare a financial report to the Board of Directors for each meeting.

ARTICLE VII - COMMITTEES

The Chairman or Board of Directors may create such committees as are deemed necessary to accomplish the purpose of the _____ Major Crimes Task Force.

ARTICLE VIII - COMPENSATION

SECTION 1: Officers and members of the Board of Directors shall serve without compensation.

SECTION 2: Except as otherwise provided in the Agreement, police assistance provided by any aiding agency shall be rendered without charge to the requesting agency or any other participating agency.

SECTION 3: The Board of Directors may approve expenditures for professional consultants for training only as required by the _____ Major Crimes Task Force.

ARTICLE IX - DISBURSEMENTS

Disbursements of funds may be made only as authorized by the Board of Directors.

ARTICLE X - PROPERTY

The equipment, property, supplies and furnishings needed to fulfill the purpose of the _____ Major Crimes Task Force will be supplied from the operating fund. Any item provided by a participating agency shall be, and remain, the property of that agency unless otherwise provided by the agency. The Board of Directors may approve expenditures for specialized equipment required by the Task Force. Any property purchased by the Task Force shall, at the time of dissolution of the Task Force, be sold at fair market value and the proceeds shall be equally distributed among Task Force member agencies.

ARTICLE XI - AMENDMENTS

These By-Laws may be amended at any meeting of the Board of Directors by a two-thirds (2/3) vote of those members present, provided the amendment and notice of the meeting have been sent to the Board of Directors not less than fifteen (15) days prior to the meeting.

ARTICLE XII - DISSOLUTION

If at any regular meeting or special meeting called for the purpose of dissolution, two-thirds (2/3) of the members of the Board of Directors vote in favor of dissolution, the _____ Major Crimes Task Force shall be dissolved within thirty (30) days, provided notice of the meeting has been sent to the Board of Directors not less than fifteen (15) days prior to the meeting.

ARTICLE XIII - EFFECTIVE DATE

These By-Laws shall be in full force and effect from and after their passage and approval by the Board of Directors of the _____ Major Crimes Task Force.

APPENDIX 3

MAJOR CASE MANAGEMENT
PLANNING CHECKLIST

Case Objectives and Priorities

Identify case priorities, such as:

1. Successfully solve the case
2. Identify and arrest those responsible
3. Disrupt perpetrator's future criminal activity
4. Allay public fears
5. Identify related crimes
6. Assist with prosecution needs

Required Resources

Estimate the numbers and sources of investigative and specialized personnel needed for the initial response.

Personnel Required	Approximate Number Needed	Personnel Source(s)
Investigative personnel		
Non-investigative law enforcement personnel		
Specialized personnel (List positions needed)		

Estimate the numbers and sources of crime scene response and management personnel needed to conduct crime scene response.

Personnel Required	Approximate Number Needed	Personnel Source(s)
Crime scene/investigative personnel		
Non-crime scene/ investigative personnel		
Specialized personnel (List positions needed)		

Single Agency Investigative Effort:
- Identify the location(s) of agency personnel resources.
- dentify the location(s) of agency technical resources.

Multiple Agency Investigative Effort:
- Identify any applicable mutual aid agreements.
- Establish liaisons with cooperating agencies.

Operational Personnel Assignments

Position Title	Person Assigned	Date Assigned	Approval
Officer in Charge/Case Manager			
Deputy Officer in Charge/Case Manager			
Primary Investigator			
Leads Coordinator			
Crime Scene/Evidence Coordinator			
Legal Coordinator			

Investigative Personnel Assignments

Name and Agency	Preliminary Assignment	Date Reporting	Date Relieved

Support Personnel Assignments
- Investigative support considerations include:
- Locating, securing, and establishing a suitable command post
- Developing a media plan
- Acquisition and allocation of technical support equipment
- Acquisition and allocation of clerical staff personnel
- Establishing a transportation and supply system
- Establishing a mechanism for developing, analyzing, and dissemination of intelligence
- Implementing physical/technical surveillance operations
- Acquisition and allocation of emergency or tactical personnel

Position Title	Person Assigned	Date Assigned	Approval
Logistics Coordinator			
Liaison Coordinator			
Technical Support Coordinator			
Media Coordinator			
Intelligence Coordinator			
Surveillance Coordinator (if needed)			
Emergency Services Coordinator (if needed)			

Non-Law Enforcement Support Personnel

Identify any non-law enforcement support personnel that would be beneficial/ needed for this investigation.

Type of Support Personnel	Source	Date Acquired

APPENDIX 4

LEAD SHEET

CASE #_____   LEAD #_____

Date & Time Received:_____ Received by:_____
Caller's Name: _____ DOB:_____ M/F: _____
Address:_____
Phone #: Home_____ Work_____ Other _____
Method of Contact: __In Person __Phone __ Written __Other

Synopsis of
Lead:_____
_____
_____
_____
_____
_____
_____
_____
_____
_____

Investigator   Date/Time
Assigned:_____ Assigned:_____

Lead Cleared: ___ Yes ___ No

Comments:
_____
_____
_____
_____
_____
_____

Additional Leads Developed:

_____
_____
_____
_____

Lead Coordinator:_____ Primary Investigator:_____

Lead Entered By: _____

APPENDIX 5

MASTER LEAD SHEET

Case Number _____
Page _____ of _____

Lead #	Date Rec.	Lead Description	Investigator Assigned	Date Assigned	Date Completed	Related Lead #s

APPENDIX 6

LEAD ASSIGNMENT CONTROL LOG

Case Number _____

Lead #	Date Received	Time Received	Assigned Investigator	Date Compelted	Ongoing

APPENDIX 7

INVESTIGATIVE SUMMARY REPORT

CASE NAME: _____ CASE NUMBER:_____

INVESTIGATOR ASSIGNED:_____

DATE OPENED:_____

DATES OF SUMMARY: _____ TO _____

SYNOPSIS:

This includes a brief synopsis of the case, enough to provide the reader with a basic understanding of the offense and facts surrounding the incident. In the case of multiple summaries, this section would reflect the activities for the period of this summary only.

CHAIN OF CUSTODY OF EVIDENTIARY ITEMS:

The date that the evidentiary items were recovered, the recovering Officer, the current location should be listed in chronological order.

DEFENDANT'S CRIMINAL HISTORY:

This information need only appear on the initial summary.

LIST OF WITNESSES:

This is optional, and can appear on the initial and/or any subsequent summaries.

TABLE OF CONTENTS:

All reports should be placed in chronological order and numbered. The list of page numbers and a brief description of the report is listed here. In the event that multiple summaries are used, it is recommended that the numbering system on previous summaries be continued on subsequent summaries.

APPENDIX 8

INVESTIGATIVE SUMMARY REPORT

CASE NUMBER: 04-2287

CASE NAME: STEWART, JOHN M. DOB: 06-14-56 SSAN:317-64-0766
              1432 South Ashland, Chicago, IL 60644
              M/W 5'09" 180 Brown Hair, Brown Eyes

INVESTIGATOR ASSIGNED: Det. Curtis   DATE OPENED: 03-31-04

DATES OF SUMMARY: 03-31-04 TO 04-30-04

SYNOPSIS:

On 03-31-04 the body of MARY ELIZABETH STEWART (Victim) F/W
DOB: 07-15-58 was found in the Blair Woods Cook County Forest Preserve.
Subsequent autopsy revealed that the cause of death was blunt trauma to the
head. Witness information indicated that a vehicle similar to one owned by
Subject (Husband of Victim) was observed near the scene of the body recovery
the day before Victim's body was discovered. Subsequent interview of Subject
resulted in a confession to the murder of Victim.

CHAIN OF CUSTODY OF EVIDENTIARY ITEMS:

Exhibit #1: Gold Rolex Wristwatch
03-31-04- recovered from Victim's body at the Cook County Medical Examiner's
Office by Detective Curtis
03-31-04- placed into the LPD Evidence Vault by Det. Curtis

Exhibit #2: Black silk women's panties
03-31-04- recovered near Victim's body in Blair Woods, Cook County Forest
Preserve by LPD Crime Scene Investigator Protsman
03-31-04- placed into the LPD Evidence Vault by CSI Protsman
04-03-04- transported to the ISP Crime Lab by CSI Protsman

04-03-04- turned over to Forensic Scientist D. Bartlett by CSI Protsman

Exhibit #3: <u>True Value Brand Claw Hammer</u>
04-01-04- recovered from the kitchen sink cabinet during a consensual search of Subject's residence located at 1432 South Ashland, Chicago, IL 60644 by CSI Protsman
04-03-04- transported to the ISP Crime Lab by CSI Protsman
04-03-04- turned over to Forensic Scientist D. Bartlett by CSI Protsman

DEFENDANT'S CRIMINAL HISTORY:

Subject has an extensive criminal history, see pages 8-11

LIST OF WITNESSES:

Lansing Police Department Detectives Curtis, Oberman, Smith
Lansing Police Department Crime Scene Investigator Protsman
2710 170th Street, Lansing, IL 60438 TX: 708/895-7133

ISP Forensic Scientist D. Bartlett, Joliet Laboratory TX:815/726-6377

TABLE OF CONTENTS:

<u>Page</u>

APPENDIX 9

INTELLIGENCE REPORT

CASE #_____

Date & Time Received:_____ Received by:_____

Evaluation of Source:
___ Highly Reliable ___ Usually Reliable ___ Questionable ___ Unknown

Source Name: _____ DOB:_____ M/F:_____
Source Address:_____
Phone #: Home_____ Work_____Other_____

Source Received Information Through:
___ Personal Knowledge ___ Hearsay/Rumor ___ Documents

Synopsis   of   Information:
_____
_____
_____
_____
_____
_____
_____
_____
_____
_____

Information:
___ Verified ___ Unverified ___ Refuted

Evaluated by: _____ Date Evaluated:_____

Disposition: ___ Follow-up ___ Dropped ___ Assigned Lead Number (_____)

Comments:

_____

_____

_____

_____

_____

_____

_____

_____

Lead Coordinator: _____ Primary Investigator:_____

APPENDIX 10

MAJOR CASE AFTER ACTION CRITIQUE

TOPIC	CONSIDERATIONS	YES	NO	INIT.
ORGANIZATION	was an adequate Chain of Command established in a timely manner			
	was the Chain of Command understood and followed by personnel assigned			
	was a comprehensive organizational structure developed and communicated to personnel			
	did the various components and functions of the organizational structure clearly defined and implemented			
	were the various assignments among investigative personnel clearly defined and implemented			
	was there an effective level of cooperation among participating agencies			
	was a formal pre-arranged agreement in place			
	was the agreement adequate to suit the needs of the investigation			
	was administrative communication among participating agencies adequate			

	was adequate legal assistance provided			
	were the investigative techniques utilized effective			
	were there any investigative techniques not utilized that should be considered for future major cases			
	have arrangements been made to provide for training for those non-utilized but desirable investigative techniques			
INFORMATION MANAGEMENT	was the mechanism used for information and leads management adequate			
	was the leads management system used to its full potential			
	if a non-computerized leads management system was used, was it adequate for investigative needs			
	were strategic briefings held on a regular schedule			
	did strategic briefings accurately reflect management of the investigative effort			
	were all personnel adequately briefed as to the progress of the investigation			
	were all personnel provided an adequate opportunity for input during strategic briefings			
SECURITY	was the security system that was utilized adequate			
	was command post security compromised in any way			
	if compromised, were problem areas addressed sufficiently			
	was information security compromised in any way			

	if compromised, were problem areas addressed sufficiently			
	are security improvements needed for future major cases			
RESOURCE ALLOCATION	**PERSONNEL**			
	were there adequate personnel assigned to the investigation			
	were the personnel assigned adequately skill for participation			
	were there any problems with individuals assigned			
	if problems existed, were they adequately addressed			
	were any training needs identified among assigned personnel			
	were adequate clerical personnel available			
	were clerical personnel suitable for investigative assignments			
	were any specialized personnel needed/utilized			
	have records been made of personnel assigned, specialty personnel, and clerical personnel for future major cases			
	EQUIPMENT			
	was there an adequate amount of administrative equipment available			
	was any specialized equipment needed/utilized			
	was there specialized equipment needed that was not available			
	were technical personnel available for specialized equipment operation/ maintenance			

	have procedures been put into place to insure equipment needs are in place for the next major case			
	have records been made of equipment sources for future major cases			
	was adequate communications equipment available			
	have records been made of communications equipment sources for the next major case			
	FINANCING			
	were adequate financial resources available			
	were those financial resources used in an effective manner			
	have additional funding sources been explored/identified			
	LABORATORY ASSETS			
	was an assignment made for crime scene/evidence duties			
	was the person assigned effective in this			
	were laboratory and crime scene requests/reports processed in a timely manner			
	was the evidence handling/processing/storage system used adequate			
	NON-LAW ENFORCEMENT RESOURCES			
	were any non-law enforcement groups/resources needed/utilized			
	if utilized, were they suitable			
	were unsuitable groups or individuals adequately addressed			

	have records been established regarding these groups/resources for use in future major cases			
	PERSONNEL SUPPORT & LOGISTICS			
	was the command post facility adequate and secure			
	were personnel support facilities adequate			
	if utilized, were lodging arrangements for personnel adequate			
	were any personnel needs that arose appropriately addressed			
	were relief assignments made in a timely manner			
	were meal services available for investigative personnel			
	have records been made of potential command post locations			
MEDIA MANAGEMENT	was an effective media liaison officer immediately assigned			
	was the media strategy adequate			
	was the scheduling of press briefings adequately addressed			
	were press releases completed in a timely and thorough manner			
	were media inquiries adequately addressed			
	were there any unauthorized leaks of pertinent information			
	were there any other security concerns relating to the media			

GENERAL OVERVIEW

If one aspect of this investigation could be improved to have made this major case investigation run more smoothly, what would it have been?

How could it have been successfully addressed/improved?

If there were problems noted during the major case investigation, have mechanisms been put into place to address these improvements for future major cases?

Overall Greatest Strength

Overall Greatest Weakness

INDEX

251

ABOUT THE AUTHOR

Daniel S. McDevitt, is a 35 year law enforcement veteran, currently serving as Chief of the Lansing Police Department, a nationally accredited 130-member department, located in the south suburbs of Chicago.

He began his career as a Special Agent with the Naval Criminal Investigative Service (NCIS). He then completed a 24-year career with the Illinois State Police, retiring as a Captain. His command assignments included Violent Crimes, Drug Enforcement, Auto Theft, Financial Crimes, Patrol, Tactical Response Team, and several other units. He participated in and supervised numerous high profile major case investigations, and commanded many multiagency task forces. Following his retirement from the ISP he served as Chief of Police in Homewood, IL.

He holds a B.S. Degree in Criminology and Psychology, an M.S. Degree in Criminology, and is a graduate of the FBI National Academy and the FBI Law Enforcement Executive Development Program. He has taught at colleges, universities, and police academies in the United States, Europe, and the Middle East for both civilian and military law enforcement personnel. He currently develops law enforcement and management courses and is an instructor throughout the United States for Northwestern University, the University of North Florida, as well as local training programs. He has authored two books *Managing the Investigative Unit* and *Major Case Management: A Guide for Law Enforcement Managers* and several law enforcement and management articles.

He retired as an Intelligence Officer with the U.S. Navy, where he held the rank of Lieutenant Commander after completing a 20 year career which included enlisted and commissioned service. He served as a Medical Corpsman, caring for Vietnam wounded Naval and Marine Corps personnel, and as an Intelligence Officer specialized in foreign counterintelligence, physical security, and analysis of terrorist operations. He was recalled to active duty for the Gulf War, and has conducted numerous physical security surveys of military installations.

He has served as a consultant for the U.S. Department of State on several occasions, planning and conducting protective service details

253

for such dignitaries as the Dalai Lama, the Vice Premier of the People's Republic of China, and others. He has also developed coursework for the State Department's Anti-Terrorism Assistance Program, and traveled extensively, consulting with host country police personnel and providing training on a variety of topics, including Major Case Management for law enforcement agencies in Kenya.

McDevitt is co-owner of REM Management Services, Inc., a management consulting firm, that provides consulting services for governmental agencies and private industry regarding personal selection, chief executive selection, policy development, promotional processes, critical incident planning, physical security surveys, workplace violence assessment, and a variety of training offerings.

Charles C Thomas

PUBLISHER • LTD.

P.O. Box 19265
Springfield, IL 62794-9265

- Payne, Brian K.—**CRIME AND ELDER ABUSE: An Integrated Perspective. (3rd Ed.)** '11, 350 pp. (7 x 10), 7 il., 18 tables.

- Violanti, John M., Andrew F. O'Hara & Teresa T. Tate—**ON THE EDGE: Recent Perspectives on Police Suicide.** '11, 182 pp. (7 x 10), 2 il., 4 tables

- Blake, William F.—**ADVANCED PRIVATE INVESTIGATION.** '11, 244 pp. (7 x 10), paper.

- Blake, William F.—**BASIC PRIVATE INVESTIGATION.** '11, 266 pp. (7 x 10), paper.

- Barker, Tom—**POLICE ETHICS. (3rd Ed.)** '11, 174 pp. (7 x 10), 1 table, $40.95, hard, $25.95, paper.

- Garner, Gerald W—**HIGH-RISK PATROL. (2nd Ed.)** '11, 266 pp. (7 x 10), $59.95, hard, $39.95, paper.

- Bartone, Paul T., & Bjorn Helge Johnsen, Jarle Eid, John M. Violanti & Jon Christian Laberg—**ENHANCING HUMAN PERFORMANCE IN SECURITY OPERATIONS.** '10, 486 pp. (7 x 10), 23 il, 15 tables, $93.95, hard, $66.95, paper.

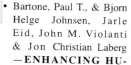

- Mendell, Ronald L.—**THE QUIET THREAT. (2nd Ed.)** '11, 254 pp. (7 x 10), 4il., 6 tables.

- Coleman, John L.—**POLICE ASSESSMENT TESTING. (4th Ed.)** '10, 298 pp. (7 x 10), 15 il., $63.95, hard, $43.95, paper.

- Covey, Herbert C.—**STREET GANGS THROUGHOUT THE WORLD. (2nd Ed.)** '10, 328 pp. (7 x 10), 1 table, $63.95, hard, $43.95, paper.

- Garner, Gerald W.—**POLICE CHIEF 101.** '10, 284 pp. (7 x 10), $60.95, hard, $40.95, paper.

- Hale, Charles D.—**THE ASSESSMENT CENTER HANDBOOK FOR POLICE AND FIRE PERSONNEL. (3rd Ed.)** '10, 238 pp. (8 1/2 x 11), 64 il., $36.95, spiral, paper.

- Harmening, William M.—**THE CRIMINAL TRIAD.** '10, 294 pp. (7 x 10), 40 il., $62.95, hard, $42.95, paper.

- Hendricks, James E., Jerome B. McKean, & Cindy Gillespie Hendricks—**CRISIS INTERVENTION. (4th Ed.)** '10, 412 pp. (7 x 10), 4 il., 1 table, $77.95, hard, $55.95, paper.

- Mendell, Ronald L.—**PROBING INTO COLD CASES.** '10, 324 pp. (7 x 10), 5 il., 34 tables, $63.95, hard, $43.95, paper.

- Rivers, R. W.—**TECHNICAL TRAFFIC CRASH INVESTIGATORS' HANDBOOK (LEVEL 3). (3rd Ed.)** '10, 494 pp. (7 x 10), 252 il., 8 tables, $113.95, hard, $77.95, paper.

- Schafer, John R. & Joe Navarro—**ADVANCED INTERVIEWING TECHNIQUES. (2nd Ed.)** '10, 192 pp. (7 x 10), $53.95, hard, $33.95, paper.

- Schafer, John R.—**PSYCHOLOGICAL NARRATIVE ANALYSIS.** '10, 220 pp. (7 x 10), 10 il., $49.95, hard, $29.95, paper.

- Slatkin, Arthur A.—**COMMUNICATION IN CRISIS AND HOSTAGE NEGOTIATIONS. (2nd Ed.)** '10, 230 pp. (7 x 10), $39.95, spiral (paper).

- Smith, Cary Stacy & Li-Ching Hung—**THE PATRIOT ACT.** '10, 284 pp. (7 x 10), 2 tables, $58.95, hard, $38.95, paper.

5 easy ways to order!

PHONE:
1-800-258-8980
or (217) 789-8980

FAX:
(217) 789-9130

@ EMAIL:
books@ccthomas.com

Web: www.ccthomas.com

MAIL:
Charles C Thomas • Publisher, Ltd.
P.O. Box 19265
Springfield, IL 62794-9265

Complete catalog available at www.ccthomas.com or email books@ccthomas.com

Books sent on approval • Shipping charges: $7.75 min. U.S. / Outside U.S., actual shipping fees will be charged • Prices subject to change without notice